P9-EDZ-710

ACTRESSES AS WORKING WOMEN

Victorian performers were drawn from various class backgrounds and enjoyed a unique degree of social mobility. Nevertheless, the living and working conditions of female performers were very different from those of their male colleagues. Their segregation and concentration in low-status jobs, like dancing, guaranteed economic insecurity. Actresses' attempts to reconcile sexuality and the female life cycle to a physically demanding, itinerant occupation while under constant public scrutiny led to assumptions about their morality – assumptions that were constantly reinforced by theatrical conventions which reflected popular pornographic images. This is an important book that brings fresh perspectives to bear on nineteenth-century theatre. It will be of interest to a wide range of specialists including historians and feminist critics.

Tracy C. Davis is Assistant Professor in Theatre and English at Northwestern University. She has written numerous articles on Victorian theatre and is co-editor of Routledge's Gender and Performance Series.

GENDER AND PERFORMANCE
Series Editors
Tracy C. Davis and Susan Bassnett

Gender and Performance is a new series that reflects the dynamic and innovative work being done by feminists across the disciplines. Exploring both historical and contemporary theatre, the series seeks to understand performance both as a cultural and as a political phenomenon. Key issues discussed will include conventions of representation, the politics of the theatre industry, the constructions of gender affecting professionals' working and personal lives, changing interpretations of gender and the contributions of women to theatre history.

ACTRESSES AS WORKING WOMEN

Their social identity in Victorian culture

Tracy C. Davis

London and New York

First published 1991
by Routledge
11 New Fetter Lane, London EC4P 4EE

Simultaneously published in the USA and Canada
by Routledge
a division of Routledge, Chapman and Hall, Inc.
29 West 35th Street, New York, NY 10001

© 1991 Tracy C. Davis

Typeset in 10/12 Palatino by
Megaron, Cardiff, Wales
Printed in Great Britain by
T.J. Press, Padstow, Cornwall

All rights reserved. No part of this book may be
reprinted or reproduced or utilized in any form or by
any electronic, mechanical, or other means, now
known or hereafter invented, including photocopying
and recording, or in any information storage or
retrieval system, without permission in writing from
the publishers.

British Library Cataloguing in Publication Data
Davis, Tracy C.
Actresses as working women: their social identity in
Victorian culture.
1. Great Britain. Theatre. Actresses, history
I. Title
792.028092

Library of Congress Cataloging in Publication Data
Davis, Tracy C.
Actresses as working women: their social identity in
Victorian culture/Tracy C. Davis.
p.   cm. — (Theatre and gender series)
Includes bibliographical references and index.
1. Theatre and society—Great Britain—History—
19th century.
2. Women in the theatre—Great Britain—History—
19th century.
3. Actresses—Great Britain.   I. Title.   II. Series.
PN2594.D34   1991
306.4'84'082—dc20   90-47664
73350
ISBN 0-415-05652-7 — ISBN 0-415-06353-1 (pbk)

CONTENTS

AUGUSTANA ^v UNIVERSITY COLLEGE
LIBRARY

Part II Conditions of work

LIST OF FIGURES AND TABLES

FIGURES

TABLES

LIST OF ILLUSTRATIONS

ACKNOWLEDGEMENTS

Research for this book has been conducted at numerous libraries and archives on two continents. Particular thanks are due to the staffs of the British Library and British Newspaper Library, British Museum Department of Prints and Drawings, General Register Office (Edinburgh), Glasgow University Archives, Greater London Record Office, Guildhall Library, Hackney Archives (Rose Lipman Library), London School of Economics (British Library of Political and Economic Science), Mander and Mitcheson Theatre Collection, Millicent Garrett Fawcett Library (City of London Polytechnic), Mitchell Library (Glasgow), Public Record Office (London), Royal Opera House Archives at Covent Garden, Theatre Museum (London), and the Victoria and Albert Museum's Department of Prints and Drawings. In North America, I am indebted to the Harvard Theatre Collection, Kinsey Institute for Research in Sex, Gender, and Reproduction, the Lilly Library (Indiana University), New York Public Library at Lincoln Centre, Queen's University at Kingston, University of Calgary, University of Illinois, University of Rochester Archives, University of Toronto, and Yale Center for British Art. Initially, the Webster endowment at Queen's University enabled me to begin work systematically. Thereafter, the Social Sciences and Humanities Research Council of Canada provided grants and fellowships at critical moments; this ongoing support was instrumental in providing the encouragement, time, and resources needed to do research.

Sections of the text incorporate revisions of articles previously published in the *American Journal of Semiotics, New Theatre Quarterly, Nineteenth Century Theatre, Nordic Theatre Studies, Queen's Quarterly, Theatre History Studies, Theatre Journal, Theatre Notebook, Popular Music,* and *Theatre Research International.*

The personal debts accrued while writing a book are always enormous. The influence of the many feminist scholars and activists who crossed my path — in person or in print — during the conception and writing of this book cannot be overemphasized. In more than one fractious situation they kept me sane, entertained, and impassioned. Without Charlene Senn, Meredith Smye, Mary Laushway Davis, Neville Davis, Miriam Stanford, Jeanne Perreault, Susan Rudy Dorscht, Susan Bennett, Garrie Ellender, Georgia Farrell, Kathleen Foreman, Jeffrey Goffin, Roberta Hamilton, and Susan Irving the task would have been joyless, and probably impossible. Professionally, Susan Bassnett, Michael Booth, Clive Barker, J. S. Bratton, Jim Davis, Jane Steadman, Richard Foulkes, Louis Knafla, David Mayer, Thais Morgan, Thomas Postlewait, and Joseph Roach commissioned, read, or responded to portions of the work in its many manifestations, and I thank them for it. Peter Davis saw the book through to completion, and in so doing was more important, in every way, than he realizes.

Every effort has been made to obtain permission to reproduce copyright material. If any proper acknowledgement has not been made, or permission not received, we would invite copyright holder to inform us of the oversight.

INTRODUCTION

This book was initially conceived as a social history of women's employment in the Victorian theatre. From that over-ambitious beginning, the project grew yet bigger. No single approach proved sufficient to tackle a question relating women's work on stage to their social existence off stage. Extensive reading in the history of women, social welfare, labour agitation, feminist politics, fine art, theatrical production, popular culture, economics, and Victorian lives strengthened the conviction that the topic is multifaceted and that conventional subject boundaries are meaningless. In order to be faithful to my findings it became clear that the complicated social existence of actresses could only be explained pluralistically, and narrative models of historical explanation were abandoned. The result is a book that poses a central question – why were actresses so equivocal in Victorian society? – five times, bringing to theatre studies five 'foreign' methodological approaches and five distinct disciplinary traditions. Only by this stratagem could a meaningful answer be approached.

While this study is concerned with women who (because they were autonomous professionals) were exceptions to their sex, it also considers factors common to all women who were self-supporting or who contributed to a family wage while bearing and raising children within or outside of marriage. I do not see how actresses' professional and personal lives can be separated; they are integrated components, and must be recognized as such in the writing of history. Only then can women be accurately assessed as artistic producers and social entities.

Employment in the Victorian theatre was ruled by distinct class and gender divisions. Community standards did not operate uniformly on all the groups: neither men and women nor the morally upright and the morally equivocal were treated uniformly. Marxist theory (which, despite doctrinaire flaws, does acknowledge an economic basis in the separation of labour from domestic spheres) and feminist theory (which, despite factional schisms, highlights the roles of both sexes and gender differences in the regulation of sexuality, the education needed for work, property and power, and women's cultural roles in shaping and reflecting society's outlook) significantly inform my analysis. I am comfortable with Linda Nicholson's characterization of socialist feminism: 'as a stance it represents less a particular theoretical position than a commitment to integrate the insights of radical feminism and Marxism.'[1] Because the theatre is an essentially public medium and social art involving the communication of ideology through living images, it tends to convey the ideology of the group that is dominant as producers and consumers of the images. I agree wholeheartedly with Lawrence Stone's list of the important historical questions for today:

> The nature of power, authority and charismatic leadership; the relation of political institutions to underlying social patterns and value systems; attitudes to youth, old age, disease, and death; sex, marriage and concubinage; birth, contraception and abortion; work, leisure and conspicuous consumption; the relationship of religion, science and magic as explanatory models of reality; the strength and direction of the emotions of love, fear, lust and hate; the impact upon people's lives and ways of looking at the world of literacy and education; the relative importance attached to different social groupings, such as the family, kin, community, nation, class and race; the strength and meaning of ritual, symbol and custom as ways of binding a community together . . . structural conflicts between status groups or classes; the means, possibilities and limitations of social mobility.[2]

Sensitivity to class and gender is a prerequisite that should be written between each line.

There is no need to justify a study of women: the struggles of the last twenty five years have settled that one question, if no more. Not everyone yet agrees that artistic activity takes place within the constraints of historical materialism and that conditions of production and consumption affect both the art practice and the practitioner, but undertaking this study of Victorian actresses has certainly convinced me of the historical logic of that principle. In Griselda Pollock's words, 'the meaning of the term woman is effectively installed in social and economic positions and it is constantly produced in language, in representations made to those people in those social and economic positions – fixing an identity, social place and sexual position and disallowing any other'.[3] This identity is constantly changing and, consequently, requires a flexible explanatory touch. I depart from Marxian philosophy by refusing to comply with its doctrinaire interpretive options. Instead, I see more affinity between feminists and advocates of the concept of *mentalité* in history. Lawrence Stone describes this as consisting of 'the deliberate vagueness, the pictorial approach, the intimate juxtaposition of history, literature, religion and art, [and] the concern for what was going on inside people's heads'.[4] This widens the scope of eligible historical sources, and delicate complicated interpretations ensue. In the case of actresses, the hard facts of theatrical legislation, business history, labour supply, legal dockets, and aesthetic innovations interact with 'soft' evidence about social beliefs, customs, and values to form the warp and woof of the cloth of history.

The different methodological approaches in this book roughly correspond to the chapters. In the first chapter, various aspects of social and labour history are addressed. Information about the organization of employment and crucial demographic and economic background is provided to lay the foundations of the arguments that follow. Women's choice to go on the stage is examined in the light of the growing 'surplus' of women needing employment, the expansion of the theatrical industry, changing attitudes to the theatre, and the gentrification of the upper ranks of the profession. This does not accept, however, the myth of the rise of the Victorian actor. Literary records, personal accounts, and professional surveys support statistical data demonstrating that the advantages of middle-class respectability attributed to the late-Victorian stage were actually enjoyed by very few performers – and even fewer women. The reality for most was a low working-class wage, social ostracism, and the constant threat of unemployment. The profession was rigidly stratified into an aristocracy of labour, reflected in the career opportunities and wages available to women; the opportunity to successfully escape the drudgery and exploitation endemic to other types of skilled and unskilled employment were minuscule in theatre, but nonetheless women persistently took the chance. Women have not been excluded from theatre history, least of all in the Victorian period, but historians have tended to focus on actresses that were extremely successful, popular, and therefore exceptional. The variety of practitioners and the bulk of unnotable women has been largely ignored, and this first chapter sets out an alternate model by specifying the nature and composition of the masses.

The second chapter incorporates research into the historical demography of the profession, relying heavily on the house-by-house censuses of Britain's largest cities (London, Glasgow, and Liverpool) to describe the social fabric of the profession in the mid-Victorian period. The growth of the industry and its social, geographic, sexual, and economic characteristics can be traced from these sources. Case histories are utilized to counteract the anonymity of statistical data. Family structures, migratory patterns, economic circumstances, and the career patterns of the working majority of performers directly resulted in calls for systematic professional welfare (unemployment insurance, sickness benefits, disability pensions, and superannuation), initially through friendly societies and charities and later as labour unions. The socio-economic and sexual balance is central to how these needs were identified and addressed. The measures taken by a sector of the profession dominated by a male middle-class clique of managers are distinct from those undertaken by women. Managers practised piecemeal philanthropy, while women recognized the root causes of hardship and addressed them directly. Each group's approach reflects their respective vested interests.

The third chapter demonstrates how economic circumstances had social consequences for women, particularly with respect to judgments about actresses' sexual morality and conduct. This is integrally related to the dichotomy of public and private spaces and beings. Women performers defied ideas of passive middle-class femininity and personified active self-sufficiency. Their visibility and notoriety in the public realm led to persistent and empirically unfounded prejudices and very real sexual dangers in their work places. All of this contradicted public relations attempts to depict actresses as home-centred, modest, self-respecting females redolent of Victorian middle-class virtues. Their public existence seemed to preclude private respectability.

The sexual equivocacy was also constantly reinforced by the theatrical conventions in which actresses were presented to male audiences as beautiful, sexual, available beings, in the compromising milieu of playhouses. The second part of the study examines conditions of actresses' work, utilizing reception theory and semiotic analyses of performance and neighbourhoods. In the fourth chapter, the effects of stage costume, gesture, and figural composition on actresses' equivocacy are detailed. There was widespread objectification of the female body, and comparisons with contemporaneous pornography reveal how this objectification corresponds to heterosexual male sexual fetishes. Popular illustrated pornography explicitly celebrated sexual commerce in content, context, and form; the frequent appearance of actresses (real and fictitious) in popular pornography demonstrates that the theatrical conventions that defied social norms were capable of receiving explicit sexual readings by spectators who were fully literate in the conventions of pornography.

The theatrical conventions in question enjoyed considerable longevity; somehow the encoded eroticism survived virtually unchanged for decades. Full understanding of the sexualized meanings in the *mise en scène* was restricted to people (invariably men) capable of recognizing the gestalt of performance in the context of the erotic neighbourhoods outside playhouses. The final chapter examines this interplay between society and theatre, and concludes by considering how the situation was perpetuated. The sexual components of performance eluded the wrath of theatrical reformers, yet never failed to attract a male audience; as long as the erotic key to decoding performance was harboured by an exclusively male literature, performance could not be received in its full import and the conventions could not be successfully challenged. As long as female performers were unwitting parties to this 'invisible' semiosis, they were subject to social ostracism and treated like sexual anathemas.

The analysis of pictorial evidence (including the physical construction of theatres, changing relationships between the audience and stage space, costuming, and placement and movement of performers) as a factor of feminist theatre history has been posited but until now has not been explored in a historical context. The visual literacy of Victorian audiences and the realization of popular and high art on the stage has been demonstrated but the function of sexualized representations has not formed a major aspect of such work.[5] Feminist philosophers and critics have discussed the phenomena of male patronage and voyeurism in fine art and film but as yet such analytical constructs have not been applied to the theatre of the past. The implications for the eroticization of the female form (and resultant status of the woman performer) are considered here – in live theatre of the historical past – for the first time. Recent theoretical writing in theatre history, socialist feminism, literature, fine art, film, cultural history, and semiotic analysis of performance all inform this work. By keeping issues of gender, class, economics, artistic custom, and social mores to the fore, actresses' stigma is understood as a socially produced meaning that served the interests of particular social groups to the disadvantage of female performers themselves.

Part I

THE PROFESSION

1

THE SOCIOECONOMIC ORGANIZATION OF THE THEATRE

Victorian performers were an unusual socioeconomic group. Unlike other professionals, they were recruited from all classes of society.[1] While performers repeatedly demonstrated that class origins could be defied by hard work, talent, or strategic marital alliances to secure some a place in the most select company, others lived with and like the most impoverished classes. Unlike other occupational groups, performers' incomes spanned the highest upper middle-class salary and the lowest working class wage, and were earned in work places that ranged in status from patent theatres to penny saloons. The heterogeneity of performers' experience, competence, salaries, and social classes made them anomalous among middle-class professionals, while the differences between their art and others' trades set them apart socially and existentially from the people of the factory, mill, and workshop. In a sense, they were everywhere and nowhere in Victorian culture, only nominally classifiable as a group, and as diverse as possible in their rank in the social pecking order.

Actresses' identity within this occupational cluster was further complicated by social constructs of their sex. All Victorian women's lives were interpreted by a male-dominated culture that defined normative rules for female sexuality, activity, and intellect. Social respectability was merited as long as women met the views prescribed for their age and class, but actresses − virtually by definition − lived and worked beyond the boundaries of propriety. Victorians were deeply suspicious of women whose livelihood depended on skills of deception and dissembling, and the circumstances of actresses' work belied any pretences to sexual *naïveté*, middle-class immobility, or feeble brain power.[2]

In his history of the Victorian acting profession, Michael Baker argues that the increased respectability of the theatre as a social institution of entertainment and culture coincided with the inclusion of acting among the professions. Educated, self-regulating, and respectable entertainers were accepted as the heart and brains of the leisure industry, resulting in what Baker calls the 'rise of the Victorian actor' to a middle-class status.[3] Baker's argument rests only on information about the most successful performers in legitimate lines of business (especially serious drama and comedy) based in the West End of London. The circumstances of the majority (including performers who were lower paid, non-legitimate, provincial, or female) are almost entirely left out of the equation. Baker dates the transcendence of (highly paid, legitimate, successful, male, West End) performers to 1883, the year that Henry Irving declined Gladstone's offer of a knighthood. Irving's subsequent behaviour and his colleagues' recognition of him in the 1880s and 90s as their foremost artistic, social, and political representative does make it appear as if the honour had been accepted, or that it was a *fait accompli* in all but the ceremony. But Irving did not accept the honour until 1895. Whatever the first and second offers of this knighthood signify about performers' status, a distinction between West End stars and the rest of the less privileged ranks remained marked long after Irving arose 'Sir Henry'.

Following the bestowal of Irving's knighthood, performers revelled in public acknowledgment of their long struggle for recognition as respectable, responsible citizens on a par with what the census designated as 'Class A' professionals (barristers, physicians, the military, and the clergy). A string of knighthoods to male West End actor-managers specializing in legitimate theatre followed: Squire Bancroft (1897), Charles Wyndham (1902), Herbert Beerbohm Tree (1907), and George Alexander (1911).[4] It is significant, however, that the first female to be thus honoured for service to the theatre (rather than raised to the honour through marriage) was Geneviève Ward, appointed D.B.E. in 1921.

Almost no actress maintained as strict standards of propriety throughout a long career as Ward. Although she managed her own company for years and enjoyed international admiration and respect, a quarter of a century elapsed between the first such recognition of the lifetime contributions of an outstanding, upright actor-manager and the granting of an equivalent honour to an outstanding, upright actress-manager. A fundamental distinction was made between Irving and Ward, and the distinction was based on gender. True, Irving was a sort of ambassador of the theatre, but so was his leading lady Ellen Terry, who received her D.B.E. thirty years later (or forty-two years after Irving's first offer of a knighthood). Terry had been the most popular and universally revered English actress of her time. She had also mothered two illegitimate children and had several marriages and numerous affairs with notable men, including, by popular rumour, the impeccable Henry Irving. Of course, by 1925, Terry had long since gone into retirement and the public that applauded her and Ward in their prime was not that which lived to call them 'Dame'. Terry's D.B.E. followed closely upon Ward's;[5] evidently, the social gulf that distinguished the daughter of itinerant players and enchanting mistress of artists and actors from the Countess de Guerbel (daughter of a scion of New York City) was at last bridged. Until the 1920s, women were prevented by their collective social status and stigmatization by the educated classes from due recognition. Similar factors prevented Charles Kean from being officially recognized for his services to the Queen in the mid-nineteenth century.[6] As long as the public regarded the theatre (or an employment subcategory within it) purely as a source of entertainment and did not take it seriously as a educative moral forum operating for the general good, performers were denied the appreciation granted to architects, sculptors, painters, and musicians.

Becoming a member of the 'actressocracy' is in no way equatable to being knighted.[7] Anastasia Robinson and Lavinia Fenton gained fortunes by wedding Charles Mordaunt (the Earl of Peterborough) and 3rd Duke of Bolton respectively, but their marriages were not sanctioned. Elizabeth Farren, Louisa Brunton, Mary Bolton, Maria Foote, Katharine Stevens, Harriett Mellon, Connie Gilchrist, Valerie Reece, and Belle Binton were socially recognized after marrying into the peerage, but permanently forfeited their careers. Irving, Bancroft, Wyndham, and Tree, in contrast, added a title which augmented their prestige in society, while continuing to do what made them meritorious. When actresses married titled gentry, their prestige and allure as performers was no longer relevant because they retired from the stage; when men received knighthoods in their own right, however, they used this official status to enhance their professional cachet, and became better box office draws than ever. Whereas the women exchanged a public life for a private life (albeit celebrated), the men became more public figures than ever, representing their profession to society. While Victorians could reason that the 'actressocrats' were chosen for an honour by one individual (who, in his crazed enamour, may have been blind to the significance of the woman's station or have been devoid of good judgment and taste), it was indisputable that the men were recognized by the monarch in her capacity as a representative of the government and all the people, and warranted general acclaim.

The social operation of gender distinctions is as apparent in the bestowal of criticism as it is with honours. The respectability of actresses was assessed on different terms from that of actors, though after Irving's knighthood it was less acceptable to say so. Victorians' failure (and perhaps refusal) to acknowledge actresses' respectability results from their defiance of socioeconomic prescriptions about genderized social roles and working spheres for 'Good Women'. Certain realms of artistic production changed significantly before Irving's career began, making possible the visually and contextually genteel accomplishments of Irving, Wyndham, Tree, and Alexander. In other realms — particularly burlesque, extravaganza, ballet, pantomime, and music hall, where women's employment was concentrated — the social stigma on female performers was perpetuated by the context in which they were presented on stage. The neighbourhoods of playhouses, costuming, and customary gestural language of the non-legitimate stage perpetuated and reinforced the traditional view of actresses. Performance genres (once they were established) changed little and reinforced rather than challenged the sexual and gender stereotypes. The circumstances of women's work conspired with socioeconomic circumstances to prevent women performers' 'rise' to social or cultural transcendence.

FAMILY DYNASTIES, RECRUITMENT, AND CAREER OPPORTUNITIES FOR WOMEN

The free trade in spoken drama (dating from the Theatre Regulation Act of 1843) took control of the theatrical industry from the hands of a few and made licences available to unlimited numbers of small and large scale entrepreneurial managers. The greater number of managements and theatres meant greater mobility of labour, a more economically competitive marketplace, and wider employment opportunities for performers. With the introduction of long runs in the 1860s came a gradual change in the nature of engagements from seasonal salaried contracts for all players to run-of-the-piece contracts for most players and waged weekly employment for players in the smallest roles. The eighteenth-century stock system dissolved in favour of companies producing single pieces, sometimes touring as number one, two, and three companies with the same piece under a single controlling management, or less often as self-contained repertory companies with two or three plays and a star. Acting style, training opportunities, and recruitment were all affected. Performers' career opportunities, which had previously tended to be focused on a provincial circuit or a particular London theatre, were decentralized and could change many times in a single year. Career pathways multiplied but the constancy of touring, the fluidity of the acting community in touring companies, and the ferocious competition for employment had an even greater effect on theatrical women than on men because of the implications for restricted variety in casting, disruptions to family life, and the premium on ties to a management giving steady employment.[8]

The localizing of the theatre community in seventeenth-century Southwark and Shoreditch, and eighteenth and early nineteenth-century Drury Lane (plus selected provincial cities) broke down in the Victorian period as the entertainment industry reached out to all corners of the nation and became as much a feature of neighbourhoods and small towns as it had previously been of large or market cities. Concentration of power in theatre-owning managerial families was challenged as more and more novices came from nontheatrical backgrounds and rose to managerial status. The erosion of family control of management and hiring expedited the opening of theatres to recruits from all sorts of backgrounds. As long as nepotism was the basis of hiring and promotion, actresses enjoyed the advantages of physical and financial security within the family compact; later, Victorian actresses from increasingly heterogeneous backgrounds were faced with the necessity of negotiating their own terms of employment, fending off unwelcome sexual advances themselves, and learning to compensate for being barred from the back rooms and club rooms of male acting society.[9]

Unlike the 'true' professions, the stage had no standardized system of examinations or qualifications, yet it was grouped on the census with the Order III professions: the clergy; barristers, officers of the courts, and law stationers; physicians, druggists, and midwives; authors and editors; artists; musicians and music teachers; schoolteachers; and engineers and scientists. These are distinct in the Victorian hierarchy from the military and civil service in

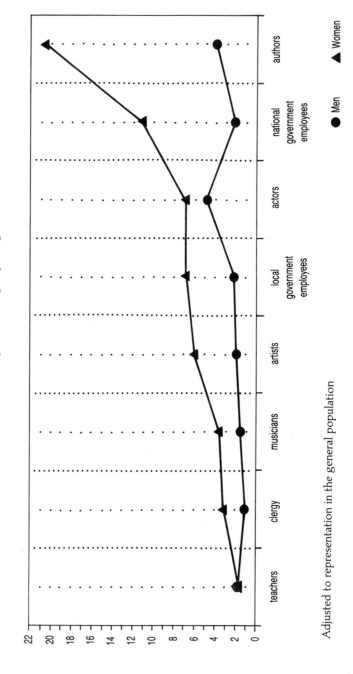

Figure 1 Multiples of increase in selected professional groups, England and Wales 1861–1911

Adjusted to representation in the general population

● Men   ▲ Women

Orders I and II. The census is a mine field of taxonomic peculiarities, and critiques of enumerators' failure to record women's occupations accurately (or to record them at all) are justified,[10] yet in the permanent absence of other comprehensive comparative data the published census is worth consideration. It shows a field into which women entered in great numbers between 1841 and 1911, equalling and then eclipsing the number of their male colleagues, despite a concurrent influx of men. Particularly in the latter period, when the spectacular increases in the acting population are more evenly shared by the sexes, it is important to read the figures in relation to three factors: (1) the influx of women into other professional groups, (2) the overall rise in population, and (3) the theatrical population in the major industrial cities.

Charting the accumulated fifty year multiples of increase into national government, local government, writing, fine art, music, acting, and teaching reveals that the theatre underwent comparatively little change in its sex ratio, second only in consistency to the teaching profession (Figure 1). The literary profession was the most affected by women's influx — more than twenty fold (X20.72) — with the national civil service next in line (X11.29). Acting had the greatest increase among men (X4.96), well above the male mean increase of X1.96; the increase of actresses is significantly greater (X7.09), though this falls below the women's mean of X9.55. Actresses' statistical growth is best compared to musicians' and music teachers' (X3.56 overall), especially when the sex ratio is involved:

	Acting (Female:Male)	Music (Female:Male)
1861	67.96:100	56.92:100
1911	101.05:100	96.32:100

Several factors slowed the increase of women musicians: certain instruments were 'off bounds' to women; until a woman virtuoso (such as Marie Hall) emerged on a particular instrument women's capacity for mastery was doubted; and women were barred from most professional orchestras (including theatres) and ghettoized in 'minor' performance types such as light concert work, soirées, and 'at homes'. Nevertheless, the cheapness of instruments and printed music, the surfeit of teachers, and the increase in the market for musicians during this period helped mitigate access problems for women and men alike, in line with the theatre.[11]

Although the sex ratio of actresses and actors in England and Wales shows a steady climb between 1841 and 1881, and a levelling off between 1881 and 1911 (Table 1), further calculations show more region-specific patterns (Table 2). The municipal patterns most closely resembling the national pattern are in London and Manchester. Liverpool follows proportionately only until 1891, when it plummets to mimic the wide curves of Birmingham and Leeds. The pattern in Scotland resembles England and Wales, though the ratio is lower, but it is extremely dissimilar to the

Table 1   The acting profession in England and Wales, from census enumerations
1841–1911

	Enumerations			Ratios	Census Increase(N)			Census Increase(%)		
Year	Female	Male	Total	Female:Male	Female	Male	Total	Female	Male	Total
1841	310	1,153	1,463	26.89:100						
1851	643	1,398	2,041	45.99:100	333	245	578	107.42	21.25	39.51
1861	891	1,311	2,202	67.96:100	248	−87	161	38.57	−6.22	7.89
1871*	1,693	1,895	3,588	89.34:100	802	584	1,386	90.01	44.55	62.94
1881	2,368	2,197	4,565	107.78:100	675	302	977	39.87	15.94	27.23
1891	3,696	3,625	7,321	101.96:100	1,040	1,428	2,756	43.92	65.00	60.37
1901	6,443	6,044	12,487	106.60:100	2,747	2,419	5,166	74.32	66.73	70.56
1911	9,171	9,076	18,247	101.05:100	2,728	3,032	5,760	42.34	50.17	46.13

Source: Published censuses of England and Wales
* The figures in the 1871 divisional table of Occupations of the People do not tally with the county or overall national tables. The amended figures here are derived from the county tables which distinguish actors from showmen and persons employed in and about theatres.

principal Scottish cities; furthermore, Glasgow's peak occurs a decade later than Edinburgh's. Edinburgh parallels Leeds and Birmingham from 1871 to 1891, but recovers a favorable ratio after 1891 while the English cities continue to decline. The meaning of these regional variations of sex ratios is, of course, subject to interpretation. The accuracy of the collected census data is highly contentious, and it may all be too flawed to be meaningful: door to door enumerations on a Sunday early in April were designed to get the best data from itinerant agricultural labourers and six-day factory workers, not performers who used Sunday as their travel day. Classifications of occupations are extraordinarily erratic, not only among the performers themselves, but by enumerators and the clerks who interpreted enumerators' schedules. Some figures, such

Table 2   Sex ratios of performers, 1841–1911 (n Women per 100 Men)

	England & Wales	London	Leeds	Man-chester	Liver-pool	Birm-ingham	Scotland	Glas-gow	Edin-burgh
1841*	26.89								
1851*	45.99								
1861	67.96	80.80	31.81	95.65	41.86	42.86	59.05	70.59	19.28
1871	89.34	108.16	100.00	101.75	95.89	78.85	79.10	33.81	58.33
1881	107.78	138.32	160.00	114.63	112.36	137.21	86.56	100.00	140.00
1891	101.96	130.92	106.25	133.33	106.14	91.14	86.83	164.15	61.54
1901	106.60	130.30	39.15	51.36	58.70	50.42	86.12	85.26	74.28
1911	101.05	121.54	33.89	100.56	34.55	39.75	71.81	65.10	89.80

Source: Published censuses of Scotland, and England and Wales
*Civic occupational data is unavailable before 1861

as Leeds', may be too small to be statistically reliable. Nevertheless, in the absence of any other source of statistical data ranging over the whole geographical area, the following interpretations are offered.

In 1871, a year of general economic prosperity and theatrical expansion, the representation of female and male performers in the major cities is the most homogeneous, averaging 9.26 per 10,000 persons, with a range of only 8.01 to 10.42 (Table 3). The tendency for theatrical agencies to locate in London and Manchester may mean that the number of 'resting' actors was concentrated in these cities, while the numbers enumerated in other centres more closely reflects not only the amount of employment actually available but also the proportion of acting jobs allocated to women. If this is true, then the marked progress toward equity in the sex ratios of Leeds, Liverpool, Birmingham, and Edinburgh between 1861 and 1871 indicates tremendous real increases in the employment available to actresses in the mid-Victorian years. The importance and reliability of the representation of actors and actresses in the general population and of the sex ratios in Leeds, Liverpool, Birmingham, and Edinburgh seems to be reinforced by the drop in both sets of numbers in these cities in 1881 (a period of general economic depression) while London and Manchester alone experienced increases. Everywhere, actresses formed a greater proportion of the profession in 1881, dominating all the figures except the Scottish total. But even in Glasgow and Manchester, which peaked in 1891, the gains were temporary; the later stability of national ratios is

Table 3 Actors in the principal cities of Britain, adjusted to representation in the general population, 1861–1911 (Number of Actors Per 10,000 People)

	London	Leeds	Liverpool	Manchester	Birmingham	Glasgow	Edinburgh
MEN							
1861	3.79	7.07	5.67	3.65	5.10	0.92	11.08
1871	4.75	4.45	5.56	4.42	5.97	6.09	6.71
1881	4.38	1.67	3.27	5.02	2.21	3.59	1.92
1891	8.38	3.59	5.99	6.33	4.53	1.91	2.18
1901	13.35	n.a.*	n.a.	n.a.	n.a.	3.30	3.07
1911	19.92	n.a.	n.a.	13.19	n.a.	3.91	3.42
WOMEN							
1861	2.67	2.01	2.23	2.96	2.02	0.57	1.72
1871	4.52	4.13	4.86	3.87	4.32	1.92	3.24
1881	5.40	2.51	3.56	5.28	2.86	3.37	2.26
1891	9.56	3.49	5.96	7.76	3.81	3.02	1.13
1901	15.13	n.a.	n.a.	n.a.	n.a.	2.67	1.83
1911	20.86	n.a.	n.a.	12.03	n.a.	2.41	2.49
MEN AND WOMEN							
1861	6.46	9.08	7.90	6.61	7.12	1.49	12.80
1871	9.27	8.58	10.42	8.29	10.29	8.01	9.95
1881	9.78	4.18	6.83	10.30	5.07	6.96	4.18
1891	17.94	7.08	11.95	14.09	8.34	4.93	3.31
1901	28.48	n.a.	n.a.	n.a.	n.a.	5.97	4.90
1911	40.78	n.a.	n.a.	25.22	n.a.	6.32	5.91

Source: Published censuses of Scotland, and England and Wales.
*not available

simply not reflected in the volatile Northern, Northwestern, and Scottish cities as the century closed.

With an expanding labour pool and changing sex ratio, the amount of employment available for women needed to undergo regular increases. In the 1860s, Clara Morris noted that advertisements for the ballet generated three applications whenever twenty were required, yet at the end of the century such advertisements inspired more responses than could be processed, and up to 200 actresses would apply for one minor part in a new drama.[12] By the end of the century, actresses were chronically over supplied. All types of 'surplus women' may have contributed to the glut, but the middle classes were best equipped to survive it. As long as the profession lacked systematic training schools with low or free tuition, middle-class recruits tutored in singing, dancing, languages, and recitation at home or in girls' schools had the best chance of getting employment in dramatic lines. At the same time, changes in audience composition, dramatic fare, and women's consciousness about work and self-sufficiency conspired to make the stage a more palatable alternative to middle-class women who formerly dismissed it.

The restriction of women's education to the 'feminine' accomplishments of music, modern languages, fine needlecrafts, and the cultivation of beauty and genteel manners prepared only a specific class of women for the theatrical world where such frivolities could be easily adapted from the drawing rooms of middle-class society to the box sets of the 1860s and after. Although the stage drew increasing numbers of middle-class recruits, the reasons for men's and women's attraction to the footlights were often different. Some circumstances (like being stagestruck) were not sex-linked traits, but others (like the fall from sexual grace, or sudden total financial self-dependence following the death of a presumed lifelong provider) were only applicable to women. According to Havelock Ellis (1894), middle-class women's socialization destined them for histrionic eminence:

> In women mental processes are usually more rapid than in men; they have also an emotional explosiveness much more marked than men possess, and more easily within call. At the same time the circumstances of women's social life have usually favoured a high degree of flexibility and adaptability as regards behaviour; and they are, again, more trained in the vocal expression both of those emotions which they [do] feel and those emotions which it is considered their duty to feel.[13]

The stage longed for and earned middle-class respectability, but there were drawbacks. As Lena Ashwell (the daughter of a clergyman cum sea captain) noted:

> [By 1929] the Theatre had become so respectable that it was the refuge for the incompetent, all those that shirked drudgery and hard work but wanted a life of ease.... I wished for the good old days of vagabondage and outlawry, when only those who had the artist temperament dared to undertake the squalor and hardship of the life.[14]

The influence of these middle-class recruits on stage manners, diction, and acting style was significant, but their influence should not be allowed to stand for their monopoly.[15] In 1892, Rudolf Dircks confidently asserted:

> The careers of histrions are all pretty much alike. They are all, or nearly all, the sons and daughters of respectable parents, who have an antipathy to the stage bordering on monomania: they all receive the usual middle-class education. ... The girl who takes to the stage has a much easier time of it [than the boy]. If she gets on at all, she does it quickly; if she is not successful within a week or two, she usually retires to the seclusion of her family circle, and is cut by the set which was wont to harken very attentively to her simple efforts at recitation.[16]

Dircks's rendition of the cultural myth of debutantes' meteoric rise to fame or quiet retreat to drawing room obscurity is a temporal implausibility. Even Irene Vanbrugh, who fits the stereotype more than anyone, sought work for six months before securing a position with J.R. Toole, and was only then successful through the intervention of Ellen Terry. Dircks is also mistaken in his conclusion that nearly all aspirants were middle-class and well educated, though the tendency for them to be so in some lines of business is demonstrable.

While the change in the sexual composition of the profession can be shown by a straightforward statistical demonstration, unless other sources of data are found the socioeconomic class of recruits cannot be represented in a set of numbers. Michael Sanderson's sample of 409 actors and 241 actresses on stage between 1890 and 1913 shows marked increases in the number of actors and particularly actresses whose social origin was among the upper or middle classes rather than the working classes (Table 4).[17] While Sanderson's figures neatly demonstrate the theses that the late-Victorian theatre experienced gentrification, that the children of middle-class theatricals looked beyond the stage for their livelihoods, and that working class encroachment was kept to a minimum, the erroneousness of the figures and conclusions should be obvious. To compile the table, Sanderson drew only upon the portion of the profession eminent enough to appear in the *Green Room Book* or to be immortalized in published biographies and autobiographies. Thus, Sanderson uses the word 'actor' generically but is actually referring to actors whose careers took specific turns; lower paid, non-legitimate, and provincial performers are not

Table 4 Occupational groupings of the parents of late-Victorian actors (by percentage)

	Debut pre-1880		Debut 1880–9		Debut 1890–1913	
	M	W	M	W	M	W
Landed or Titled	1.5	2.9	[3.2]	1.1	5.3	0.0
Professions	32.3	5.8	44.5	34.0	58.7	46.0
Commercial/Industrial	18.5	5.8	14.2	10.6	11.1	7.1
Artistic and Literary	7.7	11.8	5.8	16.0	4.2	8.8
Theatrical Occupations	36.9	70.6	29.0	37.2	18.3	35.4
Clerical/Lower Sales	1.5	0.0	1.9	0.0	0.5	1.8
Artisan/Manual	1.5	2.9	1.3	1.1	1.6	0.9

Source: Michael Sanderson, *From Irving to Olivier: A Social History of the Acting Profession in England 1880–1983*, London, Athlone, 1984

included at all.[18] Such quantitative evidence is deeply flawed: perhaps the number of middle-class recruits did increase (literary evidence suggests it did), but was this necessarily out of proportion to the growing ranks of middle-class households? Traditionally, women's choice to go on the stage was at least as much a financial imperative as an artistic inclination; what were the motivations of middle-class women from non-theatrical backgrounds, and how could anti-theatrical (and anti-women's work) prejudices be overcome?

Among the middle classes, the perception that acting was an unsuitable female occupation greatly affected the attitudes of families, peers, and audiences toward a debutante. Nevertheless, though the stage was considered anathema to middle-class women's moral upbringing, it was particularly well suited to their education and stood to benefit enormously by certain aspects of their socialization. As performers, women did not trespass on the masculine domains of science, literature, or philosophy, but the theatre required of them a curious mixture of assertiveness and self-negation, flamboyance and modesty, intellectuality and emotiveness, and active and reactive qualities. For exceptional women who were alert to the dangers and vicissitudes of life outside the home, the theatre offered a utopic world of independence, responsibility, and self-direction, but for the majority of women it offered a Pandora's Box of evils and pitfalls. As an editorial in the *Stage* explained:

> For the average trained girl to go on the stage is, in a word, hazardous. In no way has she been fitted for the career. She has always been required to give an account of her comings and

goings; she has never learnt to act without advice; she has never been taught the use of money; she has never, except in small companionships, had to fight for her own hand and order her own life. . . . [The stage] is an abrupt emancipation from the fetters – silken, it may be – of the domestic vassalage; and it is vain to pretend that so great a change of environment is unaccompanied by risk. . . . The evil is with a system of education by which the feminine nature is cribbed, cabined, and confined; so that the liberty ordinarily allowed to young men becomes liable to misconception and misuse when the stage gives it . . . to the young men's sisters fresh from home.[19]

The feminine virtue of industriousness, the study of literature, languages and music, and the preoccupation with dress and personal appearance were valuable in drawing and dressing rooms. In the theatre, however, these attributes could not be enhanced separately from the cultivation of other theatrical job skills, namely: indefatigability, worldly knowledge, self-sufficiency, mobility, and the freedom to interact with men as colleagues, admirers, pursuers, and economic equals. Therein lay the hazard.

The 4 per cent surplus of women identified in the British population in the 1850s led to a widespread recognition of the number of women who were self-supporting (by necessity or by choice) and a movement to diversify and consolidate female employment opportunities in professions and trades.[20] The arts undoubtedly offered the most accessible and suitable professional fields for middle-class women who were schooled in drawing room accomplishments (and perhaps little else) as well as some of the most desirable lines of work for lower middle-class and working-class women for whom the social stigma of acting, singing, or posturing in public was less distasteful than the rigours of manufacturing, distributive, or domestic trades. A modicum of competence, attractiveness, and good luck could provide a wage for a theatrical woman of any class or age – single, wife, or widow, alone or with children or other dependants – or it could supplement other underpaid daytime or seasonal work. Compared to teaching, the civil service, seamstressing, idleness, marriage, or obscurity, the theatre was a powerful lure for thousands of women (including those without capital, experience, or artistic talent) who entered the profession at all levels. Along with retail service, mill work, and small scale artisan trades such as watchmaking, bookbinding, and bootmaking, the theatre was acknowledged as a viable and growing trade for women.

Although its reputation was equivocal, it was a well-established field of employment for women, and possibly no more unpleasant than the traditional options. Schoolmistresses and governesses were de-classed by their occupations. As Madge Kendal asked, 'how many educated girls . . . have turned with a sigh of relief from the prospect of the stereotyped position of the companion or governess to the vista that an honourable connection with the stage holds out to them?'[21] Women who studied science were 'un-womanly' unless they derived a living by writing. Any branch of literature followed seriously and successfully by a woman branded her as a 'blue'. There were no perfect solutions. The theatre at least kept marriageable women visible, and paid while it trained.

This message was disseminated through guides to the stage, actresses' advice to newcomers, and employment manuals specific-ally addressed to women. The successful communication of these ideas to employable women is indicated by their reiteration in three-volume novels about the stage. In Mrs E.J. Burbury's novel of 1851, *Florence Sackville, or Self-Dependence,* the title character coldly considers her options following the financial ruin of her upper-middle-class family. She rejects offers of marriage that do not include guarantees of protection to her mother and sister. Being a gov-erness (like Kate Phillips) would not give her enough money to support her mother, who is too distraught to work, or her younger sister, who is too ornamental to work. When the sisters discover that only a bare subsistence can be earned by tutoring a few art and music students, Florence turns to writing fiction (like Mary Stafford). Before long, that project is abandoned because it is financially pre-carious and not really suited to Florence's disposition. Because she is tall, graceful, elegantly beautiful, well educated, spirited, discerning, and independent, she finally turns to the stage. Florence calculates the risks of a theatrical career and decides that the repercussions for her social status are not overridden by the necessity to work in an industry suited to her abilities and temperament.[22]

Fields of employment over which women exercised a controlling prerogative were usually low-paid, often seasonal, and susceptible to sudden termination when market conditions changed. For adventurous women who were willing to travel, the theatre was no more of a risk. The theatre was distinguished by several desirable characteristics unknown to any of the other occupations open to

17

women in the nineteenth century. The following conditions were unique to women's employment in the theatre:

1   In the context of career opportunities, female performers were not pioneers: the first professional English actresses emerged in 1660.
2   These professionals and their successors held exclusive rights to their occupations – men could not be actresses, ballet girls, chantresses, etc. – and competed only against other women.
3   These women neither encroached on a male labour market nor did they affect the scale of wages for men in the same trade, and so they were immune from pressures to give over their jobs to principal (male) breadwinners.
4   Public demonstration of education in the liberal arts was sanctioned and applauded in many branches of theatrical performing, and enhanced women's social and professional credibility.
5   Women and men in the theatre *generally* received equal pay for work of equal value (as assessed by box office appeal) and both had ingress to the highest ranks of management.
6   In the co-sexual work place, female performers enjoyed freedoms unknown to women in other socially sanctioned occupations.
7   The stage could be used as a springboard into marriage; this could either serve to eclipse women's original class and provide an exit to the leisured classes, or it could enhance women's stability within the trade.
8   The theatre's reputation for immorality reduced the necessity for social hypocrisy; female performers had to be worldly-wise, self-sufficient, self-determining, and hard-working and it was useless to pretend otherwise.

Rosy-eyed recruits from every class also realized that though an actress could experience as much drudgery as any domestic servant, as much insecurity and abuse as any teacher or governess, as much menial labour as any agricultural worker, the same sorts of sexual and age discrimination as women in retail trades, as much exposure to disease and depravity as nurses, and although she could know the exploitation, tedium, and physical strain of women in manufacturing and mining, the actress alone enjoyed an element of excitement and an unequalled degree of personal and sexual freedom in the practice of her trade. As Simone De Beauvoir observed: actresses might be independent and spend a lot of time with men, yet by 'making their own living and finding the meaning of their lives in their work, they escape the yoke of men . . . [and] in their self-realization, their validation of themselves as human beings, they find self-fulfillment as women.'[23] The public nature of acting and the absolute necessity of putting oneself up for general scrutiny led to an intellectual association between actress and prostitute that no other educated public woman moving in society on a pretense of her accomplishments, marriage, or breeding was saddled with. Whether or not an individual actress played on the connection between the stage and the immoral trade, acting was the only living other than prostitution in which a woman's own labour could be so financially rewarding, with the added advantage of paying regularly and predictably at such brief intervals. By comparison, the pay for literary work was irregular and uncertain. For a woman determined to maintain her career after marriage or reliant on her earnings for her own or her family's survival, the stage provided better wages than any other legitimate occupation freely accessible to a woman.

THE PROFESSION'S DIVISIONS OF LABOUR

The gender divisions of employment were overt and untransversable. Just as theatres' supplementary staff were split by custom into men's and women's employment spheres (those who built, painted, shifted, flew, lit, wired, ported, peruked, advertised, and called shows were men, and those who dressed actresses, constructed costumes, ushered audiences, and cleaned up were women), performers' specialties were defined by sex in all types of companies and for virtually all types of entertainment.[24]

The types of companies ranged from fit-ups to limited public companies. Fit-ups (or booths) were almost invariably underfinanced by one or two members who divided receipts on a commonwealth basis to compatriots who not only acted but were also the technical crew.[25] The larger sedentary companies were generally financed by a small circle of investors in cooperation with a family-based team such as the Swanboroughs, Gattis, and Batemans, or the leading performer or performance team such as Vestris and Mathews, Hare and Kendal, and the Bancrofts. Such West End theatres represented considerable investment equity and offered specialized employment, though sometimes the financial security of investors and performers had no better guarantee than in

19

a fit-up. Between these extremes of prestige lay the companies that routinely took a repertory of stock pieces around county-based circuits of theatres owned by a single individual or family (particularly in the early and middle part of the century), which usually offered seasonal contracts to proven players. The later development of numbers one, two, and three touring companies that took a single piece throughout the country following a London success usually involved contractual engagements cancellable on a fortnight's notice for small part players and longer-term contracts for the principals. The number one companies generally played for periods of a week or more in provincial cities and large towns, while number three companies might take the same piece under the same producing manager to each small centre for a single performance. Similar circuits were established between the suburban London theatres (particularly in venues also used for meetings and concerts) though it was more usual for suburban theatres to maintain a company or a piece exclusively in one venue and be quite specialized in repertoire and clientele.

London was a city of specialists. In its warehousing, manufacturing, and entertainment industries, Victorian London called on limited numbers of expert labourers for exclusive contributions to a finished product or service. Just as the 'trades which moved either to the outskirts [of London] or to the provinces tended to be those producing commodities of low value and high bulk,'[26] according to Gareth Stedman Jones, provincial and suburban theatres were less prestigious and specialized than those in London's West End (exceptions are found in Astley's circus and Sadler's Wells under Phelps). The larger sedentary companies in West End theatres could not only specialize in a type of entertainment (e.g. high class music hall, the lyric stage, or legitimate theatre) but also a genre (e.g. ballet, melodrama and pantomime, burlesque, drama, comedy, or farce).[27] The managements of West End houses were inextricably associated with their particular genre, production style, and material (e.g. the Bancrofts' social dramas at the Prince of Wales's, Harris's pantomimes at Drury Lane, the Alhambra ballet, Wyndham's society comedy, and Gilbert and Sullivan at the Savoy). By adhering to a particular product, they also determined hiring practices.

After the industrial transformation of the Northern and Midland counties, London functioned as a small-scale production and distribution centre for finished consumer goods and the luxury trades. The theatre fitted admirably into this pattern, though by the mid-century it was more labour intensive than most industries. Stedman Jones estimated that in 1851, '86 per cent of London employers employed less than ten men each. In fact there were only twelve factories recorded as employing more than 300 men, and the majority of these, significantly, were engaged in textiles and engineering'.[28] In 1860, E.T. Smith claimed that during pantomime season Drury Lane employed nearly 400 people, Her Majesty's over 300, and the Alhambra about 300, so that a single theatrical lessee retained 1000 employees in three houses.[29] A few years later, the skilled labourers of a single theatre could rival this sum. Michael Booth writes:

> At Christmas time the size of the Drury Lane company, including all staff of whatever description, would be at least double the number employed at any other time of the year except during the autumn drama. Even in 1865, in the pre-Harris years, it was estimated that the total theatre staff for *Little King Pipkin* was nearly 900, including 200 children, 60 in the ballet, 48 seamstresses and wardrobe ladies, 45 dressers, and 17 gasmen.[30]

The orchestra, front of house, carpenters, stagehands, firemen, propertymen, actors, prompters, callboys, cleaners, and management are also included in the 900. In 1891, the Alhambra's *Oriella* ballet employed between eighty and a hundred women – and this was only one turn on a long bill.[31]

The geographical mecca of most performers was London, or more precisely the West End, though there are notable exceptions. Regional loyalty resulting from familial and financial entrenchment kept Mrs Baker in Kent; the anachronistic performance style and material of booth theatres were unsuited to Victorian London, and some performers (particularly actresses from the middle classes) preferred not to be seen by London Society.[32] Establishment in a London theatre in any performing capacity did not necessarily result in the professional (and hence domestic) stability that it implies; London was the chief market of hiring for the lucrative provincial summer tours and long overseas tours of months or years duration for which performers forfeited the stability of a permanent residence. London engagements could be the most secure for those in the lowest ranks, particularly dancers and choristers, who could find employment in houses specializing year-round in an appropriate type of entertainment (e.g. the Crystal Palace, Alhambra,

Empire, and Gaiety), whereas employment in such capacities in the provinces was rare between pantomime seasons.

Some specializations rendered performers more employable than others. The theatrical specializations open to women were many, and in contrast to lines of business they crossed types of entertainment as well as genres. 'Lines of business' designated the employment opportunities in legitimate theatre making up the personae of The Drama (comedy, serio-drama, and melodrama): walking lady, lead, heavy, ingenue (juvenile business), character, utility, supernumerary, old woman, and soubrette. Farce included a few of its own lines, such as character comediennes, but the usual one-act format subordinated the farce to the main piece (The Drama) and utilized the same company of players.

The progression from walking ladies, who 'have been said to derive their appellation from the fact of their being always ready to escape from their father, aunt, or guardian, and walk off with their lover',[33] to leading business was natural. Walking ladies are the Jessicas, Colleen Ruaidhs, and Mrs Quesnels of the Drama and are trials for bigger business such as Portias, Colleen Bawns, and Rebellious Susans. Leading business generally, though not necessarily, meant dramatic roles; exceptions are Eliza Vestris, the young Marie Wilton, and Ellen Farren. The progression from leading lady to heavy business (Emilia, Gertrude, Lady Audley, etc.) was an honorable concession to maturity and experience. As financial circumstances and personal following allowed, leading or heavy business could be coupled with management.

Ingenues provided the love interest in the plays, minimally differentiated. Character actresses, however, played the low comedy, dialects, some adventuresses, and eccentrics. Utility designates the competent actress who took minor parts, often double or triple-cast in stock companies and spectacles. 'Utility' and 'character' are sometimes used interchangeably, but both are distinct from the supernumerary (or walk-on) who did not speak and was engaged by the night rather than by the week. The amount of employment for supers is difficult to determine, as they were usually excluded from the bills.[34] Leman Rede observed that old women was the safest line for an actress in 1836, but only if she was not actually old; for young actresses, the old women line was a character specialty.[35]

The soubrette could cross from the Drama to musical genres. She was typically a 'short, somewhat stout, white-toothed, sweet-breathed, snub nosed, black-eyed, broad-hipped Hebe who played

... "the Chambermaid." She possessed a good voice, could sing by ear, and had a saucy way of tossing her head that was half-boyish, half-hoydenish, and wholly captivating.' When Robertson wrote this in 1864, the soubrette had already been transformed from supporting business to a sexual beauty with star billing; she had been 'eclipsed by a more vivid, more dazzling, more spangly star – the Burlesque Actress, who now rules the hours between nine and twelve p.m., as sure as legs are legs'.[36] Musical ability, either as a singer or lady-pianist, was never a disadvantage, and burlesque specialists thrived when they combined a good voice with the preferred physical proportions. The re-invented soubrette found plentiful employment in burlesque, pantomime, and (in the last years of the century) musical comedy in the Gaiety style.

Lines of business decreased in importance as the stock system degenerated, and actresses complained of being locked into a part rather than a type. Minimal training, challenge, and artistic development often plagued the young women who found sub-sistence but not fulfillment by speaking a few lines in the same piece (on tour or in the West End) for weeks, months, or years in succession. In 1896, Davenport Adams observed that just as utility walking gents and ladies had disappeared (replaced by boring juveniles and insipid ingenues), singing soubrettes similar to the young Vestris and Mrs Keeley were recruited into musical comedy, not Drama, and refined singers from the Royal College of Music and the Guildhall usually could not act – walking on and off was the extent of their stage ability. Sentimental balladists were plentiful, but seriocomic ones were almost all in the music halls.[37] This was a consequence of streamlining bills to a single dramatic piece without song, a trend instigated by the Bancrofts.

'Specialties' preceded and outlasted 'lines of business'. Specialties are defined by the skills required for employment (acting is presumably a requirement of all). Skill at dancing, for example, was a requirement of burlesque artists, ballet girls, pantomime boys (who were frequently soubrettes or, in the later decades, music hall stars), and aerial figurantes (flying specialists). A good singing voice was required of choristers, minstrels, extras, and sometimes the ballet. Competence at singing and dancing was not *always* a requisite of the chorus, particularly at the Gaiety.

The Gaiety Girl had not suffered the agony of a long classical ballet training; she may not even have come up through the rigours of pantomime. She had to be able to walk well, move elegantly, and wear expensive costumes with dignity and poise. In a sense, *the chorus*, at the Gaiety, were choristers – ladies who sang their hearts out, unseen, behind a convenient 'flat'. The Girl, meanwhile, sat (beautifully) while the star did a number – perhaps moving an elegant arm in time to the music, pointing a neat foot in one direction, then another, and walking sinuously around the stage.[38]

Among dancers, therefore, the Gaiety Girl is a special case. Equestriennes were not limited to the circus ring, but were engaged as specialty acts in legitimate and other non-legitimate theatrical forms, just as gymnasts, tightrope walkers, and animal trainers sometimes found employment in circus, music hall, and melodrama. Whenever it was advantageous, music hall artistes such as singers, comediennes (though there were few non-singing female comics), topical vocalists, and specialty dancers crossed back and forth between the halls and the theatres featuring pantomime or burlesque.

WAGES

It has already been pointed out that women could make as much money as men in the Victorian theatre. When box office appeal was the deciding factor in contract negotiations, the drawing power of the performer was the most important consideration. Managers' assessment of the public demand for a performer determined the quotient of expenditure to profit.[39] Performers who had some bargaining power in this respect could set very favorable terms: in 1801, managers vied to pay Mrs Billington £3,000 for the season, plus a clear benefit; toward the end of her career, Maria Foote is said to have received £951 16s. for three nights in Nottingham; in the 1880s, Lillie Langtry received £250 a week for appearing with the Bancrofts in *Ours*; and in the 1890s, Ellen Terry earned £200 a week, though Letty Lind was reputed to be the highest paid English actress of her era.[40] As Cyril Ehrlich points out for the music profession, reports of salaries could be inflated or deflated in order to make a particular impression, but the range of earnings was certainly great.[41] The exorbitant salaries of a few late Victorian performers do not reflect the standards of the whole century or the whole of Great Britain.

The earliest payrolls of Manchester music halls totalled less than £50 a week, though later popular performers like G.H. Macdermott earned £20 a turn, and in 1893 yearly earnings for individuals were as high as £1,500.[42] According to George Foster, Ada Reeve did a nine week tour of South Africa for £5,000.[43] In 1875, Charles Booth recorded wage rates at working men's clubs between 3s. 6d. and 5s. a turn, small music halls at 20s. a week for the worst acts and £3 to £7 a week for stars, and West End halls at £4 a week for padding or first turns and £25 a week for later turns. This meant that for a good performer whose evening rounds consisted of 'two early turns at £9 each, two good turns at £25 and one late turn at £12 . . . £80 a week for five turns per night, would be possible'.[44] This indicates that the halls could be considerably more lucrative than theatres.

Early in the century, annual salaries at the Haymarket ranged between £75 and £2,365 for singers and £40 and £1,537 for dancers.[45] By comparison, the incomes of legitimate performers seem remarkably low: Sarah Siddons never made more than £12 a night; John Phillip Kemble, as manager and leading man of Covent Garden, received £6 a night; and George Frederick Cooke and Eliza O'Neill made £5 and £6 a night respectively. The highest salary received by Ellen Tree before she went to America was £15 a week.[46] Performers' salaries increased markedly between 1870 and 1885, when a popular soubrette/burlesque actress could expect between £10 and £20 a week without being a pre-eminent exponent of her line of business. By 1885, a leading comedy actress could earn between £20 and £40 a week, and a popular prima donna in opera-bouffe could make from £40 to £50 a week.[47] Katti Lanner — ballet teacher, choreographer, and contractor to leading companies from 1877 — listed the pay rates of child dancers as 1 to 2s. a performance, older girls as £4 to £8 a month, free-lance adults as £12 to £18 a month, seconda donnas as £20 to £25 a month, and star soloists as £750 to £2000 a year.[48]

Such rates were not universal. Many players earned less in a year than others earned in a week, and the benefit system (while it was in place) rarely made up the difference. Ann Catherine Holbrook states that in 1809, provincial wages averaged £1 6s. 3d. a week,[49] and Leman Rede's list of wages in principal provincial theatres in 1836 shows a range between 18s. and £2 10s., with most between £1 and £2.[50] This indicates that there was no effective change in the first third of the century. Before she married Charles Calvert in 1856, Adelaide Biddles and her sister Clara earned a combined salary of

£2 7s. playing lead and walking business at Southampton.[51] One source states that in 1853 the maximum rate was £3 to £6 a week,[52] but Mayhew indicates that in 1856, 15s. was a common wage in fit-ups.[53] The same low wage is recorded in the 1890s, when touring actresses could be paid as little as £2 a week for utility parts in a number one company, 30s. in number two and three companies, and as little as 15s. in fit-ups under provincial managements.[54]

The earnings of popular performers could rise very quickly. Marie Bancroft's first London salary was £3 a week (1856), which climbed to £15 at the Adelphi (1857–8).[55] Marie Kendall was paid 30s a week for singing 'My Old Man is one of the Boys, and I am one of the Girls' at the Bedford Music Hall, where she showed such promise that her next engagement was as a principal boy at £15 a week.[56] As a leading article in the *Stage* points out, 'there is nothing to prevent an artist who is getting £2 10s. a week obtaining £80 a week a few years later'.[57] Fitzroy Gardner, Tree's business manager, tried this principle in 1907:

> I have just been looking through some notes on salaries paid about ten years ago by managements with which I was connected. Of fifteen names on one list there are eight of actors whose weekly salaries are now on an average over 100 percent more than they were then, and one against whose name £4 stands on my notes but who is now receiving £50 or £60. Among other notes I find against the name of an actress, now refusing engagements at less than £25 a week, a remark entered in my book only five years ago, 'Decidedly promising. Asks £4, might take less.'[58]

Of course, those who fell by the wayside or whose careers took a downward turn were no longer in Gardner's purview. Salaries did not necessariiy follow a predictable upward curve. Few contemporary managers other than Tree, Wyndham, Alexander, Edwardes, Hollingshead, and Irving could afford to pay high salaries at all, and the highly paid formed a minority even in the best establishments. Gardner estimated that only a quarter of the 600 actors, actresses, and choristers employed yearly in the West End were paid as much as £10 a week. Touring wages, he observed, had recently declined so that in suburban and provincial companies (including fit-ups) visiting permanent theatres, town halls, and assembly rooms no more than 100 of the 6,000 or so performers earned as much as £10 a week. 'Considering the large proportion of

£1 and £1 10s. salaries, especially in the "fit-ups", the average provincial company salary may be roughly estimated at £2 5s.[59] Rates varied from theatre to theatre, but in the lowest paid lines of business there is little overall increase until the end of the century. In 1851 supers were paid 1s. a night, in 1870 Kate Phillips made her first appearances at the Lyceum for 9s. a week (including matinees),[60] but in 1894 one source gives extras' wage rates as 15s. to 20s. or as high as 21s. in the best theatres.[61] In 1895, the Choristers' Association advocated the minimum wage of £2 a week in the provinces and 5s. a performance in London;[62] this seems to be a call for standardization and not just a rise in wage rates.

Wage rates for the rank and file were determined by a common scale reflecting the type of company, location or touring circuit, and performer's line of business; capitalist managers exacted the most work for the least pay, and both men and women were exploited and under-rewarded. As with other highly skilled crafts, London drew the cream of provincial talent.[63] The surplus of skilled and unskilled labour in London ensured that wage rates remained low for dancers, choristers, and supers alike. The distinction between wage rates in major and minor (or suburban) houses is the same distinction that is made between the West End and the provinces. West End theatres offered the highest salaries, though of course the increased cost of living and dreadful housing conditions in London meant that the advantage was effectively obliterated for performers in the lowest ranks.

Following from these basic observations about Victorian pay scales for common players, three generalizations demand close examination:

1 *The principle of an equal wage for work of equal value*
Cicely Hamilton, whose acting experience was gained prior to the First World War, and mainly in the 1890s, insisted that the concept of equal pay for men and women was not applicable to the lower ranks.[64] Leppington's table of wage rates documents that in 1891 the weekly wages of male chorus singers started at the ceiling rate of female choristers: 30s. to 40s. for men compared to 25s. to 30s. for women.[65] The best comic opera houses could pay more. Though the Gaiety management insisted its rate was 30s., in 1896 a female singer successfully sued for back pay of 35s. a week,[66] which is still lower than Leppington's rate for men. The female choristers' work was not of an inferior class, just lower paid.

Leppington's table shows that male and female supers were each paid between 1s. 6d. and 2s. a night in first-rate theatres, and 1s. to 1s. 6d. in most minors. Although the wage rates seem to indicate parity, women supers were only provided with their wardrobe in West End and touring original-cast productions. Otherwise, Hamilton claims that women were always expected to supply their own gowns for modern plays, and occasionally for period plays also:

> In companies (such as Edmund Tearle's) which ran costume plays, clothes would be provided for the men of the cast, [but] the women often had to find their own – and, if their dresses were not considered suitable, the management looked at them askance.[67]

Even when the basic rate was at par, the take-home pay was different for men and women. The plenitude of female novices for this kind of work (especially after 1871) meant that employers could choose only those who agreed to put up with the inequity. In this respect, the theatre was no different from manufacturing, distributive, and agricultural trades that devalued women's labour and got away with paying women at a lower rate because competition for their jobs was so high. The situation endured because there was only isolated resistance from a disorganized labour force.[68] Experienced actresses frequently complained about the preference for moneyed and well-dressed women who usurped the tradition of apprenticeship into the craft by quite literally dressing their way onto the stage, or outbidding women who actually worked for their livings, but since it was in managers' interest to hire the best-dressed supers, the complaints were disregarded.

The notion of equal pay for work of equal value is also contradicted by the practice of joint salaries. Married couples in provincial touring companies, for example, were sometimes paid the single wage of £3 10s., whereas a comedian made £2 alone. Instances of couples in severely reduced circumstances (or unsuccessful in finding employment in separate companies) accepting joint engagements are peppered throughout the nineteenth century. In 1809, Holbrook described the hardship of a jointly salaried family:

> A married couple, whose united salaries amounted to [£]2 10s. per week, travelled in three months 280 miles: [£]14 was thus wrested from them [for fares]; of [£]30 only [£]16 remained, which reduced their income to [L]1 6s. 8d. taking from this 8s. or 10s. weekly for lodging.[69]

While there were advantages to working in the same company (child care, maintenance of family life and conjugal felicity, lower expenses, and likely a more pleasant working situation for the woman) the financial penalty could be substantial. In 1891, another couple took the pitifully low joint salary of £1 15s.[70] In such cases where neither performer commanded enough box office clout to have bargaining power with the manager, the husband and the wife were hired as an exploitable conjunct unit, not as autonomous individuals.

Nevertheless, the concept of acting as a serious career and independent livelihood for single women of middle and low ranks was accepted by the law courts in two separate cases of 1893. A Birmingham actress named Ada Juneen gave up the stage and sold her wardrobe and jewels upon engagement to an Australian resident named Charles Buxton. Juneen waited between four and five years then sued Buxton for breach of promise to marry, demanding £5,000. A New South Wales jury awarded her £1,500 in damages.[71] In another case, Harriet Richardson (a chorus singer) sued Mr Anderson (a senior partner in a firm of wine and spirit merchants) for misleading her about his marital status. She suspended her theatrical engagements for a year in anticipation of marriage, forfeiting as much as £104 if she had been employed during the entire period; when it was disclosed that Anderson had a wife living, a jury awarded Richardson £150.[72] In both cases, Juneen and Richardson were compensated for loss of professional momentum, as well as income. They are distinct from the Marjoribanks case of the same year, wherein Miss Watkins (the Gaiety Girl known as Birdie Sutherland) sued the son of Lord Tweedmouth for breach of promise to marry and won £5,000 in compensation, plus costs.[73]

2 Theatrical and industrial wage rates for women

The lowest paid performers did not necessarily make more than other working-class women with comparable experience in a trade. Very few ballet dancers, perhaps only 1 per cent, made large wages (even Genée was paid only £15 a week when she joined the Empire in 1897, and she retired on £70 a week).[74] The highest figure given for corps dancers is £6 (1897). Most ballet dancers made between 10 and 15s. a week for dancing in the back row, 15 to 30s. for the middle rows, and 35 to 38s. as coryphées in the first row.[75] The rates for chorus girls (who sang and danced – or at least postured) are no higher. Most ballet girls served an apprenticeship or studied dance in their childhood or teenage years, and yet they joined the corps for the same wages that women expected as cotton workers, tailors, or milliners.[76]

For unskilled women from the lower classes, the stage seemed to offer an exorbitant rate of pay for comparatively light and varied labour. To a Liverpudlian fruit picker receiving 7 or 8s. a week or a jam factory hand earning between 8 and 10s. a week in season,[77] the ballet dancer's 10 to 38s. seemed a fortune, and the London comedy actress's £20 to £40 truly was one. In fact, the average annual income of performers lucky enough to be employed forty two weeks in the year was calculated to be only £105, or £2 a week.[78] An even lower estimate (provided by the Actor's Association in 1914) was £70 a year, which was reduced by half after job-related expenses were deducted, leaving a weekly wage of approximately 12s. 6d.,[79] a typical figure for working-class women of the period[80] and well below the £100 mark associated with a membership in the middle class.[81] For the actress who was constantly putting up in temporary lodgings while in the country, buying omnibus fares while in the city, eating from other women's kitchens, dressing to look respectable, paying for stamps and telegrams, or helping to support a child, parent, or husband, 12s. 6d. (or even £2) a week indicates constant distress. Other statistics demonstrate just how widespread the distress was. Between 1888 and 1895, the Actors' Benevolent Fund dispensed a yearly average of £1,821 of relief to 870 needy legitimate actors and actresses. This represents more than 10 per cent of the pool each and every year.[82]

Many dancers made another wage while working in the theatre. It is impossible to determine whether the theatre was their principal employment (supplemented by daytime or seasonal work) or whether the theatre was their secondary employment (one form of seasonal work among several). Up to two-thirds of the dancers and aerial figurantes in regular employment at the Alhambra and Empire music halls were dressmakers, tailors, shop girls, and factory hands;[83] in such cases the aggregate wage was relatively good, though the personal toll of a double working day must have been enormous. Dancers' additional costs of tights (8 to 10s. for a pair of worsted, and 30 to 40s. for good silk) and shoes (2s. 6d. to 5s. every three or four weeks)[84] substantially consumed any second wage. During periods when daytime rehearsals of a new piece and evening performances of an old piece were called, dancers and choristers who normally worked two jobs lost the daytime wage. The lost wages were not made up by the theatre, for rehearsals were unpaid everywhere until very late in the century; for actors and actresses this could mean three to four weeks unpaid labour prior to the opening of each new piece, but dancers and choristers in comic opera (well-trained terpsichoreans and musicians) could be in full-time unpaid employment for eight to ten weeks before each original production. Gardner calculated the out of pocket costs of a three week rehearsal (lodgings and board extra):

> Among the many hardships suffered by the 'small people' of a London company is not only the non-productiveness of rehearsal periods, but the expense attached thereto. For instance, the daily railway or omnibus fare and frugal luncheon, costing together an average of eighteen-pence a day, will have amounted to about 30s., or perhaps nearly a week's salary, by the time the salary commences.[85]

Auxiliaries, such as choristers and dancers, were disqualified from receiving help from the Actors' Benevolent Fund, their wages prohibited most of them from subscribing to insurance plans, and the one theatrical charity for which they were qualified (the Dramatic, Equestrian, and Musical Sick Fund benevolent branch) gave away a mere £258 in 1883. Only highly paid actors could force managements to compensate them for spending weeks in rehearsal.[86] Half pay, when granted, was bestowed as a favour not a right. Choruses were often reduced after a few weeks, and if the show closed prematurely choristers faced another unremunerative rehearsal period.[87] Persistent lobbying by the Choristers' and Actors' Associations in the 90s resulted in only 6s. on £1 1s. salaries being granted (for dancers and supers), and 12s. 6d. on £3 salaries.[88] Matinees sometimes paid only half the rate of evening per-formances, if anything, and further restricted daytime employment (including the hours available for tutoring young dancers).

Actresses of the legitimate stage also had professional costs apart from their performing wardrobes. Like women in other trades where personal appearance was considered important, actresses were required to look their best at all times. Maude Royden draws a parallel between the situations of actresses and office typists. Although she exaggerates when she says that the discrepancy between income and expenses necessarily led to prostitution, her point about a budgetary deficiency is salient:

The position of typists and chorus-girls is similar in the need of both for wages largely in excess of the sum necessary for food and shelter and clothing. The wages of typists who have no special commercial training or knowledge of foreign languages vary from 7s. 6d. to £1 10s. a week; but in all cases they must dress like respectable middle-class girls. The chorus-girl or beginner on the stage cannot earn more than £2 2s. or £3 3s. a week; but she must present an appearance of physical wellbeing and must wear 'smart' striking clothes.[89]

With the addition of travelling expenses, personal accessories, stationery, and postage, the actress's advantage was soon whittled away.

For an actor earning £67 10s., Daisy Halling and Charles Lister calculated an average yearly expenditure:

Lodgings	£13	0s.
Washing	5	4
Wardrobe	10	0
Newspapers and Tobacco	5	0
TOTAL	£33	4s.

Actresses would not have as high an expenditure for the last item, but would have had higher outlay on wardrobe.[90] The difference between £67 10s. and £33 4s. would disappear on insurance premiums, incidental travel expenses, and food, while the rest was laid by for the inevitable periods of unemployment. The result for most actresses was an average yearly wage considerably less than that of lower-middle-class working women. Comparing Halling and Lister's clothing allowance of about £15 and Clara Collet's statistics on the incomes and expenditures of educated working women, it becomes clear that actresses dressed no better than school mistresses who expended between £10 and £16 a year on wardrobe (out of £100 to £130 salaries), and considerably worse than a female clerk who spent £41 and a journalist who spent £42 on clothing (out of £227 and £338 salaries).[91] The education needed for any of these jobs was comparable. A few actresses could make a great deal more than teachers, clerks, and journalists, but most made a great deal less in real terms.

While adult theatrical wage rates were usually lower than those for comparably educated and experienced women from the middle and lower-middle classes, children gained a considerable financial advantage through theatrical employment. Statistics show that children's wages were of real benefit to them and that the rate of pay was exceptionally attractive, especially for girls. An 1897 study reveals that boys could expect between 1d. and $1\frac{1}{4}$d. per hour for delivering milk, coal, or newspapers, or for working in a shop. One barber's boy earned 2s. 6d. plus food for working more than thirty hours per week. In contrast, girls tended to remain in domestic industries, and there a 10-year-old might earn 6d. and food for minding a baby for forty-two hours a week. A 7-year-old girl helping a landlady to clean for several hours a day earned only a few pennies a week. One 11 year old girl working every night for four and a half hours in a shop earned a total of 1s. a week. Another girl received 2d. and her food for turning a mangle for three and a half hours daily and for ten hours on Saturdays. Matchbox makers working in all their out of school hours and on weekends made 6d. per gross. At the top end of the scale, a 12-year-old brushmaker earned 3s. for her week's labour. Rates of pay higher than 1s. a week were exceptional for female children.[92]

In the late-Victorian theatre, however, male and female children could earn between 3d. and 6d. a night for dancing in provincial pantomimes,[93] or between 6d. and 1s. in London. As they became more experienced, child pantomime supers could earn up to 8s. a week at Drury Lane or 3s. at minor theatres, and between £1 and £3 for chief parts at Drury Lane, or 10 to 20s. at the minors.[94] Children on one musical tour received 15s. a week, and the principals earned between £2 and £5 plus travelling expenses.[95] These rates of pay are comparatively generous, even though wages were only paid from the last week of rehearsals, leaving from two to five weeks of labour unpaid. When they could get them, managers preferred girls to boys because they were more attentive to authorities; along with the custom of using females for boyish and adolescent parts, this gave girls the competitive and pecuniary edge, as well as valuable experience for adult careers.

3 Theatrical wages and provision for unemployment
Whereas women in manufacturing trades could expect from four to six weeks of pay to be deducted for illness, slackness of trade, and half-time seasons, performers' off-time was much greater.[96] Estimates of the average number of weeks performers were in work vary, but Halling and Lister concur with an American source that suggests that thirty weeks is a reasonable figure. Gardner is more pessimistic, stating that twelve weeks were to be expected

(presumably the pantomime season) and agreeing with an anonymous dancer who states that half of all performers are employed
only six months in the year.[97] This phenomenon was endemic
throughout the ranks:

> A case occurs to me of a versatile young actor, who has had
> excellent Press notices, whose salary is about £8 a week, but
> who has recently 'rested' for thirteen consecutive months; and
> another one of a clever, cultured, small-part actress who, after
> working for fourteen out of eighteen months, waited in vain
> for another engagement for six months, and was then obliged
> to accept a situation in a milliner's workroom, where, I believe,
> she now remains; and of a lady of the first rank in the
> profession, who has received and earned £80 a week, who
> 'rests' over forty weeks in the year.[98]

The number of 'resting' performers was, therefore, substantial.
Hibbert generously estimates that of 3,000 (actually 4,057) women
in London who called themselves actresses (including dancers and
supers), no more than two-thirds had regular work. Taking a £2
wage (which is what the Actors' Association lobbied for) as a good
case, a twelve week working year would give an average weekly
wage of less than 10s. The Women's Trade Union League estimated
the average wage of a manual worker to be 7s. 6d., taking into
account the huge disparities between East London homeworkers
whose wages sometimes dropped to 2s. 6d., and the relatively
affluent unionized Lancastrian textile workers whose wages averaged
higher than 15s.[99] A woman could survive on 10s. a week, but the
wage table of an upholsteress indicates the scale of economies.[100]

Room	2s.	6d.
Coals and Wood	0	9
Light	0	$1\frac{1}{2}$
Bread, butter, milk, tea, and sugar	2	$4\frac{1}{2}$
Sunday dinner	0	9
Daily dinner at home	1	6
Washing	0	6
Clothes and boots	1	0
Doctor, if ill, or omnibuses in bad weather	0	6
TOTAL	10s.	0d.

The annual clothing allowance of £2 14s. barely sufficed for an
upholsteress, but seriously jeopardized an actress's employability.

The unemployment problem was particularly acute for women in legitimate drama, where the ratio of roles for men and women was approximately two to one, but the genres where women found more employment than men (burlesque, extravaganza, ballet, and pantomime) were those that either engaged a corps for an eight to ten month season or hired only during the Christmas period. In either case, the competition among women was ferocious and the summer was always a slack season. Established actresses exhorted women in tedious but steadily-paying jobs in industry and service trades not to give up their livelihoods for the stage; their laments about the unemployment rate for untrained women were ceaseless.

The evidence clearly shows enormous variation in wage rates for different performers, with extreme hardship at the lower end of the scale. Women's sufferings were particularly acute, for their basic rates of pay were lower, their professional expenses were higher, and their competition for employment grew more intense in the latter decades of the century. Undeterred, they continued to crowd into the profession from all walks of life, even though the only time their wages were likely to exceed industrial rates was in childhood. Hardship was greatest for women in precariously financed itinerant booth companies, but every performer shared the uncertainty of employment termination endlessly throughout their careers no matter what type of company, line or business, or geographical location they played. Low and uncertain wages could have particular consequences for women, and undoubtedly fuelled popular beliefs about their characters. The theatre blossomed as an employment sphere for women after 1843, and the allure of footlights grew more intense as starring wages escalated in the mid-century, but it was no panacea for 'surplus women' and an unattractive alternative in real terms to the drudgery, exploitation, and hazards of needle and domestic trades, teaching and retailing, or industrial and manufacturing jobs.

2

SEX, GENDER, AND SOCIAL DEMOGRAPHY

HISTORIOGRAPHY AND THE WEST END ACTOR

The competitive employment market that characterized the 1880s and 90s led managers to establish systematic training schools compensating for the loss of the stock system and certifying that at least a few debutantes had knowledge of the basic principles of stage art and an adequate smattering of the middle-class graces and accomplishments useful in genteel drama and comedy. Even those who were trained and experienced found difficulty obtaining work when they reached an unfashionable age, and their difficulty only increased with the onset of true maturity. The career patterns of women and the reasons for their unemployment were, therefore, different from men and almost entirely beyond individuals' control. With the influx of women into the theatre from the 1850s onward, the profession was forced to deal with the welfare of an essential, large, and identifiable sector of the work force that voiced specific problems about their wage rates, unemployment, training, re-cruitment, and working conditions. From mid-century the socio-economic characteristics of employment conjoined with a new demographic reality to highlight certain difficulties and provide a lever for change.

As the theatrical industry expanded, enormous numbers of employment opportunities were created. There were far more jobs than could possibly all be filled by the children of theatrical parents, and the nepotic tradition was weakened. The theatrical life was alluring and active recruitment was not necessary to enlist apprentices; instead, performers actively discouraged would-be newcomers, partly in the attempt to limit oversupply by dissuading the least suitable novices. Anti-enlistment propaganda concen-trated on themes that also reveal the class dynamics of green room

36

politics. While managers argued that 'it is from the drawing-room, not from the factory, that our future actresses *must* come',[1] performers complained that the influx of the moneyed, titled, and bored must be curbed or else bona fide actors would find it impossible to obtain minor parts. It seems that with increasing production costs managers gave preference to women who could supply their own 100 guinea costumes and men whose family names attracted a curious upper-class audience. Bona fide performers wanted to foster an image of gentility, but not by the perverse use of affirmative action on behalf of this under represented group.

As the theatrical repertoire diversified, people from all walks of life increasingly perceived performing as a viable occupation. Paradoxically, another anti-enlistment theme urged the ambitious self-confident individualists accustomed to long factory shifts, physical labour, obsequious service, seasonal employment, and financial want to stay away from the theatre even though their life skills were ideally suited to making a living on the overcrowded mid- and late-Victorian stage. Managers and actors united in their attempts to discourage new recruits 'from shop and factory, from the loom, from dress-making, even from domestic service.... Impressionable young women for the greater part, with no education to speak of and little discrimination to help them in realizing their position'.[2] This was, in some respects, a gesture of protective kindness, though the citation of begging letters rattling with split infinitives, misspellings, dialect words, and *naïveté* also had a condescending purpose to demarcate the successful performer from the bumptious pretender. Apparently, the system of sponsored mobility was never intended to include the working class. Historians have assumed that the exercise of choice in encouraging or discouraging certain classes of recruits is indicative of the theatre's rising status and the gentrification of the profession, yet by the last decades of the century there is much empirical evidence suggesting that in such exhortations performers were actually appealing to their own socioeconomic group – or the group into which they were born – to follow a more traditional path.

The evidence is found through detailed analysis of the manuscript censuses of 1861 and 1881. These documents show that however respectable actor-managers and leading players became by the late-Victorian years, the rank and file maintained a different demographic profile, dwelt in neighbourhoods dominated by the artisan and semiskilled labouring classes, and were lodgers rather than owning or renting their housing. In other Victorian industries the owners, shareholders, and superintendents were distinct from those on the factory floor, in the workshop, and down the pit. It should not be surprising, therefore, to find that those who have been catalogued and lionized are noticeably different from the majority of practitioners. The theatre was a classed work place which institutionalized socioeconomic and demographic differences in its hierarchies. As the theatre expanded, the impulse to aggrandize the West End increased exponentially. The historical demography of West End stars should not, however, be substituted for that of the industry as a whole.

The movement known as the New History, as advocated by Lawrence Stone and the adherents of the *Annales* tradition, studies the masses rather than small elites;[3] through sixty years of experimentation New Historians have adapted techniques from the social sciences to carry out such enquiries. Implicit in this, according to Stone, is the belief that 'explaining the workings of the institution to which . . . [individuals] belonged, will reveal the true objectives behind the flow of political rhetoric, and will enable us better to understand their achievement, and more correctly to interpret the documents they produced'.[4] One of the techniques – known to classical historians as prosopography, to sociologists as career-line analysis, and practised as historical demography – accumulates uniform data on a group in order to compare variables such as age, mortality, fecundity, occupation, religious faith, and economic status. Quantitative data is used to understand the group's social structure, internal dynamics, and changes over time. Furthermore, it may aid in 'the determination of the degree of social mobility at certain levels by a study of the family origins, social and geographical, of recruits to a certain political status or occupational position, the significance of that position in a career, and the effect of holding that position upon the fortunes of the family'.[5]

Michael Baker's *The Rise of the Victorian Actor* (1978) and Michael Sanderson's *From Irving to Olivier: A Social History of the Acting Profession 1880–1983* (1984) both begin with the premise of investigating the socioeconomic constitution of the acting pro-fession. Both suggest that in the last decades of the nineteenth century the number of performers with a good education and elevated social position steadily grew, and both set out to describe the causes and consequences of this change. Unfortunately, however, the statistical portions of their analyses are extremely weak. In each case, only performers who were prominent enough to publish an autobiography or to be listed in *The Green Room Book* or *The Era Almanack* are actually considered; this leads to prosopography of the actor-manager and leading player classes, which should not pass for a study of the acting profession as a whole. Additional shortcomings are evident. Baker and Sanderson both rely on statistical data from the published censuses of England and Wales yet neither attempts to investigate the accuracy of the data or so much as adjusts the figures to take into account the 220 per cent rise in the population of England and Wales between 1841 and 1911. Furthermore, both historians refer to the census figures showing numerical parity between women and men in the profession, yet neither takes the trouble to include a balanced number of the sexes in his samples. These methodological flaws spawn misgivings about Baker's and Sanderson's assumption that disproportionately male samples of celebrated London-based performers adequately represented actors and actresses in any or all regions of the country. Their conclusions regarding the profession's growth, changes in the socioeconomic sphere performers enjoyed, and class-based analyses of the industry's demography must, therefore, be rejected.

Unlike Baker's and Sanderson's approach, which strings together data on the elite from easily accessible sources, New Historians advocate the systematic assemblage of data that stands up to scientific and logical scrutiny. This is not to be done at the expense of non-quantifiable evidence but in addition to it, regarding all documentation on its own merits. As Stone argues:

> Proof of an important historical argument is most convincing when it can be demonstrated from the widest possible range of sources, including statistical data, contemporary comments, legal enactments and enforcements, institutional arrangements, private diaries and correspondence, public speeches, moral theology and didactic writings, creative literature, artistic products, and symbolic acts and rituals.[6]

A valid study can only spring from a sample of performers that is as true to the social, economic, sexual, and professional demography of the theatre as possible. Using geographical residence (the organizing principle of the census) rather than fame as the criterion for inclusion is a step towards this. Some theatre historians believe that the leaders – not the masses – characterize the profession, and write history in defiance of principles accepted in mainstream historical studies for several decades. A far more progressive stance involves looking beyond the West End of London to suburban and provincial centres and encompassing the broadest spectrum of performing specialties that comes under the rubric of 'actor' as the term was colloquially understood in the nineteenth century: including, in other words, specialties that range from tragedienne to danseuse, marionette manipulator to serio vocalist, Negro comedian to patentee, and equestrian artiste to heavy villain. The terms themselves reflect prejudicial stratifications which are the historian's responsibility to uncover, not perpetuate. Sanderson acknowledges that dramatic performers liked to promote the separateness of their specialties, but the fact remains that all these types performed in the theatre and they were all actors, which makes substituting the elite of the legitimate stage for the whole industrial work force a rather dubious exercise. Demographic historians are justifiably suspicious of the comprehensiveness, taxonomic peculiarities, and tabulations of the decennial censuses. Nevertheless, the censuses provide the only alternative to anecdotal and elitist accounts of the constitution of an occupation as territorially dispersed and socioeconomically stratified as that of performing. By examining the census records, one draws on a sample of performers that is as true to the social, economic, sexual, and professional demography of the theatre as possible. Furthermore, the records of any area of Britain can be chosen for scrutiny.

Technically, the occupational statistics in the published censuses of England and Wales should provide the most comprehensive samples possible. The reports of 1841 to 1911 show a regular increase in the raw numbers of performers, with an average decennial increase of 45 per cent overall (see Table 1, page 10). The increase in the number of actresses is especially remarkable, as the ratio of females to males jumps from 27 per 100 in 1841 to 108 per 100 in 1881, levelling off to 101 per 100 in 1911. This implies that the number of actresses increased by 764 per cent in the forty year period between 1841 and 81, with an astounding aggregate increase of 2,958 per cent in the seventy year period from 1841 to 1911. This is in a profession which, theoretically, had been wide open to women since the Restoration. If the 1841 and 1851 data is put aside (for the science of gathering and tabulating the census was comparatively crude prior to 1861), an increase among actresses of

1,029 per cent is evident between 1861 and 1911. But no matter how true these figures are in spirit, they are misleading in detail. A simple statistical manipulation such as prorating the acting population to the general population in each census year makes the rate of increase among actresses fall to 709 per cent between 1861 and 1911, which is 320 per cent less than otherwise thought.

When used properly, the published censuses provide otherwise unrecoverable documentation, but before accepting the results it is incumbent upon a historian to prove the reliability of the data. Comparisons between the published reports and the enumerators' manuscripts demonstrate the importance of using the primary sources from which the published censuses are abstracted. To this end, the particulars of every theatrical employee residing in the London parishes coinciding with the West End theatre district and the enormous parish of Lambeth,[7] and in central Glasgow[8] and Liverpool[9] have been transcribed from the manuscripts of 1861 (the first year in which occupational data is used in the published census) and 1881 (the most recent census made available under the hundred years rule). Remarkably, none of the occupational totals published for London's parishes in 1861 accord with totals taken anew from the manuscript, and no factor consistently accounts for discrepancies. The margin of error is enormous: the published census misrepresents the acting profession by a range of − 25 per cent to + 16 per cent. Faulty addition may not be the sole cause of the inaccuracies. The explanation may lie in the census supervisors' inconsistent classification of performers' specialties. For example, holograph marks suggest that vocalists (whether concert singers or panto choristers) were just as likely to be classified 'musicians' as 'actors', with contradictory interpretations apparent even in neighbouring registration districts. Wide variations in local classifying practice seem to have stemmed from inadequate direction in the unwieldy office of the Registrar-General. Therefore, having noticed that a good number of music hall performers declared themselves as vocalists, all vocalists are included in this study for the sake of consistency and greater accuracy. This provides a sound data bank of consistent, controlled evidence for a cross-section of Britain's theatre centres in the most populous cities. Every performers' name, address, age, birthplace, living arrangements, marital status, family grouping, and occupational self-description is known and manipulable as a variable. Significant refinements and corrections of the published reports are possible.

Whereas the published reports show that the numbers of actresses and actors both grew significantly, data from the manuscript censuses reveals that their demographic profiles were distinct: actresses were more likely to be enumerated in their county of birth, a lower percentage were born outside the UK, they were clustered in fewer and lower age cohorts (15 to 29 years compared to 20 to 44 years), and they were far less likely to remain on stage after marriage. While actresses' demographic profile remained fairly consistent from 1861 to 1881, their male colleagues' differences grew more pronounced. This means that when discussing the mid-Victorian theatre there is empirical justification for setting actresses and actors apart for separate analysis.

Adding the variable of 'region' to that of 'sex' in an analysis of the manuscript census graphically depicts how the historiography has been skewed by the metonymic substitution of successful West End performers for the Victorian stage as a whole. Data on performers' ages, for example, demonstrates something about the actual amount of work available, but this can only be credibly deduced outside London. Because of the concentration of agents — the brokers of theatrical employment — in London (especially Lambeth and Covent Garden), provincial figures are the most reliable indicators of the actual numbers in employment; theoretically, then, provincial data (excluding Manchester, which was another rendezvous for 'resting' actors and their agents) gives the truest reflection of the actual numbers and types of men and women that the industry could sustain. Age pyramids of performers in Liverpool and Glasgow show this clearly. The roughly equal numbers of women and men vying for work in 1881 (according to the published census) do not reflect equal chances of employment (according to the manuscripts). The *dramatis personae* of the Victorian dramatic repertoire was weighted two to one in favour of men, and the age range of female parts further limited the sorts of women who could make a living. The concentration of over 75 per cent of Liverpool's and 63 per cent of Glasgow's actresses in the 15- to 29-year-old age group illustrates the near monopoly of ingenues among working actresses in 1881; the census was taken in early April, but it is safe to assume that during the pantomime season this concentration was probably much higher. Although the census also reveals a large percentage of men in their 20s entering the profession, there was more work for them as they aged to maturity, and so it is no wonder that their age range is broader.

42

Lambeth was riddled with theatrical agencies during this period[10] and it is likely that many unemployed performers were recorded there, yet its age demographics are strikingly similar to the provinces. It is the men of Westminster who are exceptional: by 1881, what was formerly a bell-shaped pyramid of age cohorts changed to a pattern more reminiscent of women's (in other words, they entered the profession in their 20s and were gone by age 39). This probably reflects the migration of successful, established, mature actors away from their working neighbourhood and into the higher status residential areas of the Regency aristocrat, the Victorian entrepreneur, or the bourgeois family. Thus, there was mobility for men working in the West End, but not for women. Single women – who found the battle for employment only intensified as they aged – could rarely afford to make this move either in the geographical or hierarchical sense.

In correlations of marital status to age the data is frustratingly erratic, but limited observations can be made. Except in one population, the number of widowed performers was too small to support generalizations among either sex; in Lambeth in 1881, however, twenty widowed women represent a wide spectrum of ages. The diminution in the number of actresses over the age of 30 is logically attributed to marriage, yet the data does not entirely support this interpretation. The percentage of unmarried actresses typically peaked at ages 20 to 24, and married actresses at 25 to 29, so there was overlap between marriage and continuance of careers. The vast majority of 25- to 29-year-old married actresses (71.43 per cent) had a spouse in some branch of theatrical or musical employment, and only 8.34 per cent of married actresses aged 30 or over had spouses who were not connected with the performing arts. Marrying within the theatre undoubtedly increased women's ability to maintain a career even if couples could not always find engagements in the same companies or on the same tours. The rigours of bearing and rearing children do not seem to have deterred women from continuing their careers in London or the provinces. Half of all married actresses are enumerated with dependent children, and 74 per cent of these women are under 35 years of age. Forty-nine per cent of married actresses had only one dependent child, but 22 per cent had two children, and 30 per cent had more than two.

The manuscripts reveal variations in the rate of professionalization, clearly setting West End males apart from performers elsewhere. Professionalization is important to the industry's demography for several reasons. It is thought that the disintegration of the stock system in the 1860s, together with the comparatively minimal skills needed by actors in long running tours of the 70s and 80s, broke down the centuries-old tradition of family-based companies and made the stage more accessible and attractive to the middle classes who did not have theatrical connections. The resultant need for training schools and the lobby for some system of accreditation is seen as integral to the justification of acting as a profession comparable to law, medicine, and the clergy, and hence to its cultural importance, the social status of its practitioners, and the stability of its labour pool. A professionalized stage with an infrastructure of amateur activity to feed it allows for more British talent to develop, reducing the need and taste for theatrical immigrants particularly in dance, circus, and variety, integrating the theatre more fully into its parent culture and de-exoticizing practitioners. Whether the competition inherent in an expanded marketplace fostered national or just local patterns of recruitment and migration towards work is indicative of the system's complexity and demographic sophistication.[11] The specification of birthplaces on the manuscript census allows for systematic testing of these propositions rather than mere impressionistic speculation.

The most significant change in numbers of foreigners shows up in Westminster, where foreign-born men dropped from 39 per cent of the acting population in 1861 to 25 per cent in 1881. Yet this remained by far the highest foreign population, for elsewhere it fluctuated between 0 and 9 per cent among men and women on both censuses. This may be accounted for by foreigners' familiarity with the West End as a hotel district even though their employment may have been elsewhere, but this does not explain why foreign-born actresses were as likely to reside in the West End as Lambeth or why British-born actors resident in Westminster show patterns of migration from their counties of birth unlike that of men and women elsewhere.

The proportion of actresses born *and* enumerated in London Middlesex was steady, while the number of actors from the immediate area decreased. Irish actresses figure highly in Westminster in 1861, probably a result of the influx of the unskilled destitute poor to this area in emigrations of the 1840s and 50s; by 1881 they were displaced by Surreysiders likely to be from a slightly higher socioeconomic stratum.[12] In Lambeth, London-born performers of both sexes dominated each census. Among men, the 10 per cent drop in Londoners is almost entirely due to the declining influence of London Middlesex, usurped by a large contingent from the industrial Northwest. Among women, the reduced numbers from London Middlesex was made up with Surreysiders. Antithetic to the Westminster Irish, this may be interpreted as a displacement of women born into the skilled working class by women from the semiskilled working class, a pattern that is peculiar to this parish but one which does not seem inconsistent with the repertoire and audiences of the theatres and music halls located in Lambeth. Overall in 1881, locally born women were more prevalent than locally born men. Why, if London was the mecca of ambitious performers, were only male actors increasingly from outside the metropolis? Both the Northwest and West Midlands were areas of heavy industrialization, crippled by the recession of 1873 to 1896; perhaps the inevitable gravitation toward the theatrical heartland was compounded by a shortage of work for men in Lancashire and Warwickshire.

In Glasgow, the tendency to record most English births as 'England' without specifying the county makes comparison difficult; nevertheless, it is clear that Glasgow's English-born performers were far out of proportion to the English representation in the general population in 1881.[13] In Liverpool, patterns of in-migration are traceable. In 1861, women from the Northwest comprised virtually half of Liverpool's actresses, with approximately 10 per cent from Ireland and 10 per cent from London Middlesex; by 1881 the local contingent from the Northwest decreased to about 30 per cent, while actresses from London Middlesex doubled to 20 per cent as the West Midlands and Scotland displaced Ireland in importance. These results are consistent with London in that women still tended to come from the immediate locality in greater numbers than men. In 1861 men from the Northwest and Ireland dominated Liverpool's stage, but by 1881 they were displaced by performers from London Middlesex, and the Northwest actually sank to second place, followed (as among the women) by the West Midlands, with Ireland and Scotland in close proximity. Considering London's concentration of theatres and its long tradition of professionalism, it does not seem unreasonable that a large proportion of provincial actors should continue to hail from the capital, yet the rapid decline in local recruitment of men is inexplicable unless perhaps Liverpool's theatrical entrepreneurs could not afford to gamble with too many billings at less than star level. The predominance of Northwesterners in Westminster certainly suggests that there was a pool of local talent in Lancashire, should Liverpudlians care to sustain it. The exchange of personnel between London and the Northwest was never equitable but it shows a more unbalanced pattern in 1881, with sizeable fluctuations in recruitment patterns throughout the United Kingdom.

Altogether, this provides ample evidence to discredit homogenizing views of the mid-Victorian performing population. The historiography of the Victorian theatre is acknowledged to be largely based on London's West End,[14] with an unacknowledged bias toward male actors of the legitimate stage. Yet the manuscript census suggests that the actors who worked in Westminster were the exception rather than the rule: their age range and birth places are as different from their colleagues' across the Thames as they are from Liverpudlian and Glaswegian samples. If the social history of the acting profession is based on Westminster, then either the West End is anomalous or the history is bad.

THE FEMALE SURPLUS QUESTION AND THE SEX RATIO

The demographic redefinition of the mid-Victorian theatre coincided with a political and social crisis known as the Surplus Women Question. The 1861 census demonstrated that due to emigration and declining fertility and marriage rates the majority of the adult population were women, amongst whom an increasing number were reliant solely on their own wage packets. The limited career opportunities for urban women of middle-class and working-class backgrounds not only had to be broadened, but living wages – rather than 'women's wages' – must be provided. Feminists concerned about the Surplus Women Question recognized that for working-class women alternatives must be sought beyond the obvious choices of service and sempstressing and 'the less common occupations in which women still hold a more uncertain footing . . . [such as] serving in shops, working in mines or mills, aiding in manufactures . . . and occupying subordinate positions in theatrical exhibitions'.[15] Their argument rested on the observation that in the theatre working-class women were either incapable of competing effectively or could never rise above menial status. 'Accomplished girls' with middle-class tutelage in drawing, singing, reading, and reciting were also advised that their partial mastery of skills left them ill-suited to compete in the professional marketplaces of art, music, and theatre.[16] Such advice was overwhelmingly ignored. The manuscript censuses show that the sex ratio among performers in large urban centres averaged approximately 110 women per 100 men as early as 1861 – twenty years before the published census shows a majority of women – so the feminists agitating around the Surplus Women Question in the 1860s recognized an employment ghetto that was already firmly established.

Labour historians accept that an industry's changing sex ratio is usually related to capital's ability to dictate wages, which in turn is related to the valuation of labour and the excess of workers over jobs. Probably more than in any other industrialized sector, theatrical employment was characterized by many necessary gender divisions, and its influx of women may be a significant deviation from the usual industrial scenario. Questions of wages and unemployment have already been discussed in Chapter 1; subsuming this information, how did the theatre accommodate the enormous change in the sex ratio which occurred with great rapidity in the years following the 1843 Act for Regulating Theatres? Within the realm of economic history, two areas should be closely scrutinized. First, how did the industry's product (in this case its repertoire) change to accommodate women, and what were the long term effects? And second, did possession of the means of production (capital investment and control of management) come to be shared by women, the majority of participants in the enterprise of performance?

Although the dramatis personae and traditions of performers' apprenticeship in the British theatre suggest a steady ratio between the sexes from the Restoration to the Regency, the development of ballet, music hall, pantomimes' transformation and processional scenes, burlesque, and extravaganza in the early Victorian period radically changed the proportion of employment. The mid-Victorian crisis of 'female surplus' in the general population forced unmarried women to look for livelihoods in a variety of trades, while the changes in dramatic repertoire permitted the stage to absorb female recruits in growing numbers. Unlike some industrialized sectors, it is unlikely that the theatre was actually retarded in its development by a shortage of women (who would work for low wages), but the mushrooming of certain genres of entertainment employing women should not be ignored. Whereas the increase in theatrical activity is partly a function of the overall increase in the British population and its willingness to dispose of income on this form of recreation, the increase in employment for women is related to the broadening of repertoire. This may in turn reflect social as well as aesthetic changes within the theatre. It is significant that the new employment fields for women were concentrated in low-status lower-paid non-dramatic specialties: ballet dancers, aerial faeries, panto choristers, extravaganza supernumeraries, and burlesque beauties. This concentration of women in relatively or totally unskilled parts of the labour process was precisely the scenario feared by feminist critics of the Surplus Women Question.

Competition was fierce and unemployment rife, so capital could dictate the terms of female labour's compliance. This is nowhere more apparent than in the age profile of actresses, for like shop girls and barmaids they were virtually unemployable after their looks faded. Older actresses' inability to find employment was a fact of life according to the theatre's own sick and annuity funds.[17] Presentational conventions objectified younger women, maximizing anatomical display and minimizing individual expression and the need for talent, rendering experience and seniority irrelevant. The days of the Georgian theatre – in which everyone knew everyone else in London and managers had to scour the provinces for new talent – were over. After the dismantling of the stock system, a line of business was less important than the line of a leg. The growth of the agency business testifies to the employers' market and the depersonalization of theatrical hiring below starring ranks, with the development of mass calls, generic advertisements, and audition through a proxy rather than by direct trial in dramatic and non-dramatic lines. Music halls' weekly change of bill is a literal version of the concept of replaceable cogs in an entertainment machine, but as far as lesser-skilled and female labour is concerned the principle was as much in evidence in pantomime, burlesque, extravaganza, and touring dramatic companies.

Some economic historians argue that innovation is greatest in eras of labour surplus. This appears to be true in the mid-Victorian theatre, for a surplus of performers coincides with the innovations of burlesque, music hall, and lyric opera under the formative reigns of men like John Hollingshead, Charles Morton, and Richard D'Oyly Carte. On stage and backstage theatres became analogous to the industrialized factory, growing increasingly specialized in what they offered. As in textile and heavy manufacturing trades this involved newly mechanized procedures, required highly specialized labourers, diluted the skills of the majority, induced a greater intensity of labour, and increased the scale of production. Great competition existed between closely complementary enterprises, but in the employment sector this only affected the hiring of star performers. In contrast to the handicraft system of manufacturing where membership in a craft was strictly controlled through a journeyman process and apprentices learned all aspects of the trade while working toward full competence, capital-intensive industrialized processes discouraged entry control and used unskilled labour without offering any prospect of further training. Breaking down the stock system eliminated ancient customs of apprenticeship and long training; unskilled young adults could easily slot into the production process, but for the vast majority of such recruits there was nowhere to go – neither up the hierarchy nor into a more demanding line of business – and so the system took them in regularly when youthful and spat them out permanently when mature.

Overall, the theatre gained a reputation as a truly artistic pursuit and a respectable calling, but the majority of its women employees remained stigmatized. A separation seems to have occurred between the 'respectable' performing classes and the vast pool of labour whose names were never recorded on playbills. This class is analogous to the casual labour pool which preoccupied social reformers such as Henry Mayhew and Charles Booth. Concentrated in the inner cities of large conurbations, casual labourers were seasonally employed and chronically poor. Irrespective of their skill levels, the supply of their labour so exceeded demand that work could not be relied upon and employers could easily replace even qualified personnel, reducing their incentives to encourage steadiness of habit and other middle-class virtues. Tension between the metropolis's casual labourers and the geographical personifications of capital grew to a head in the 1880s, when marches from Southwark, Camden Town, and the East End led to angry occupations of Trafalgar Square in 1886, culminating in the Strand's Bloody Sunday riots of 1887.[18] Like this 'residuum' of casual labourers surrounding London's core, female performers were predominantly locally born. Among theatre workers, the great unfamed seem to have been demographically, geographically, and circumstantially likened to the vexatious body of troublemaking 'residual' labourers. But because they were women, actresses' threat was rendered into sexual terms (promiscuous conduct and opportunistic predation) rather than the terminology of the economically demoralized. The repertoire to which they had access did nothing to challenge these impressions, and the long term effects were entrenchment of hiring practices, sanctification of the new repertoire and its presentational conventions, and ghettoization of women into low-paid jobs without chance of promotion. As long as this endured, neither the visible part of their work nor the community to which their work likened them permitted such women to project what Victorian culture recognized as 'respectability'.

With the expansion of the theatre industry and the increased scale of production came growing demands for capital investment. It became increasingly difficult for the manager, leading performer, and financier to be the same person. By 1880, when the new Companies Act permitted public stock issues for any limited liability venture, the scale of investment was astronomical. Wages played a minute part in the escalation of costs, and rank and file wages factored even less, for they changed only in number, not quality. The salient question is whether women were able to acquire the reins of management, raise capital, and take charge of the means of production. The answer is a qualified no. Even women at the apex of the hierarchy operated under restricted conditions.

Marie Saker made a living but acquired no capital as a manager in Liverpool. Upon her retirement, she remarked:

> For the last two years there have been exhibitions, and, consequently, there has been a falling away in attendance at the theatres, and the Alexandra has suffered. A woman cannot manage financial affairs so well as a man, and so I felt afraid, and worried myself about the matter until I am now almost ill with nervousness.[19]

This belief in women's unsuitability for management was shared by the judge who revoked Sarah Ann Squier's licence for the Trocadero in 1891,[20] and however despicable it is in principle it does have justification insofar as financing is concerned. Before 1880, money had to be put up by wealthy entrepreneurs; since wealth was concentrated among men it was less accessible to women, for they could not join gentlemen's clubs, masonic societies, or political parties. They could not possibly have had the equivalent social resources of the Gatti brothers, George Edwardes, Herbert Beerbohm Tree, George Alexander, and Henry Irving in the West

End, or Benjamin Conquest and Morris Abrahams in their respective East End communities. Whatever their success in raising start-up capital, women's sphere of contacts capable of underwriting the expenses of a new and lavish production on the short term were reduced. Lillie Langtry had other resources, and she flourished. Emma Cons was among the first to issue a stock option and, never needing additional funds, her books remained forever in the black. Women managers were quite common in hostelry, restaurant, and retail businesses, but not in medium or large scale concerns producing finished goods or services, such as theatres. There is no other division of industry in which women operated the equivalent of a large manufacturing plant, so manageresses' existence is laudatory and remarkable, but their participation was limited. The concentration of women's employment in low-paid specialties ensured that they could not proportionately aspire to management, and the circumstances of the business world further restricted their chances of assuming an equal footing.

The first known English manageresses included Miss Elizabeth Leigh and her mother, Mrs Mynns, briefly noted in connection with London fairs as early as 1687 and 1703 respectively.[21] More is known of Tryphosa Brockell, the daughter of a clergyman, who married an actor in 1749. Together, she and Henry Miller established a continuing theatrical dynasty when both their daughters went on the stage. Brockell's second marriage, to the Yorkshire manager J. Wright, also resulted in theatrical offspring. When Wright died in 1771, Brockell ran the company which became the foundation for the York-Richmond circuit.[22] In many respects this story is typical of women's succession to management: Brockell was well placed in a theatrical family tree and became manageress upon her husband's death, inheriting theatrical real estate and executive power simultaneously. Her prototype is mirrored in Mrs Baker (a manageress of the Canterbury Circuit c. 1769–1815), Mrs Wild (who owned a travelling theatre in Yorkshire and Lancashire c. 1820–51), Mrs Nye Chart (at the Theatre Royal Brighton, 1876–92), Ellen Poole (at the South London Palace of Varieties, 1882–95), and Marie Saker (at the Alexandra Theatre Liverpool, 1883–8). Victorian women rarely had such lengthy tenures in management. Typically, like Louisa Swanborough, Anne Vagg, Mrs Bateman, and Helen D'Oyly Carte they were lessees for short interim periods in lieu of a male relative. Countless widows became managers of public house music halls, remaining just long enough to sell the business as a going concern,[23] connoting neither a desire to manage nor an ability to do so. Other women began or soon became joint managers with male partners – notably Mary Moore and Charles Wyndham at Wyndham's, then the New Theatre, and Marie Wilton and Charles J. James at the Prince of Wales's (1869–71, superseded by Squire Bancroft as sole lessee). Other long serving manageresses were exceptional in one way or another: Lillie Langtry was only briefly a lessee at the St James's (1890) and Imperial (1901–3), preferring to make her fortune in America; Sarah Lane succeeded her husband at the Britannia, running the theatre from 1871 to 1899, but like Sarah Thorne at the Theatre Royal Margate she maintained a stock company decades after it ceased to be fashionable or viable elsewhere; Kate Santley failed to make the tiny Royalty Theatre pay, though she was lessee for a quarter of a century; and Emma Cons ran an extremely unorthodox theatrical venture at the Royal Victoria Hall and Coffee Tavern from 1880 to 1913. Jennie Hill's intermittent brief stints in management have been explained by her inability to match the model of male fellowship and camaraderie integral to music hall sociability,[24] but the reasons why Fanny Josephs, Marie Litton, Matilda Wood, and Violet Melnotte repeatedly but only briefly took theatres has not been fully discovered. The successes of Lena Ashwell, Agnes Littler, Gertrude Kingston, and Annie Hornimann belong to the twentieth century.

THE FEMALE LIFE

The fact remains that the vast majority of women could not aspire to management for even the briefest term. Demographic data from the manuscript censuses suggests that among actresses neither marriage nor childbirth were the decisive factors in determining when they retired from the stage. The termination of an actress's career seemed to have more to do with her age than her family life. Employment was markedly restricted to glamourous functions demanding young recruits. In other words, the development of a woman's career was largely decided by factors beyond her control and unresponsive to her talents or determination. She could not decide what proportion of jobs she would qualify for, or how the industry would capitalize to effect her, but she could exercise some choice over whether to try to integrate reproduction and family life with a career. Yet there were consequences. The adjunct of a family made a woman an awkward employee, and the system was not kind to encumbered persons whether they sought eminence or just a living. Frustration and tension must have been inevitable, and there are stories to be told.

The rapidity and volume of female influx in the mid-Victorian period not only means that the composition of the acting population changed, but that the problems of women and families in professional life were increasingly obvious, and pressure to institute reforms relating to them was potentially greater. For an actress determined to maintain her career after marriage, or reliant on her earnings for her own or her family's survival, the stage could provide a higher wage than any other legitimate occupation freely accessible to a woman. On the negative side, however, it could also lead her (and her dependants) far from emergency financial aid, medical attendance on credit, relatives who looked after children without charge, comfortable and healthy lodgings, and her rightful parish Poor Law relief. Pregnancy and confinement precluded work, and nursing interrupted it. Proper day care and schooling for the children of touring performers was difficult to arrange, if not impossible on the wages. Whereas the stock system found it convenient to regard the family as an employable unit and allowed for a semipermanent residence, the long provincial tours of a single play that characterized the latter part of the century had less use for married couples and broods of children, no matter what their respective skills backstage or on stage. Parents' alternative was to deposit children with an institution, if they could afford it, or a guardian, if a suitable one existed. As Sydney Paxton wrote in 1887:

> The *great middle class* of us, who, whilst earning a respectable and comfortable living, cannot afford to keep up two establishments, and consequently have to travel our children with us, and let them pick up their education as best they can .... It is but seldom now that we make a stay of any considerable length in a town, save, perhaps, at Christmas time. It would surely be a comfort to know that the children could be left comfortably and satisfactorily, without the responsibility of taking them from place to place at all hours of the day and night.[25]

Arranging for the care of elderly performers was also difficult. Demand for elderly performers' services was low even if they were able to tour. After fifteen years managing a theatre in Scotland,

Aston Carle and his wife became chronically unemployed. Carle wrote:

> There is a rage for young actors; I am sixty, my wife twenty years younger. I suppose that is the primary cause, coupled with our long absence from the English market. At any rate, it is no want of exertion and from, I swear, no fault of our own.... I want to know what we have done, after an honourable career, that the street or workhouse should be our doom?[26]

If performers were forced through illness or unemployment into retirement, the wages of theatrical progeny (if they had any) were not necessarily sufficient to support the elder generation comfortably. Younger stagers' migrations after employment could leave parents alone for long periods, eliminating the advantages of shared accommodations and requiring (as with the young) hired attendants.

It is not easy to find the language or evidence to explain and document the intersection of the private and public lives of women coping under these restraints. The discovery by Carolyn Heilbrun that distinct narrative traditions of telling women's lives did not exist prior to 1970 helps explain why. Until recently, the only model for writing about the lives of women has been derived from biographical and autobiographical writing about men, where imperatively,

> Above all, the public and private lives cannot be linked.... We hardly expect the career of an accomplished man to be presented as being in fundamental conflict with the demands of his marriage and children; he can allow his public life to expand occasionally into the private sphere without guilt or disorder.[27]

Clive Swift, writing about marriage and the actor in the 1970s, unwittingly gives a ludicrous demonstration of the masculinist notion of a performer's home sphere:

> It's not so much a matter of families preventing us performing great exploits ... as the fact that great exploits will be performed (given the slightest opportunity) however many wives or children we have....
>
> But the actor's lot – his independence, his travelling, his uncertainty, make the family hearth a pleasant prospect. It

represents a warm island in a cold sea. And the roles of bread-winner and father are attractive ones.

One cannot pronounce upon the requirements of the human heart. There are no better dads than actors. They respond to their children in ways that more conventional chaps don't. And love, of husband and wife, has been what men have lived and died for. But acting threatens. It makes fierce demands: takes us away when we are needed and keeps us domiciled when we should be in the world (for often the actor is at home during the day).[28]

For a Victorian actress, maintaining the boundaries of a private life and professional life involves an entirely different set of circum-stances, negotiated through entirely different social, biological, and familial pressures. Not least of all, the demands of a simultaneous day job (rehearsing) and night job (performing), or touring, must have created acute pressures for women with children, particularly if their husbands were unwilling to tend the hearth in vestal sanctity. According to the censuses, most married actresses' spouses were in the performing arts, but this may not have provided professional flexibility if many were paired with the likes of Clive Swift. For actresses, events such as conception, gestation, the timing of parturition, nursing, and child rearing – so easily accommodated by leisured middle-class women with servants and by husbands who regard their only important realm as the public sphere – were necessarily momentous obstacles to integrate with a theatrical career. The public and private lives were, for the actress, inseparable. Each woman made her own choices and devised her own reasons. Lacking models for describing this invisible knit, history has ignored it.

The autobiographies of Victorian actresses, like their con-temporaries in all autobiography-spawning walks of life, are peremptory on the subjects of motherhood, the never ending negotiations of married life, the decision to remain single, the personal dimension of divorce, and the socially disreputable aspects of courting. Adelaide Calvert mentions that the early years of her marriage were punctuated by six 'domestic incidents' (confine-ments) during which times only her husband worked, but each birth seems by implication to have been as easily accommodated as the purchase of a new hat.[29] Biographies are rarely better. Naomi Royde-Smith's *Private Life of Mrs. Siddons*, which remarkably claims the subtitle *A Psychological Investigation*, is curt on the subject of

Sarah Siddons' pregnancies and family life, and only breaks the masculine narrative of professional credits and plaudits to describe Siddons' daughter's entanglement with the painter Thomas Lawrence.[30] Hunt's biographical note on the burlesque star Valerie Reece is a classic example of how the male model understates crises and eclipses the significant events in an actress's life:

> MEUX, Lady (née Valerie Langdon; stage name, Valerie Reece); d. of Charles Langdon; m. Henry Bruce Meux (heir to Sir Henry Meux, 2nd baronet, and principal proprietor of Meux's Brewery), November, 1878; appeared in burlesque and various other of the lighter productions at several of the West End theatres; retired from the stage on her marriage, which, in view of the fact that the bridegroom was the heir to a fortune estimated at something like three millions sterling, was nothing short of a society sensation; her husband, on succeeding to the baronetcy, on the death of his father, 1883, at once settled £20,000 a year upon her; on his death, in December, 1899 (without issue), hers was the only name mentioned in his will, and she inherited everything he had possessed, including some 15,000 acres of land (mostly in Wiltshire), a substantial interest in Meux's Brewery, an estate in Herts, houses in Park Lane and Paris, and some priceless jewels; resides mostly at Theobald's Park, Waltham Cross, her Herts estate; has devoted herself largely to facilitating the training and education of promising aspirants to the stage, and in many ways deserves the respect of the profession for her liberal but unostentatious charities.[31]

Whatever scandal, wealth, the peerage, childlessness, widowhood, her abandoned profession, teaching, and charitable work meant to Reece exists only in silence.

Common players who tell their own lives are occasionally more realistic. In their stories, more of the aspects that were crucial to their lives — inseparably meshing in the public and private person — are voiced. Catherine Holbrook expresses the anguish of theatrical motherhood:

> An Actress can never make her children comfortable; ill, or well, even while sucking at the breast, the poor infants, when the Theatre calls, must be left to the care of some sour old woman, who shakes or scolds them into fits: or a careless wench, out of whose clutches, if they are freed without broken

or dislocated bones, 'tis wonderful. The mother returning with harassed frame and agitated mind, from the various passions she has been pourtraying [sic], instead of imparting healthful nourishment to her child, fills it with bile and fever, to say nothing of dragging them long journies [sic], at all seasons of the year, all hours of the night, and through every inclemency of weather, frequently on the outside of coaches, in open chairs, etc.[32]

In a description of a stormy night-time journey across the Irish Sea, an actor in a first class touring company eloquently portrays the women's circumstances:

No cabin or sleeping places for ladies, who were on the deck, crying and seasick, occasionally one or two falling asleep for a few minutes. The principal ladies were best off, for the chorus ladies gave up to them the bales of *saturated rope, which had only been used a short time before in the harbour, for them to lie or sit upon* in their cloaks and shawls.[33]

Terrestrial travel could be just as harrowing. Before the advent of the railway, one Midland manager who 'made a rule never to engage married or old people' herded his troupe over 500 miles in one season. They went by foot: 'coaching in those days was no trifling matter, and salaries being on the lowest scale, actors were obliged to walk.'[34]

Without a state welfare system or wages high enough to permit subscribing to insurance funds, hardship scraped these lives at every turn. Doubly disenfranchised by Parliament and their occupation, actresses eventually keened to each other and shared their troubles, discovering much common ground.

Heilbrun predicts that unless women band together, neither the telling nor the circumstances of their lives will profoundly change:

I do not believe that new stories will find their way into texts if they do not begin in oral exchanges among women in groups hearing and talking to one another. As long as women are isolated one from the other, not allowed to offer other women the most personal accounts of their lives, they will not be part of any narrative of their own.[35]

As actresses became more numerous, banding together was precisely what happened. Out of widespread hardship, personal remembrances of crises, and a will for female solidarity, change ame possible. As Heilbrun found in the fiction of Kate Chopin, Doris Lessing, Susan Glaspell, and Jean Stubbs, so also in the last decades of the nineteenth century 'we read, among much else ... stories of women who, feeling trapped in a script they did not write but were slowly beginning to analyze, looking about them for a way out, a way on to a different life'.[36]

PROFESSIONAL WELFARE

Numerous schemes attest to performers' sensitivity to the difficulties women, men, and families faced in all branches of theatrical life: most just ameliorated hardship but a few also addressed its fundamental causes. The profession's politics are reflected by the constitution and actions of these schemes. For example, instead of creating a united front, there was a tendency among some of the institutions newly created toward the end of the century to deliberately entrench the profession's hierarchical distinctions, perpetuating rather than mitigating poverty and hardship among the lower ranks.

The earliest schemes were small-scale friendly societies: providential organizations based on the concept of self-help. These theatrical funds at first served the needs of a particular theatre (such as Covent Garden from 1765, Drury Lane from 1766, Edinburgh from 1827, the Britannia from 1860, and the Strand from 1875), a specified district (such as the York circuit from 1815), or an occupational group (such as the General Theatrical Operatives' Sick and Benevolent Society, established in 1870). Typically, after contributing for several years members were entitled to sickness pay, medical costs, and superannuation, and their dependants could claim funeral funds and widow's, widower's, or orphan's pensions. Local funds were usually open to all theatrical employees, but most members of unstable companies and unaffiliated workers were without protection. Other schemes helped to fill this gap: the Royal General Theatrical Fund (created in 1839 and incorporated by royal charter in 1853) was open to dancers, pantomimists, and chorus singers everywhere in Great Britain and Ireland; and the Dramatic, Equestrian, and Musical Sick Fund (established in 1855) served members of all branches of the theatre including orchestral musicians, technicians, and circus performers. These friendly societies are typical of the occupation-based savings funds of the working class, emphasizing concern over unemployment, sickness, accident, and old age by regulating thrift.[37]

Expectations of women's career patterns are evident in the regulations of some of these societies. The Covent Garden Theatrical Fund did not accept new female members over 35 years of age, but paid superannuation to women after their 55th year; men, however, could join up to their 40th year but did not qualify for superannuation until they were 60 years of age.[38] The Royal General Theatrical Fund claimed that women's earlier unemploy-ability necessitated different retirement ages, but as the *Rules* state: 'The reason that Females are declared eligible as claimants at 55, is, that at that age they are considered professionally *in*eligible [original emphasis] for the general range of theatrical business, and their chance of obtaining engagements therefore considerably lessened.' Women were offered memberships at the same cost as men because 'by the adoption of a distinct scale of payments for the Female Members ... those payments would be so large as to amount, in most cases, to an absolute prohibition', perhaps closer to the annual premiums of ordinary life office schedules.[39] The Royal General Theatrical Fund's records show that its dedication to women was real: returns between 1,000 per cent and 2,270 per cent are recorded. One annuitant, Mrs M.A. Barry, paid £78 6s. and was repaid £1,763 over a period of 31 years; a Mrs Leclercq, who joined in 1855 and contributed £120, received £1,240 between 1867 and 1887; and Miss Adelaide Stoneham, who paid £93, received over £917 up to her death in 1890.[40]

Some theatrical providential societies also maintained bene-volent branches, but most organized theatrical charity came from societies created and run by actors exclusively for the benefit of non-subscription paying colleagues. In the 1850s, the Dramatic, Equestrian, and Musical Sick Fund created a benevolent branch, and the ill-fated Royal Dramatic College was founded. The Actors' Benevolent Fund was created in 1882 to relieve actors, actresses, managers, and stage managers by making small loans in times of emergency. Although it calculated loans according to the number of the applicant's dependants and provided much needed interim aid, it did not address the particular needs of women and children, and consistently kept aloof from movements to correct the root causes of poverty and to permanently improve the lives of professionals. The Actors' Benevolent Fund was created and perpetuated by the male actor-managing elite of London's West End. In addition to luring donations away from more egalitarian and wide-serving societies, it rejected practical schemes like establishing a boarding

59

AUGUSTANA UNIVERSITY COLLEGE
LIBRARY

school and orphanage for theatrical children, and creating a co-operatively owned agency.

In contrast, the proposals of Kittie Carson (née Claremont) pragmatically addressed the needs of all theatrical employees and recognized the connections between women's careers and family lives. In November 1891, Carson gathered together sixty concerned actresses; for the first time in the British theatre (and possibly unique among Victorian charities, including needlework guilds) she proposed a means to assist her co-workers regardless of their income, job classification, marital status, geographical location, and tenure in the industry. She publicly acknowledged that the theatre was not a middle-class haven, that women in all divisions of theatrical work were her colleagues and deserving equals, and that women of her own profession could and too often did suffer privation. Specifically, at first, Carson appealed to the sensibility of middle-class actresses to recall or imagine the difficulties faced by their less privileged colleagues during the time of confinement and the first six months of maternity.

> We do not hear much about these cases in London, but in the provinces there is, I am sorry to say, much sad trouble. During such illness a woman is helpless. All her little stock of money is going out, and frequently none is coming in. Our less fortunate sisters connected with the stage have frequently to live from hand to mouth. How is it possible for them to save for the day of trouble? Sisters in art! Why, let the poor woman be actress, chorister, extra, dresser, or cleaner, she equally deserves our warmest sympathy, and, what is more effective, our aid. . . . It is so easy to save when you have £30 a week for a salary, but how difficult it becomes when husband and wife together earn only as many shillings.[41]

Within weeks, Carson's newly-formed Theatrical Ladies Guild had 130 members. Subscriptions were nominal (1s. and two articles of cast-off clothing) but strategic. Most importantly, the actress members of the Guild contributed their time and labour at weekly meetings to cut and sew garments for newborn children, recognizing that women who constantly travelled or struggled for daily survival had no time to sew infants' clothes. The events leading up to an application could involve prolonged and complicated hardship yet the need could be remarkably simple, as this woman's request for a walking dress for herself and clothing for her 7- and 5-year-old children shows:

> My husband was for years at —, but continued illness in the form of rheumatism has deprived him of the use of his hands. . . . I have wandered about doing what I could – a short engagement, for which I got very little money, set me up for a time till my youngest child was born. I had to cut up some of my own things, bad as they were, to provide it with clothing. . . . When I was strong enough I joined Mr. —'s company, with whom I was for four weeks, getting an average of 10s. a week, and sometimes my eldest child was able to earn a little more by going on when required. But business was terribly bad, and I had no money to send my husband. Then I secured an engagement at — where I had to walk. It was very wet, and when I arrived I was very ill from cold and want of food. . . . All seemed bright again, when business fell off, and again my share dropped down to a few shillings a week. I have pawned all I can possibly do without, and now am looking forward with some degree of hope, for Mr. — has promised to give me an engagement. But I cannot join him for want of clothing. I do not want money.[42]

From June 1892, clothing for six-month old infants, children, and adults was also dispensed for a small charge, depending on an applicant's ability to pay, along with tickets for the Convalescent Dinners Society and admittance to maternity hospitals and a seaside convalescent home.

The radical nature of the Guild is apparent in the report of the first annual general meeting, in February 1893, when 320 of the 355 members gathered on the stage of the Lyceum Theatre. Mrs Theodore Wright urged that women doctors be employed in maternity cases. More surprisingly, Geneviève Ward chastised members who claimed that the Guild encouraged immorality, and she successfully 'pleaded for deserving women to be still helped, without reference to husbands'. Fanny Brough, the President, emphatically assured everyone that the Guild would continue to assist single mothers – which was more than the Royal Maternity Charity was prepared to do.[43] In so many ways, these actresses had at last made certain stories thinkable and the realities of performers' lives utterable. This in no way adversely affected membership. In 1893–4, the Theatrical Ladies Guild had a similar proportion of eligible professionals to the Actors' Benevolent Fund (11 per cent compared with 10 per cent), but the growth of the Theatrical Ladies Guild is remarkable considering that time rather than money was the principal commitment. By 1896, membership had grown to 700; they assisted 57 maternity cases; clothed 35 men, 78 women, and 115 children (25 of the adults secured engagements thanks to the revitalization of wardrobe); sent 4 women to convalescent homes; and gave away 20 coal tickets, 54 bread tickets, 96 dinners, and 198 Christmas dinners.[44] The Stage Needlework Guild was formed as a subsidiary in 1897, and the Needle and Thimble Guild in Edinburgh worked along similar lines for women in its region.

Carson's charitable work with and for women continued unobtrusively throughout the 1890s. In 1892, it was disclosed that she aided a chorister named Mabel Harrison, who was detained in Holloway Prison for three months following a suicide attempt. The case attracted attention when it became known that the Deputy-Chaplain of the gaol neglected (or refused) to see Harrison 'because she had been an actress'. Carson visited her, arranged for the care of her child, secured a stipend from the Adelaide Neilson Fund, and found her an engagement upon release.[45] In July 1894, Carson's name also turns up as the organizer of a country excursion for mothers and children connected with London theatres. Food, gifts, and toys were all donated to the picnic and ramble, seemingly a regular event and comparable to the field-days sponsored by religious women for children in urban parishes.[46]

Carson's second great cause, taken up in 1896, was to establish an actors' orphanage. As early as 1887, the *Stage* took up cries of 'Why Not an Actors' Institute?', printing a host of correspondence debating the pros and cons of an orphanage and residential school for actors' children. An informal nationwide poll of actors concluded that an orphanage was 'essential to, and justified by, the present state of the theatrical profession'.[47] One touring actor pleaded:

> I have seen the hardships attendant upon dragging little ones round the country – the poor mothers unable to find rooms because the stern landlady 'will not take in children'; and I was once in a well-known provincial company where one of the rules governing engagements read 'no dogs or babies allowed to travel with the company'. Is the widowed mother to be deprived of the means of earning a living because she cannot afford to leave her baby of a nurse, and managers refuse, and I

will not say unjustly, to allow her to travel her little one about with her?[48]

The proposal for an orphanage touches on issues of class as well as sex, pointedly demonstrating dissatisfaction with the self-styled spokesmen of performers in the Actors' Benevolent Fund. The *Stage* contended that 'to a small but influential body of artistes, whose lives fall in easy places, the question of an Orphanage is of no paramount concern' because they do not suffer the effects of overcrowding and increased competition.[49] Sallie Booth suggested that as long as the fees were affordable for actors of the lower and middle ranks the institution would be well supported, but it should not take on a grand country building or expensive London offices: 'the great stumbling-block in the way of the popularity of the Actors' Benevolent Fund is that it costs more than £600 a year to give away £3,000.'[50]

Although the idea met no active opposition it was not carried out. The issue simmered for another decade until on the instigation of Kittie Carson and Margaret (Mrs Clement) Scott, proceeds of an enormous bazaar endowed more positions in an already established orphanage.[51] The most desperate cases could be dealt with and the matter was dropped.

The Victorian period is characterized by the creation of thousands of charities; the influx of women into the theatre did not cause theatrical charities to be formed, but the two phenomena are related. Following a decade when the number of actresses increased by 90 per cent, crucial issues of housing, protection of girls and young women, and recreational facilities for children, women, and families were tackled by the Theatrical Mission. Unlike the Three Arts Club (a residential facility founded *c.* 1912 by and for middle-class female painters, musicians, and actresses),[52] the Theatrical Mission in Covent Garden catered to working-class women and families from 1873. In addition to waiting rooms, it offered inexpensive buffet services, residential facilities for young women and the children of touring parents, meeting groups (religious, social, and temperance), classes in sewing, singing, and kindergarten, a library, provident bank, and savings funds for clothing, employment, holidays, and emigration. Like the Theatrical Ladies Guild, it also loaned bundles of infant clothes *c.* 1892.[53] Some members of the profession were leery of this evangelical unsectarian venture, but if the Mission's purpose was to denounce the theatre and dissuade people from the stage it was hugely unsuccessful, for theatrical workers and their families used the facilities and returned to their work places by the thousands. In 1890, attendance was 18,000, with twice that number visiting during the Christmas season. Library loans rose to 5,000 annually.[54]

In the 1890s, when there was a 74 per cent increase in the number of actresses, there were several attempts to improve social amenities for female performers, who were excluded from clubland and would be compromised by attending public eating houses. The Theatrical Girls' Club, founded in Manchester in 1890, provided a social facility for the year-round use of young theatrical women in and out of engagements,[55] and the Rehearsal Club, founded in 1892 and situated in Cranbourne Street, London, offered a place where ballet-girls, female choristers, and extra ladies could rest, dine, read, and socialize between rehearsals and performances.[56] The Actors' Association, founded in 1891, incorporated a cooperative agency with a legal referral service, meeting rooms, and men's and women's writing rooms. In 1892, choristers formed their own association which provided club-like premises for this female-dominated group, and advantageously combined recreational and dining facilities with rooms where female members could meet with prospective employers without compromise or risk.

In the Actors' and Choristers' Associations are found the beginnings of the labour unions that coordinated new providential funds and life insurance plans on equal terms for the women and men who, by the 1890s, comprised the profession in roughly equal numbers throughout the nation. If the disproportionate wave of female influx in the mid-Victorian period had influenced the creation of self-help and charitable societies, it was no longer a force for change. There was, if anything, greater competition for fewer jobs, but workers could join trade unions (or their direct antecedents) which took action against the unfair employment practices that formerly were the cause of much distress. The unions subsumed and conglomerated the obligations of earlier friendly societies; this trend toward collective self-help on a broader basis was reformist in its approach to the distress caused by an inhospitable system, as well as realistic about the mobility of contemporary performers who were no longer tied to a circuit or resident for a long time in a stock company. To a certain extent, the conditions giving rise to the need for relief could be checked. Later on, however, closed shops and mandatory memberships did more to ensure that protection was universal.

Performers were not unanimous in their views about union-like organizations and collective self-help. Change came slowly and only after tremendous struggles. The labour aristocracy remained an insuperable impediment to groups on the lower tiers, though major successes were achieved by the Choristers' Association. Women, by virtue of their proportional numbers in the profession, infrequent rise to management, exclusion from approved means of circulating with the upper ranks of society, limited access to speaking roles, and concentration in choruses and corps de ballet, found it particularly difficult to be accepted into the middling and upper strata. In December 1892, this class of performers (perilously squeezed between the 'respectable' working class of the dramatic stage and the 'unrespectable' class consisting of untrained non-specialists who decoratively filled in the *mise en scène*) called meetings and declared the creation of a new organization. A Choristers' Union was created to define and protect the rights and professional integrity of trained and experienced lyric performers. They unanimously agreed upon their grievances, and expeditiously drew up a list of objectives:

1 To be paid for all rehearsals.
2 To fix the number of 'a week's' performances as six.
3 To receive full payment for extra matinee performances.
4 To regularize the scale of payments for understudies.
5 To establish all contracts as 'run of the piece' (preventing indiscriminate dismissal of those who helped develop a show throughout rehearsals).
6 To improve dressing room accommodation to guarantee minimum standards of sanitation for all company members.

The first general meeting of the Choristers' Association on 9 February 1893 was held on the stage of the Savoy Theatre, though D'Oyly Carte was careful to broadcast that this in no way signified his endorsement of the Association's aims or methods.[57] Aida Jenoure (a Savoy chorister and recently Nita in *The Mountebanks*), John Child, Courtice Pounds, and Richard Green were voted in as vice-presidents, while W.S. Gilbert himself took the chair as honorary president. Membership rose to 322 in the first eighteen months, and by June 1894 new members were being signed on at the rate of 86 per month. In the end, the Choristers' Association rivalled the Actors' Association in services and outstripped it in efficiency.[58] The Choristers took premises where they could gather, set up a benefit fund (friendly society) to insure against sickness and to save for retirement, and for the remarkably low quarterly subscription of 2s. 6d. supplied free legal services for members in dispute with managers (usually to recover wrongfully withheld wages), provided medical attendance, and set up a register system to circumvent agents' fees (finding 300 engagements for members in 1895 alone). By acting collectively, choristers could finally exert pressure on managers to pay fairly, could act against lessees whose dressing rooms spread cholera and bronchial infections among touring casts, and could help to stem the influx of incompetent and inexperienced newcomers. What better guarantees against unemployment could there be?

In 1895, the Association moved from Duke Street (The Adelphi) to Chandos Street, where the spacious offices included a rehearsal room and an anteroom where choristers could meet with managers. Unlike the Actors' Association, the Choristers' Association put women's concerns foremost. Aside from Jenoure, Jennie McNulty (a Gaiety Girl) was elected to the helm, and they dedicated almost an entire floor of the new premises exclusively to women members, providing four small rooms for writing, reading, and relaxing, two large rooms where rehearsals could be conducted, and a lavatory. It was, in other words, a predominantly women's club, and its guarantors were George Edwardes, William Greet, Henry Lowenfeld, W.S. Gilbert, and Arthur Sullivan. Nevertheless, there is nothing in the *Stage* (a pro-union trade paper) to suggest that the managerial class exerted any influence in the Choristers' Association. In the Actors' Association and the Actors' Benevolent Fund, however, the prominence of actor-managers in the decision making posts led to considerable hostility, with the conflict of interests and the conservatism of their politics blatant to ordinary wage earning members almost from the outset. By supporting schemes like the Actors' Benevolent Fund instead of providing insurance and pension benefits directly to employees, managers abnegated responsibility to their own employees and weakened extra-contractual obligations. Thus, the Choristers' Association circumvented two obstacles at once, for like the Orchestral Association and the Theatrical and Music Hall Operatives' Trades Union, it was constituted of a uniformly waged stratum and thus was capable of collective action in a single interest for the mutual benefit of all members rather than setting one category against the others and fragmenting labour's representation before management.

Both W.S. Gilbert and Leopold Wagner recommended that singing in the chorus was a good entrée to the higher ranks of the profession, and Selwyn Tillett notes that in the *Ruddygore* chorus 'among all the men who can be positively identified there is not one (with the possible exception of Pearce) who could not sustain a principal part or string of parts as an understudy or in his own right'.[59] Yet remembering George Foster's allegation that Drury Lane's chorus girls were re-engaged year after year so that 'a number of old chorus girls gradually [found] themselves being pushed back row by row until they found themselves in the very back row of all,' and Arthur Sullivan's observation that 'you can never get ten chorus girls capable of singing a little solo each',[60] mobility between the chorus and leads should never be assumed. During the 80s and 90s, the theatre's new well-endowed schemes for sickness benefits, emergency relief, and superannuation drew a line between actors and choristers, benefiting legitimate performers to the exclusion of the rank and file on the lyric stage while only the nearly moribund Royal General Theatrical Fund and Dramatic, Equestrian, and Musical Sick Fund benefited the chorus. In 1891, the Actors' Association (the 'official' voice of the profession) attempted to ensure respect by excluding choristers. Why, if there was mobility between the chorus and principal roles, were actors determined to differentiate their lines of business, and why did choristers feel themselves to be so isolated and unprotected as to establish their own proto-trades union to fulfil precisely the same functions as the Actors' Association precisely one year later?

The Actors' Association conclusively proved that actors had no intention of sharing their rising status with colleagues who could not even command a place on the bill. Recognizing its unjustified ostracism, the Choristers' Association took a stand in opposition to the fundamental contractual differences separating the chorus from leading actors: lower wages, usually no rehearsal pay, no bargaining power, no share of benefit performances, ultimate replaceability, and the worst dressing and sanitary facilities allotted to members of any touring company. But the Choristers' Association also stood against the public's erroneous image of the chorus as undisciplined, undignified, sexually corrupt, and unscrupulous social climbers solely intent on ensnaring the eldest sons of the peerage. The Chandos Street office embodied respectability in its conception, floor plan, facilities, and ethos. The demographic 'face' of the chorus was no different from the acting profession as a whole, so its professionalism was expressed by creating a collective identity demanding recognition, respect, fair treatment, living wages, and insurance (rather than charity of any stripe).

3

THE SOCIAL DYNAMIC AND 'RESPECTABILITY'

No matter how consummate the artist, pre-eminent the favourite, and modest the woman, the actress could not supersede the fact that she lived a public life and consented to be 'hired' for amusement by all who could command the price. For a large section of society, the similarities between the actress's life and the prostitute's or *demi-mondaine*'s were unforgettable and overruled all other evidence about respectability. She was 'no better than she should be'.

Actresses enjoyed freedoms unknown to women of other socially sanctioned occupations, but in order to convince society that they were distinct from the demi-monde and to counteract negative judgments about their public existence, they endeavoured to make the propriety of their private lives visible and accepted. This was not entirely successful. The conspicuousness of the actress at work and at home defiles the bourgeois separation of public and private spheres. The open-door policy adopted by some performers was wise in theory but paradoxical in effect: by providing proof of their respectable 'normalcy' actresses showed disregard for privacy, modesty, and self-abnegation. Either way, the bourgeoisie disapproved.

Actresses were symbols of women's self-sufficiency and independence, but as such they were doubly threatening: like the middle classes generally, they advocated and embodied hard work, education, culture, and family ties, yet unlike prostitutes they were regarded as 'proper' vessels of physical and sexual beauty and legitimately moved in society as attractive and desirable beings. Most independent women were expected to prove that their desire for work was not self-indulgent or hedonistic,[1] placating fears of the New Woman, but the actress also fought against residual fear and loathing of an older model of female rebel. Society's ideology about women and prescriptions of female sexuality were constantly defied by the actress whose independence, education, allure, and flouting of sexual mores (unavoidable conditions of the work) gave her access to the male ruling elite while preventing her from being accepted by right-thinking and – especially – feminine society.

Like most prejudices, this depended chiefly on ignorance, fear, and the perception of exceptions as general rules. In Henry F. Chorley's 1845 novel *Pomfret*, the English characters reveal their stock of prejudices when an eminent opera singer, Helena Porzheim, comes within their sphere. Although Chorley exaggerates for a slightly comic effect, the assumptions and rumours that he details about Porzheim are a checklist of upper-middle class Anglo-Saxons' social anxieties:

> She was the daughter of a noble family somewhere in Austria, who had been cast out by her relations for wishing to go on the stage. She was the niece of a Jew rope-dancer. . . . She had stilettoed one of her lovers at Milan with her own hands. Two duels had been going to be fought about her, had not Government interfered, and sent her out of Lombardy with an armed escort. One duel *had* been fought with pistols, in her own coach, as she drove from the theatre; and both combatants were dead. One was an Englishman. There had been no duel at all; but she had certainly embezzled large sums of money, and lost them all at play. . . . She had slapped his Majesty of Wurtemberg in the face in his own box. She travelled with loaded pistols in her *cabas*. She never spoke to women. She belonged to the Greek Church. She had previously injured her eyes while playing at *Tarocco* [Tarot]. She never stirred a mile without a physician, a secretary, and two adopted children.[2]

Porzheim's singing and acting transfixes the Pomfret circle. Their social encounters demonstrate the unjustified persecution of a wholly modest woman, yet Mrs Pomfret's views on artists such as Porzheim are intractable: 'There is something in the publicity of the lives these people must lead, which must end in the total destruction of everything like delicacy. They may have great virtues, I will concede; but they are best seen from a distance.'[3] Only the younger generation sees the machinery of class privilege and cultural habituation that perpetuates actresses' stigma. Miss Pomfret argues:

It is merely a question of education: and so long as people of our class, dear mamma, keep aloof from them, so long will it be so. More forbearance, more companionship – or else one had better join at once with the sectarians who denounce all such gifts as sinful and ensnaring. Think of the charity of those people – the poor families sustained by the women; think of their generosity – their self-denial – and then of your common-place, insolent people of wealth.[4]

Stigmatization was not just the work of a lunatic puritanical fringe, but was also at the heart of orthodox response. In Porzheim's case, public opinion was reversed when a Russian princess granted her patronage, adopting the prima donna like a leisure-time toy. Acceptance by a high-born woman is the only signal that society valued sufficiently to suspend its habitual revulsion, suspicion, and unease about the performer.

The significance of *women's* acceptance of the actress cannot be over-stressed. Actresses had always been accepted by male society, as a whole, though their role within it was tightly prescribed. The willingness of *high-born* women to fraternize with actresses is also significant. Actresses had to overcome the perceptions that they 'de-classed' themselves by acting and that they schemed to social climb through the self-advertising vehicle of the stage before the upper classes could sympathize or respect them. The social and economic classes of performers and their critics are relevant to any discussion of anti-theatrical prejudice, but along with the social construction of gender they are vitally important in judgments of the actress.

ACTRESSES' DEFIANCE OF SOCIOECONOMIC PRESCRIPTIONS

The Victorian public had a voracious appetite for biographical information about actresses. What they discovered when Fanny Kemble and Marie Bancroft published their memoirs, Rose Leclercq and Alma Murray were interviewed in newspapers, or Helena Faucit and Madge Kendal were immortalized by authorized biographies was that by working in an inherently scandalizing realm (the theatre) actresses defied socioeconomic prescriptions about Good Women, yet by going home as respectable daughters, wives, or mothers they denied ideological prescriptions about Bad Women. Actresses could choose to continue their careers when marriage and finances gave them the option of retiring. They could publicly proclaim the rewards of an artistic bohemian life. They could advocate a bridge between conventional domestic felicity and careerism. The actress biographies regularly featured in the *Era*, *Stage*, and *Graphic* frequently tell a rags-to-prosperity story of hard work, talent, and beauty. However much the upper echelons of society resented and resisted actresses' success, the transversal of social class and apparent obedience to conventional womanly roles was consistently fascinating for general and theatrical readers.

The surplus of women, breakdown of family management trusts, and relaxation of social strictures combined in the latter half of the century to cause a change in the social background of at least some newcomers to the profession. More came from non-theatrical backgrounds, particularly the middle classes, where concerns about respectability and female chastity were obsessive. Middle-class women, by virtue of their upbringing and social environment, were presumed to be chaste at the time of their entry to the stage. Surrendering unmarried daughters to the co-sexual profession of acting (knowing its reputation) was traumatic for parents, especially as chastity was regarded as a prerequisite for female marriage, and marriage (rather than any trade) was regarded as *the* female livelihood. For the middle classes, an acting career was a version of The Fall from virtue. Daughters were forced to hide their dramatic inclinations from their families, and in many cases to sever all familial connections when they embarked on an acting career. The account of this woman, who enjoyed playing in an amateur theatrical club before she turned to a professional career early in the century, is typical:

> My father's aversion to all dramatic entertainments was very violent. . . . Should he discover my connexion with them, his anger, I knew, would be inexorable, and this dreaded and inevitable discovery was at length made. One night I imprudently acted in both play and farce, and did not, consequently, reach home until a very late hour. I knocked timidly at the door, and was dreadfully alarmed on its being opened by my father. His face was pale with rage, and, in spite of my dear mother's tearful entreaties, he thrust me from the door, and locked it upon me, leaving me, long after midnight, alone and unprotected in the street. My distress was fearful, and my situation shocking. I, a young girl scarcely seventeen years of age, a wanderer and a stranger in the then badly

lighted, and inefficiently guarded streets of London. I ... had not proceeded many paces before my grief overpowered me, and I despairingly rested on the steps of a door.[5]

This is certainly not the sort of 'excitement' stage-struck girls expected of the theatre, but it was a sort discovered by many from the middle classes. The family of this young woman never spoke to her again, though fortunately she possessed the talent to make a living on the stage.

Few parents of the privileged classes were as co-operative as John Stuart Mill and Harriet Taylor when Taylor's daughter, Helen, decided to try the stage in 1856, though their distaste for the experiment was evident at every step. Mill and Taylor were horrified lest someone of 'their set' should see Helen on the stage, so a London engagement was unthinkable. Nevertheless, they provided her with lessons from the eminent Fanny Stirling, as much money as she needed for travel, subsistence, dresses, and servants, her brother's time as chaperone and protector, and active ongoing emotional support. Thus equipped, Helen Taylor travelled to the nether regions of England and adopted a stage name (*Mrs* Trevor). Helen's class values instilled in her a fear and loathing of contact with her colleagues (the under classes) and in treating them like untouchables she behaved like a counterspy in buskins. With all the comfort and privilege her money gave her, Helen's experience was far from typical, peppered with tedium and disappointment rather than excitement, and completely devoid of the artistic fulfillment she sought. With the secret intact, she returned home to assist Mill in a secretarial capacity.[6]

Another middle-class aspirant, author of *The Diary of an Actress*, wrote about the effect that her mid-century debut had on her family. Her sudden disappearance from the family circle branded her as a disgraced and lost woman. After many months, one of her sisters condescended to pay a brief visit, but her other sister was intractable:

She does not wish to be brought down to my level, or to hold any communication except by letter. She has even told me that men might not like to marry her girls when they grow up, if they thought they had an aunt who was an actress.[7]

This young woman experienced all the 'excitement' from which Helen Taylor was secluded, including poverty, insecurity, and acute social isolation broken only by (unwelcome) sexual advances. Not surprisingly, she wondered if her suffering was worthwhile:

Would it have been better for me if I had married – *anyone* – married, and been happy in a quiet home? But no; I should have been tormented by the abiding sense of having missed my true vocation. I always felt I could not be happy in the life which suited my sisters. I fear I have too much of the combative element in me, ever to be satisfied with a quiet domestic sphere.[8]

Like many aspirants, she contemplated a stage career in the context of other female options. Like many from affluent homes, she crossed the boundaries of class at the expense of eternal expulsion from her natural sphere, then unceasingly sought genteel companions in her adopted sphere. Yet unlike Helen Taylor, this woman asserts that an artistic life gives sufficient compensation for the hardship, isolation, and sexual skirmishes.

Flora Mayor, the daughter of an Anglican divine who held successive chairs of Classics and Moral Philosophy at the University of London, chose to try the stage after she took a degree at Newnham College, Cambridge. Her father's objection was spiritual and moral, while her mother (who flung Flora's professional photographs across the room) rejected the project on the grounds of snobbery. Toward the end of 1902, Flora consented to join her first provincial tour, a step she had resisted for six years because she thought that touring was more de-classed than brief stints in third-rate residential companies. Her sister wrote: 'I do think your life sounds so detestable, it makes me quite depressed to think of you being on an equality with these beastly people ... *how* can you stand it.'[9] Ultimately, Flora could not stand it. Her intellectuality put off the managers, and the squalor and incessant self-denegration of the trooper's life put off Mayor. Nevertheless, like Helen Taylor forty years earlier, she had the courage to try the experiment and the financial and familial cushion to abandon it. She retired in expectation of marriage, but after her fiancé's premature death she settled for being her brother's housekeeper, and made a small name for herself as an author.

For middle-class actresses who took to the stage following a reversal in family fortunes (that mainstay of Victorian fictional plots) the choice of career was usually calculated according to the monetary, rather than artistic, returns that were expected. In *The Actress of the Present Day*, a novel of 1817, the narrator describes Mary Irwin's dilemma:

Sometimes she had thoughts of becoming a governess in some family of distinction, but that precarious and humiliating situation ill suited her independent spirit; the sudden and alarming death of her father [by suicide] at length determined her. She beheld her destitute prospects, and saw the shyness of former friends degenerate now into total neglect and contempt. 'I cannot fall *lower* in their estimation; and their opinion and regard I hold in equal indifference: it matters little what line of life I may engage in for them.'[10]

In one of Geraldine Jewsbury's novels, the actress-heroine, Bianca Pazzi, learned her craft from the age of fifteen; she entered the theatre thinking of herself as an illegitimate child and orphan, though the reader knows her birthright puts her in the upper-middle class. She passes the benefit of her experience on to an aspiring young singer:

'Strong and sterling qualities of character are needed to make the brightest genius of any more worth than the gold and purple clouds of evening, which turn to leaden coloured mists. . . unless you cultivate an iron resolution to follow a purpose once conceived steadily to the end, an industry and perseverance, which are proof against all self-indulgence, a spirit of loving-kindness and single-mindedness, you will find your genius of little worth, except to lead you into splendid mistakes.'[11]

Whatever the social price, Jewsbury advocates the value of work in an occupation such as acting as the cure for (middle-class) women's lethargy, ennui, and wastage.[12]

Although novelists asserted strongly, early on, and repeatedly that society's view of actresses required revising, Annie Edwards's depiction of three prominent stereotypes held the popular imagination. In *The Morals of May Fair*, Celeste is a vivacious French brunette in her late twenties, natural on stage, unnatural off stage, worldly, and fond of gossip. By marrying into the *nouveau riche* and retiring in France she is accepted by respectable society. Fridoline keeps her national and family origins a secret, is a masterful soubrette, and lives a reclusive blameless life in Hampstead; she works with the secret ambition of supporting her *demi-mondaine* mother in retirement in their native Norway. Rose Elmslie, an Englishwoman, took to the stage at the age of fourteen when her clergyman father suddenly died; she is a flirtatious, deceitful, feminine magnet who ensnares noble lovers, takes to drink, is hissed off the stage, and dies ignominiously in the back streets of the Haymarket.[13] These fictional actresses were Helen Taylor's contemporaries, but their types lingered in the popular imagination even as the middle-class Laura Hansen, Mary Kingsley, Kate Phillips, Janette Steer, Cynthia Brooke, Jane Grey, Gertrude Warden, Miss St Quinten, Lillie Langtry, Rose Norreys, and Flora Mayor went on the stage in succeeding decades.

Class issues certainly affected actresses' marriage prospects. It is misleading to assert that more marriages occurred between actresses and the aristocracy (or even between actresses and the upper-middle class) in successive decades, simply because there were more actresses to be chosen among. It is likewise misleading to assert that class prejudice against such marriages gradually dissolved, because opposed marriages took place in each decade (though among the upper classes, *men* increasingly came to regard the stage as a viable marriage market in which to shop). *Punch* joked about the desirability of actresses revitalizing the aristocratic gene pool, which in the republicanized late-nineteenth century stood to profit by an infusion of strength, vitality, and good looks.

Aspirants from the labouring classes had a different perspective on the merits and demerits of an acting career. They were less discouraged by perceptions of the theatre as morally equivocal and of actresses as unwomanly. For them, the possible monetary gains and marriageability more easily outweighed the disadvantages that the stage shared with most other varieties of female labour. Though the risks were high, the ill-paid precarious living that the stage afforded was not necessarily worse than a lifetime of mill, factory, sweated, or domestic labour. Ill-educated shop girls, laundresses, and seamstresses tried to enter the profession by the dozens: some graceful, beautiful, and talented, some awkward, hideous, and completely without ability. Those who met visual criteria were still handicapped by aural criteria: working class accents, rural dialects, and faulty grammar were completely unacceptable on the legitimate stage in all but character business, for the profession vigorously promoted an image of its gentility, refinement, artistry, and exclusivity. Meanwhile, as the middle-class ethos prohibited an easy surrender of middle-class daughters to the stage, the growing middle-class audience demanded their presence. This social hypocrisy became an issue of ever-increasing salience. The legitimate and illegitimate theatre became split by repertoire as well as class, not only in the auditorium but also on the stage.

The Drama's preference for middle-class newcomers was an aesthetic matter that involved more than just a question of 'aitches', the purveyance of shabby gentility, or a woman's ability to outfit herself with a theatrical wardrobe and purchase her debut. Without middle-class actresses, acting was unquestionably an art of imitation; with middle-class actresses, the stage could be populated by women who not only looked and sounded like gentlefolk, but who walked and performed life's little ceremonies like them too, because they were, indeed, gentle and everyone could clearly see and hear that they were. When theatres were deregulated in 1843, hundreds of jobs were created for lower-class performers, but the reforms of the 60s and after made employment for an entirely different sector. The cup-and-saucer drama introduced at the Prince of Wales's was based on the domestic lives of the middle class, and attracted a new audience of well-to-do playgoers who preferred to see their lives portrayed by their own caste, rather than by their servants dressed and coached in imitation of their caste. By the 1860s, of course, the prominent theatrical families had been prosperous long enough to be accepted as middle-class, and to impart the appropriate niceties to actress-daughters such as Marie Wilton and Lydia Foote (niece of the Keeleys).

As long as the drama was devoid of literary merit or social relevance, and as long as performers were of lower class or itinerant theatrical backgrounds, the public readily believed in actresses' immorality and worthlessness. Under such conditions, acting was indeed a vocation to be dreaded by every middle-class woman – and her parents. With a different type of play and a different audience, however, the theatre became an attractive career for middle-class women, though the idea of one's daughter exhibiting herself before one's peers was still loathsome to parents.

The prejudice endured, though resisted. The popular association of actresses and prostitutes is not a straightforward issue of class and gender, for neither actresses nor prostitutes represented a single class of women who uniformly broke specific cultural taboos. Among actresses, a vast range of incomes and grades of 'respectability' arising out of social background, training, talent, luck, charisma, opportunism, market demand, and professional specialty are involved. A number of actresses with impeccable professional and personal credentials were not implicated at all (Madge Kendal,

Marie Bancroft, Helen Faucit, Caroline Heath, and Ellen Kean), and a select number of others including Ellen Terry, Agnes Boucicault, Lillie Langtry, Marie Lloyd, and Mrs Patrick Campbell were exempted due to their considerable and enduring popularity.

The performers singled out as exemplars of the madonna/whore dichotomy tend to be in the lowest paid and least prestigious specialties involving the greatest anonymity and impersonalized lines of business. Their low wages, late hours, and sexual attractiveness damned them circumstantially, and effective rebuttal was choked. When aspersions were aimed at a low status group, a ripple effect implicated all other female performers: the distinctions between chorus singers, ballet-dancers, supernumeraries, and principal players that were so important to the profession were of little concern to the general public. A united front of all actresses against the allegations would not have worked to the advantage of the more privileged women, who were loath to suggest that centre stage was at all equatable to a place in the back of the chorus. The more prestigious groups were affected, but they also commanded respect and provided a useful function to society women who regarded them, like the *demi-mondaine* in France, as models of fashionable couture augmented by artistic *éclat*.[14] Such mannequins did not talk back.

ACTRESSES AND PROSTITUTES

Logistic evidence shows that identifications of the lower theatrical ranks as prostitutes were erroneous. Open prostitution for any type of female performer was out of the question, as theatrical and prostitution districts were one and the same and recognition by a manager meant instant dismissal without a recommendation. Henry Mayhew insisted in 1862 that ballet girls' bad reputation was well deserved in most cases, and grouped them among the small class of clandestine prostitutes who were 'in the habit of prostituting themselves when occasion offers, either for money, or more frequently for their own gratification',[15] but he does not explain how, if they did not accept money, they could be called prostitutes. Evidently, he accepted the common equation of women's extra-marital sex with promiscuity, rampant desire, and prostitution. Mayhew can be interpreted as including ballet girls among the many country girls and daughters of professional men seduced and abducted into secluded prostitution, but if this is his intent he mistakes their social background: most London ballet girls came from theatrical families or were the daughters of artisans and lower-middle class tradesmen from the metropolis, and many lived in the family home.

If there is foundation in the rumour (which Mayhew repeats) that one in three London operatives practised occasional prostitution, ballet girls' reputation was not exceptional among their class yet they bore a disproportionate share of malediction. According to the census of 1861, actresses were scarce in most areas of the country: as low as 21 per 1,000,000 women in Monmouthshire and Wales (14 actresses in total), while the Northwest (Lancashire and Cheshire, the provincial region where actresses were proportionally greatest) there were only 123 actresses per 1,000,000 women (186 in total). Among urban areas, London had the greatest proportion, with 344 actresses per 1,000,000 women (514 in total), yet a few parish breakdowns show how insignificant their numbers are in relation to the rest of the female population.[16]

	Actresses as % of Women	Dancers as % of Actresses	Dancers as % of Women
Lambeth	0.0866%	24.44%	0.0211%
St Martin's	0.1851%	21.43%	0.0397%
St Mary-le-Strand	0.1898%	3.85%	0.0073%
AVERAGES	0.1538%	16.57%	0.0227%

The small numbers among actresses and even smaller percentages of dancers are rendered minuscule when compared to other female occupations in the areas:

	Seamstresses as % of Women	Domestic Servants as % of Women	Laundresses as % of Women
Lambeth	7.55%	13.30%	5.25%
St Martin's	7.47%	22.52%	3.15%
St Mary-le-Strand	8.53%	13.80%	4.49%
AVERAGES	7.85%	16.54%	4.30%

It is often claimed that non-theatrical women falsely reported that they were actresses, giving the word a euphemistic double meaning and discrediting true performers, but neither the figures derived from the house-to-house hand enumerated census schedules nor admittance registers of Magdalen homes and other records relating to delinquent women offer substantive evidence of this practice.

Other statistical sources further serve to discredit the notion. The Society for the Rescue of Young Women and Children has no record of a theatrical woman residing in its refuge home between 1855 and 1857,[17] nor does Mayhew's list of the trades of women taken into custody for disorderly prostitution in the 1850s include one theatrical worker.[18] Extant records of the Middlesex police courts are either incomplete or demonstrate that prostitutes were only cleared from a narrow zone (summary convictions were only processed in the Westminster police court for arrests in Knightsbridge and Chelsea during the years 1860 to 1862); in either case, the lowest class of prostitutes was involved, prison sentences invariably resulted, and no stage involvement is indicated.[19] In an 1890 study of the trades of female inmates at Millbank Prison only nine actresses are registered among 14,790 cases (0.0608 per cent), while in a later study 0.9638 per cent of active prostitutes interviewed gave their former occupation as the stage.[20] Lock hospitals and any records relating to the enforcement of the Contagious Diseases Acts are a dead end: the only London district under their jurisdiction was Woolwich (ten miles distant from Charing Cross).

Louisa Turner gave up ballet for prostitution, recognizing that the life of a coryphée was rarely profitable,[21] yet documented cases of Victorian women who simultaneously pursued careers in the theatre and prostitution are lacking. Untold numbers were kept mistresses at some point in their careers, but prostitution, not mere immorality, was the charge. Worldly knowledge was a *sine qua non* of actresses, as their working conditions were not conducive to sexual *naïveté*, and it is possible that this professional necessity led to erroneous conclusions. For women who were not born into the profession, constant touring facilitated intrigue in the provinces, while in the large cities the possibility of disappearing into the human sea may have made illicit encounters (and even long-term liaisons) feasible, but without a commercial exchange such relationships cannot accurately be construed as prostitution. With a commercial exchange in the form of lavish gifts or a regular stipend (particularly in cases of great wage disparity between actresses and their 'friends'), the situation resembles matrimony in all but its impermanence and lack of legal endorsement — hence the social judgment of prostitution.

Considering actresses and prostitutes as parallel rather than convergent professions is a useful strategy for dealing with the morass of prejudice and soft evidence. The parallels are easily charted. Female performers found themselves in proximity to the prostitutes that patrolled public houses, public gardens, theatres, and concert halls. The testimony of J. Balfour, an investigator of working class society and morality, to the Select Committee on Public Houses (1854) is confusing, but his confusion demonstrates the parallel in operation. Balfour explains that the Eagle Tavern (a public house in Islington) is a notorious site of procurement, where common street-walkers solicit clients (Cremorne Gardens in Chelsea and Manor Gardens near Camberwell were looked upon in the same way, as being among the haunts of prostitutes identified by William Sanger and William Acton).[22] The Eagle Tavern, as Balfour describes it, is licensed by the Lord Chamberlain for dramatic entertainments, and 'the same performances as you would see at the Princess's [then managed by Charles Kean and noted for a Shakespearean repertoire] or any other theatre' may be enjoyed. Following the nightly performances 'the gardens are open with alcoves, and boxes on each side, and lads and young persons are taken in there, and plied with drink'.[23] Balfour states that the manager, a former actor named Conquest, oversees the goings on, and the place is orderly, though:

> No gentleman, well dressed, can promenade there without being solicited by a female to go to houses of accommodation outside. . . . I had not sat down above five minutes when I was solicited twice, and told that there were houses outside for me to go to.[24]

In the 1850s, the Eagle was a variety saloon, adjacent to a pleasure garden and the Grecian Theatre. All three enterprises were managed by Benjamin Oliver Conquest. The Eagle had a music and dancing licence, but it was the Grecian that the Lord Chamberlain licensed for the performance of plays. Apparently, the tavern, pleasure gardens, and theatre (which were owned and overseen by the same manager) were fixed so closely in Balfour's mind that he blended them into one indistinguishable entity.

The work places of actresses and prostitutes were, therefore, close in fact and fancy. At the end of the Regency, the drama was thought of as debased, with theatres and audiences correspondingly low in taste and decorum. No theatre, however lofty in patronage or repertoire, was free of prostitutes in the auditorium. The following comments were made at the time of the Select Committee on Dramatic Literature of 1832:

If there are any places in the world where indecency is openly and shamelessly exhibited, it is within the walls of the great monopolist houses, sacred to the holy worship of the 'legitimate' drama. It is there not only exhibited, but encouraged; not only encouraged, but defended, as a means of attraction far more potent than the charms of that fair incognita the 'legitimate' drama. . . . Two-thirds of the house cannot if they would, escape the odour of [the Lord Chamberlain's] fry of fornication, or avoid tumbling over the phocae that roll in and out of his Protean hall.[25]

Thirty-four years later, in testimony before the next Select Committee on theatres, Frederick Strange, the managing director of the Alhambra music hall, testified that he had counted the prostitutes in his establishment: 'They average 3 to 100, or a little over, certainly not 4 per cent. If I have 3,500 people in the place, there are very few over 100 whom we know to be women of the town.'[26] Strange took no measures to exclude these women as long as they were well dressed, reasonably behaved, and sober. The Magistrates, County Council, Lord Chamberlain, and Metropolitan Police were indifferent to the custom, and the Alhambra had more than 1,500,000 visitors annually.[27]

The presence of prostitutes in places of entertainment was not a characteristic limited to blood tubs or the resorts of the poor. In an unusual attack by the middle class upon the immoral tendencies of the middle class, Laura Ormiston Chant campaigned to close the Empire Theatre (the Alhambra's neighbour in Leicester Square) demonstrating that prostitutes and actresses shared the most prestigious variety theatre in the Commonwealth as late as 1894 (see Chapter 5). Chant succeeded in blocking the Empire's licence renewal until partitions were erected between the promenades and the auditorium, but prostitutes were confident that Chant's victory would be minor. A riot broke out the first night the screens were in place; the temporary barriers were smashed, and pieces were paraded in triumph through the streets.[28] Despite Chant's campaign for flimsy canvas screens and restricted access to the bars, the prostitutes stayed stalwartly at their stations.[29] A year later, when George Edwardes appealed to the Music Halls Committee because the partitions caused crowding at the remaining bars and 'many were kept away owing to a sense of want of freedom', the Empire's licence was restored unconditionally. The temples of Bacchus and

Venus remained united until after World War I, when a new audience with different theatrical tastes abandoned the Empire.[30]

Theatres were also linked to prostitution and other illicit activities by their location in particular neighbourhoods. During the daytime, prostitution centred on the principal middle-class shopping areas of Bond Street, Oxford Street, and Regent Street, but in the evening the street market in prostitution shifted to the theatre districts. Prostitutes shared the Haymarket with Her Majesty's, the Pavilion, Comedy, Criterion, and Theatre Royal Haymarket, and were most in evidence between 11 p.m. and 1 a.m., just as the theatres emptied. Towards the end of the century, the hub and radii of the street prostitution market moved south from Piccadilly Circus to Trafalgar Square,[31] nearer the Strand where dressed (pimped) prostitutes were said to make the street 'literally impassable' between 7 p.m. and 2 a.m.[32] – in other words, while customers made their way to and from the Lyceum, Gaiety, Vaudeville, Adelphi, Olympic, and Drury Lane Theatres. The eastern end of the Strand was infamously associated with the pornography shops on Holywell Street (Booksellers' Row). Holywell and the less famous Wych Street surrounded the Globe and Opera Comique, providing a notorious detour in much the same way that the by-streets of Leicester Square, another pornography district, coloured the experience of pedestrian theatre-goers in search of Daly's, the Prince of Wales's, Alhambra, and Empire.

An additional parallel is found in the analogous work situations of actresses and prostitutes. As Samuel Johnson noted: 'The drama's laws, the drama's patrons give/ For we that live to please, must please to live.'[33] The theatre must, in other words, satisfy the criteria of the audience or it will not flourish. A simple model of the consumer economy prevailed. Theatre and prostitution both provided entertainment as commercial enterprises, not public services. Recognizing an opportunity in the marketplace, entrepreneurs created a product that simultaneously fit and moulded consumer preferences. The paying customers tacitly agreed to suspend disbelief while a particular desire was gratified. Significantly, in both contexts, the vehicles of gratification were women whose identity, sincerity, and appearance were illusory but whose success relied on not giving away the hoaxes of the consumer's control or full reciprocity of enjoyment. In occupational terms, both actresses and prostitutes developed a line of business, found a niche, and moved up or down economic and professional scales implicating the retention of dignity, amusing as long as they could and as long as they were patronized. Aging or a decline in the physical attractiveness, dexterity, or health of a rejected woman usually signalled the end of her career as a prostitute or an actress. But just as a prostitute with the financial resources and business acumen could become a madam, actresses could also go into management for themselves; other prostitutes frequently became servants in brothels, just as some former actresses, such as Sarah Terry, made a new career in wardrobe.

Both acting and prostitution are erroneous 'professions'. They feature none of the self-regulatory controls, educational quali- fications, or social status of 'The Professions'. Nevertheless, no other occupations could be so financially rewarding for single, independent Victorian women of outgoing character, fine build, and attractive features. The only job qualifications for prostitution were being of the female gender and being willing enough to give sexual services for cash. Talent, ability, training, and even beauty were dispensable. The stage was usually more demanding: good looks were a definite asset and training in speech, dance, or music was usually necessary for steady work, though the wages of a completely unskilled, unattractive but able supernumerary could keep body and soul together. Some women, particularly young attractive women, got occasional engagements as supers to supplement other unsteady or low-paid work; this sort of theatrical employment, unbound by a contract, was an alternative to clandestine, occasional prostitution among sweated labourers and other lower-working-class women. The daytime occupations of Alhambra and Empire dancers and aerial figurantes in dressmaking, tailoring, retail sales, and factories allowed them to supplement their earnings and still gain an honest livelihood. The work of ballet girls (particularly in the back of the corps) was probably the hardest, the hours the longest, and the financial rewards the least of all theatrical specialties. Even in times of steady theatrical employment, their wages suggest that they, among all theatrical workers, needed a supplementary income the most. During periods when a chorus or corps de ballet was engaged in unpaid daytime rehearsals of a new piece and paid evening performances of an old piece, the need became greatest, for no time remained to work at the second waged occupation. No doubt, during these times prostitution offered a temporary replacement for piece work, but when would the women have taken their customers in the course of a fourteen-hour theatrical day?

Some prostitutes were born to their work and apprenticed by parents, relatives, and guardians,[34] while others (14,000 out of 16,000 according to the Millbank Prison sample) chose prostitution because they had 'nothing to do' (no trade or skill), or because of the possibility of high earnings, or self-employment, liberty, and 'being a lady'.[35] According to William Greg, vanity and the love of dress and admiration led women into prostitution:

> They are flattered by the attentions of those above them in station, and gratified by a language more refined and courteous than they hear from those of their own sphere. They enjoy the present pleasure, think they can secure themselves against being led on too far, and, like foolish moths, flutter round the flame which is to dazzle and consume them.[36]

Similar language is used to describe young women who enjoyed the attention and material comforts of a theatrical life. Greg's warning is usefully compared to Winifred Emery's description of the social life of a successful ingenue:

> The young actress finds herself gradually in the midst of a literary and artistic circle ... where she meets, and perhaps talks to, the cleverest men and women of the day. ... She is admired, complimented, and inundated with letters from people of all descriptions: photographers asking for sittings, admirers, male and female, pleading for autographs, unfortunate individuals wanting pecuniary help, anonymous communications, and invitations to numerous 'at homes', balls, and parties.

In order that her wardrobe might always be fresh, the actress 'has to pay long visits to her dressmaker',[37] and her adoring public plagues her for information about her holidays, health, and gowns. In moralists' view, the actress rebels, like the loathsome unwomanly woman, 'against the imprisonment of a domestic and monotonous career';[38] like the *demi-mondaine*, she is marked as a social adventuress, flaunting her beauty to accrue influence and wealth; and like the prostitute, she must perpetually stoke the fires of admiration, or perish. The incompatibility of *naïveté*, modesty, and theatrical ambition was interpreted as unfeminine, anti-family, and anti-male tendencies in women who chose to contravene their properly gendered upbringing. John Styles' description of the process resounded long after his 1806 tract went into a third edition:

> Transform her character: let modesty, the guardian of every female virtue, retire; let the averted eye which turns disgusted from the remotest approach of evil grow confident; let that delicacy of sentiment which feels a 'stain like a wound' give place to fashionable apathy; let the love of home and taste for the sweetly interesting employments of the domestic scene be exchanged for the pursuit of theatrical entertainment, and the vagrant disposition of a fashionable belle, and the picture is reversed; the female is degraded, and society has lost its most powerful, captivating charm.[39]

In this sense, the actress's contravention of men's rules for feminine behaviour likened her to prostitutes not only in terms of her public profile, but also in her perceived anti-domestic choice. She was criticized for doing exactly what men did: turning outside the home for social intercourse, intellectual stimulation, and occupational fulfillment.

In the 1880s and 90s, humanitarians believed that White Slavery (the systematic abduction of unwilling women) was responsible for much prostitution. Coercion, seduction, and deception had occasionally been thought to account for careers in acting too, though rarely with justification. The similarity between acting and prostitution was not abduction, but rather an economic choice with social consequences. Analogies with White Slavery exist, but Duchatelet, Greg, and Mayhew agree that low wages inadequate for subsistence (or the maintenance of dependants) was chief among the causes of prostitution,[40] and in the majority of cases, economic necessity was probably the most direct antecedent of either career. For aspiring actresses, financial need often combined with family trade or the perception of the stage as the least degrading of employment alternatives; Marie Lloyd, for example, claimed to have 'had a narrow escape of becoming a school teacher',[41] and delighted in her delivery from such a fate.

SEXUAL HARASSMENT

Women's decision to go on the stage became more of a free choice between equatable options as property, inheritance, and marriage laws were rewritten and as colleges, universities, and professions became more accessible. Many of the newcomers turned to private tutors for assistance in developing their skills, and to theatrical agents for help in getting their first and subsequent engagements. Some received valuable service from qualified professionals but others were defrauded, robbed, and physically endangered by unscrupulous charlatans. At the same time that the White Slavery scare was at its height, theatre professionals launched a campaign to expose and prosecute tutors and agents who took financial and sexual advantage of debutantes.

A classic example concerns 'Dr' Yeo Wellington, a clerk responsible for school and group bookings at the Olympic Theatre. In 1892, he took an office in Wellington Street, the Strand, and advertised to prepare actresses for the stage, making unauthorized use of Olympic note paper to respond to queries. A legal report in the *Stage* states that he promised Queenie Lorraine a part in a production of *Jack of Hearts*, and wrote a contract for £8 a week on condition that Lorraine supply him with a £5 bonus. When it was discovered that Wellington never rehearsed the play, never let a theatre, and illegally possessed *Jack of Hearts*, he was committed for trial.[42] At County Sessions he was sentenced to nine months imprisonment with hard labour for this and similar offences.[43]

In the following year, George Henry Gartley, an Adelphi super earning 15s. a week, advertised in the *Stage* for pupils. The police seized hundreds of letters and a cash book revealing that between March and December 1893, twenty-eight people paid or agreed to pay 178 guineas for his services. Among them was a woman who had experience dancing in the ballet at a New York casino; Gartley gave her two lessons of a half hour each, costing 2 guineas; two more guineas were to pay for her introduction at the Comedy Theatre. Another woman, Kate Fidler, responded to Gartley's advertisement for amateurs to join a 'long tour of an established success'. She had never been on the stage, though two of her sisters were actresses in Americ. She was told that her salary would be 2 guineas a week plus expenses. Later, Gartley informed her that the tour was postponed and a premium of £4 was needed; she sent £1 on deposit and received a script for a part and a note that the tour would commence on 9 January. The entire business was transacted by post; they never met until Fidler testified at Gartley's hearing.[44]

Early in 1894, another case of a fraudulent agent was heard at Bow Street. George Edward Bishop carried out business at four addresses and was shown to defraud many aspirants, including a woman who paid £30 for costumes she did not receive.[45] No doubt there were many untried cases in which credulous young women answered advertisements, had a few brief lessons or meetings to arrange their debuts or provincial tours, and then never saw the charlatan or their hard-earned savings again. If the novices did not discover the fraud until they were sent out of town, they could, like any deceived, abandoned, or impoverished woman, become very desperate and vulnerable indeed, as National Vigilance Association *Reports* demonstrate.[46]

In the case of John James Gardiner, a trial for fraud and conspiracy was combined with charges relating to sexual assault on at least four women. Emily Nelson, a barmaid, paid Gardiner and his associate Harry Roberts 10 guineas to be taught step-dancing. The trial report states that at her second lesson,

> Gardiner said that he thought she ought to wear a short dress, and suggested that she should have tights for her lessons. . . . Gardiner was very rude to her on each occasion she went there. Several times he behaved offensively. The first time he did so . . . she smacked his face and pushed him across the room to get away.

On another occasion he showed her a photograph of a nude woman. Deeply insulted, Nelson insisted that the balance of her lessons be taught by Roberts, though his conduct proved to be no better:

> On one occasion he came into the room after the lesson. . . she was putting her shoes on. Roberts sat on her knees. . . put one arm around her neck, and asked if she would go to Brighton with him the following Saturday. She said, 'Certainly not.' She tried to push him off. He asked if he could come up to her room.

When Nelson complained, she was sent to Rose D'Almaine, whom she did not know was Roberts's wife, and her course of training was completed.

Lily Holton, a 14-year-old kitchen maid in Cavendish Square, also went to Gardiner for lessons. He initially insisted on 16 guineas, which she obtained from her stepmother.

> She saw Gardiner, who gave her a song 'Come, come, don't say no.' He played the tune once on his violin, gave her the song, and told her to go home and learn the words. This was

the first lesson. He never taught her singing, but only played the violin as she sang. . . . After a fortnight Gardiner asked her if she would like to learn to dance. She said yes, and he told her to bring a short skirt and shoes. She bought shoes, and her stepmother made her a white skirt. She took it to Stamford-street, and Gardiner said it was too long. She said she could not have it shorter, and he wanted her to wear tights. Roberts on one occasion kissed her, and afterwards assaulted her. She left the house as quick[ly] as she could. She was afraid to tell her stepmother, lest she should take her away, as she had paid £21 [including £10 for costumes], and wanted to learn.

Holton was young, but not entirely naïve or without ability. When she obtained an engagement at the Mulberry Tree music hall in Stepney Green, she return to Gardiner for the final components of her wardrobe:

Gardiner measured her for tights round the ankle and the calf of the leg. He wanted to measure her round the thigh, and she refused. He then said that if the tights did not fit, it would not be his fault. He said he always had to measure all the ladies, and could not tell whether to get a large or small size if he did not measure them.

She eventually received proper tutelage from Daisy Lorne and a Mr Haynes.

Matilda Rosalie Goure, aged 19 and the wife of a dairyman, also responded to Gardiner's advertisement. He stated that his fee for teaching her and securing an engagement as an actress was 15 guineas. They purchased the text of *A Happy Pair* at French's and she was instructed to learn a page each week. After successive weeks of memorization and recitation without any elocutionary instruction, Gardiner insisted she pay another £30 for an engagement. About this time, Roberts took an interest in her:

[He] came and asked her how she was getting on, and whether she thought she would like the stage. She said she thought so. He asked her age, and she said nineteen. He said she was a dear little thing, and put his arms around her waist and tried to kiss her. She told him he was a married man, and to get away. Gardiner. . . said he wondered why a nice little thing like [her] wanted to go on the stage instead of the music hall, as he was sure she would look well in tights.

Though Gardiner neglected Goure's elocutionary training, Roberts undertook to teach her stage movement. He 'came in once and walked up and down the room, and said that she would have to do that [as demonstrated]. He also said she would have to thro[w] herself on the sofa, which she declined to do.' The testimony of Fanny Norris, aged 28, reveals what happened when more worldly-wise women resisted Gardiner's and Roberts's ploys from the outset. When Gardiner said it would take three months and cost 12 guineas to prepare her for the theatre,

> She half rose to go, and he rose, crossed over, and put his leg across the arm of her chair so as to prevent her rising. He asked her if she knew any married women who got their living at night time. He put another question, and placed his arm around her waist. She tried to get away, and after a hard struggle got into the middle of the room, where he tried to unbutton her dress. She felt choked, and could not scream. . . . She got to the handle of the door, but could not turn it. He caught her by the wrists. She sank down on a chair by the door and he made improper proposals. She got to the door a second time after a struggle, and he opened it by touching it in a way that made her think it had been fastened by a spring. She ran into the street.[47]

Of course, such ploys are not unique to the theatre. Similar scenarios can be recited from almost every branch of women's employment where men are in positions of power and authority and women are forced to go alone in search of instruction or where they are sequestered alone for any sort of private interview. The risks for theatrical women are obvious, but the evidence of abuses and assaults is rarely recorded.

Sarah Lane (originally Sarah Borrow) began her career as a music hall singer and later became associated with the Britannia Theatre, Hoxton, managing it from her husband's death in 1871 until her own decease in 1899. Two scenes in *Sam and Sallie*, a biography thinly enveloped in fiction, depict classic scenarios of sexual harassment. The descriptions are hyperbolic, but the situations are entirely plausible, and written by the Lanes' nephew. In the first incident, 'Sallie' Borrow's employer, 'Isaac Woolf' (manager of the Bedford Saloon), makes numerous advances to her. She manages to keep him at a distance until one day he finds her alone in her dressing room:

He seized her in his arms and began to kiss her bright red lips. Sallie was taken by surprise, but being strong and vigorous she successfully struggled to release herself. Having an umbrella in her hand she struck him a heavy blow on his nose which bled freely. Then, amid a volley of curses from Woolf, she fled.

That same night she returned, attended by her brother William.

Woolf had a swollen face and an ugly plastered wound, and glaring fiercely upon her said: 'I suppose you've come to apologize, young woman – look what you've done to me.'

Sallie answered firmly: 'No. I've come to do nothing of the sort. I've only come to tell you I've done with you and the Bedford Saloon for ever.'

'Yes,' added William, 'and you are lucky to get off so easily; if you insult my sister again I'll give you something more to teach you better manners.'

Woolf offers to let the affair drop, and to raise Sallie's salary, but she refuses to continue beyond the end of her weekly contract.[48] On the second occasion, she is performing at the Sun music hall in Knightsbridge under the name Sarah Wilton, singing and dancing between plays as well as acting in melodramas. One fateful night, the audience is full of Life Guards and the Life Guards are full of liquor.

The attendants, though doing their best, were quite inadequate to maintain order and Sarah Wilton's appearance now was the signal for especial disorder. It appears that a Life Guardsman had made a bet that he would publicly kiss Sarah Wilton in full view of the audience.

He had well primed himself with hot brandy and directly she came on and started her song, he staggered to his feet and, pushing off an attendant, the uniformed Life Guardsman climbed from the pit to the stage.

There was a buzz and a roar of excitement at this unexpected happening; the orchestra ceased playing, the conductor was aghast, and Sallie stopped singing and stood fascinated with terror! He came staggering towards her and grasping her arm shouted: 'Come on, Miss Wilton, I've got to kiss you, darling!'

But at this moment the stage manager, a little old man, rushed from the wing and thrust himself between them, only to be roughly thrown aside and hurled to the floor by the drunken soldier.

Momentarily, he had released his hold of Sallie, and she turned to fly, but, unsteady though he was, he managed to clutch her again before she could escape, and gathering her in his powerful arms, despite her frantic efforts, he thrust his lips towards her face, but now two arms as strong as his clutched his throat and dragged him from the terror-stricken Sallie.

Her rescuer was Sam Lane, who happened to be in attendance; he sprang forth from his box at the first sign of trouble. The soldier was knocked over and ignominiously wedged in a kettle drum: 'The audience, on its feet and aroused to intense excitement, now burst into thunders of applause, as though it had all been a prearranged sensation provided for its delectation and amusement.'[49]

For drunken Life Guardsmen, unscrupulous managers, and corrupt agents, the distinction between a prostitute and an actress was of little importance because they were both types of women whose public lives, financial fragility, and independence signalled vulnerability and the likelihood of successful, undetected exploitation. But spectators and stage door johnnies are not the only men reported to inappropriately handle actresses. H.G. Hibbert describes a incident at Astley's during a performance of *Mazeppa*:

> [James] Fernandez agreed to decide a bet made by some noble sportsmen, as to whether the lovely form nightly posed on the back of a moderately wild horse, to traverse an ingeniously terraced 'rake,' was all [Adah Isaacs] Menken's, or partly due to what the costumiers call 'symmetricals', in plain English, padding. Fernandez, to secure his evidence gripped the actress with a cruel firmness when he lifted her to the horse that night; and, deeply enraged by his incomprehensive conduct, she cut his cheek open with a short riding whip she carried.[50]

Sexual harassment of leading players was probably much less frequent than of ballet dancers, chorus girls, and other auxiliaries. According to Leopold Wagner, the difference did not arise because leading actresses were perceived more respectfully, but because managers made them less accessible. Many theatrical commentators discounted the popular view that ballet dancers were promiscuous, but Wagner attests that on stage and above stage they were accosted by their colleagues:

With 'ladies of the ballet' and the 'show girls' [chorus line] in a burlesque the conditions are by no means favourable. Actors of the lower order do unfortunately expect to have 'a good time' with these auxiliaries, because they are drawn from an inferior class of society, and rarely possess the firmness to sedulously shun their advances. Even the scene-shifters and 'property men' look forward to the pantomime season as a period of licence, during which they may play havoc among girls who do not stand on their moral dignity; but they draw the line at the *corps de ballet*. We have observed, too, particularly in minor houses, that the *figurantes* in a trans-formation scene do not always receive that careful handling while being strapped up to the lofty irons [to be flown] which common decency demands.[51]

Very few such reports come to light. It is difficult to prove, on the basis of a handful of reports, that sexual harassment was prevalent among any group of performers or from whom it came. The evidence is couched in generalizations, but it may be significant that the reporters are all men. In 1897–8, the profession had an opportunity to directly confront this issue when Clement Scott, critical doyen of the *Daily Telegraph* since 1871, expressed his views in the famous interview 'Does the Theatre Make for Good?,' published in *Great Thoughts*, an evangelical Christian magazine.

Scott spoke frankly, summarizing his thirty-seven year con-nection with the stage as a critic, author of plays, adaptor of French comedies, and in-law to a theatrical family. Many of his colleagues, employers, and friends were influential actors, managers, and playwrights. He spoke out of conviction, not malice or opportun-ism, for he had nothing to gain by offending and no patronage to win by obsequiousness. He asserted that in the shockingly overcrowded profession, middle-class women from non-theatrical families found the acquaintance of or a personal introduction to a respectable actor-manager indispensable to break into the theatre at a level that was not detrimental to their self-perception as well-bred, well-mannered women. Scott was the instrument for many such introductions, but in *Great Thoughts* he stated that young women who insisted on going on the stage contrary to his advice and without his introduction would necessarily confront situations that were injurious to innocence. Speaking in a middle-class, fatherly friend-of-the-family persona, he bluntly claimed that the atmos-phere of theatres was so impure that women were either corrupted from without or could not avoid acceding to the pollution through their innate weaknesses:

> It is nearly impossible for a woman to remain pure who adopts the stage as a profession. Everything is against her. The freedom of life, of speech, or gesture, which is the rule behind the curtain, renders it almost impossible for a woman to preserve that simplicity of manner which is after all her greatest charm. The whole life is artificial and unnatural to the last degree.... But there are far more serious evils to be encountered than these. These drawbacks are the things that render it impossible for a lady to remain a lady. But what is infinitely more to be deplored is that a woman who endeavours to keep her purity is almost of necessity foredoomed to failure in her career.... Temptation surrounds her in every shape and on every side; her prospects frequently depend on the nature and the extent of her compliance, and, after all, human nature is very weak.[52]

Following the publication of 'Does the Theatre Make for Good?' all of Scott's transgressions – real or supposed – were dredged up and published in the English and American papers. The *Daily Mail* of London fanned the controversy to the detriment of its rival paper, Scott's *Telegraph*, by encouraging performers to write in condemnation of the interview. Many did just that, arguing that though actresses encountered temptations, so did all young women who pursued their livelihood away from home. Volunteers arose to escort Scott through the theatres of the nation (as if he had never been in one) to reveal the true nature of backstage behaviour. Scott's statement that 'no one is pure, no one is beyond temptation, and it is unwise in the last degree to expose a young girl to the inevitable consequences of a theatrical life',[53] was repeatedly contradicted by professionals, including Fitzroy Gardner, Edward Chester, Joseph Jefferson, Lionel Brough, Charles and Daniel Frohman, Frank Benson, Frank Lindo, Arnold Golsworthy, Herbert Shaw, William Lockhart, George Snazelle, Charles J. Bell, Henry Fielding, and five church ministers. Only two women, Adelaide Calvert and Adelaide Farren (both daughters, wives, and mothers of performers), responded. This preponderance of male correspondents in a profession overstocked with articulate public women seems a little odd. A note in a reprinted edition of the interview seems odder still; it explains that when advance proofs of 'Does the

Theatre Make for Good?' were sent to leading actors and actresses, none responded. Apparently, the bare score of denials that appeared in the press were written in response to another edition of more than a hundred copies specially printed and distributed by the *Daily Mail*. The interview was widely known, and it was certainly contentious, but the controversy did not, therefore, arise spontaneously, but only through calculated manufacture by a newspaper bent on pursuing a good story.

If the profession hesitated over the first printing, why did the majority of performers – particularly the women who were implicated – not respond to the second special printing either? The story about Gerald du Maurier's, Henry Ainley's, and Herbert Beerbohm Tree's discussion of the 'Scott' issue over dinner at the Garrick Club is pertinent:

> Suddenly, to everyone's amazement, a generally silent, and constantly bibulous member blurted out that Scott was quite right, and that most actresses were (he used an Elizabethan word). There was consternation; the man had drunk, of course, more than was good for him, and allowance had to be made.... 'Look here,' said Tree, tapping him on the shoulder, 'of course we know that you have had – well' – he looked significantly at the empty champagne bottle – 'and that you wouldn't have said it if you hadn't; but how would you like it if we declared your sister was ...?' 'She is,' said the alcoholic member, stoutly; and the deputation broke up in confusion.[54]

The successful, prosperous, middle-class male segment of the profession eventually reacted to Scott, wrote indignant letters, and hounded his editor to discontinue his reviews (though not his weekly column) in the *Telegraph*, but how much of this response is the posturing of duty, habit, or self-interest? The letters that discount Scott's views in *Great Thoughts* point to specific instances of humility, specific exemplars of virtue, but the pleas of denial are by necessity general.

Once again, the commentators on sexual harassment are men. Does the *Great Thoughts* controversy provide any insight into the prevalence of sexual harassment? Three interpretations are possible: the question is discounted by lack of evidence on either side; lacking sufficient sociological or legal data the patchy evidence is inconclusive, and the question is unanswerable; or the question is answered – affirmatively – by the conspicuous silence of women. The last suggestion is the most fruitful. Silence can speak, particularly on topics of sexual blackmail, coercion, attack, and collusion. Although Scott's unfavourable reviews of acting inspired hundreds of vitriolic personal rejoinders throughout his career,[55] evidently there was something about the *Great Thoughts* interview that caused actresses to lay down their pens. Perhaps it was the truth.

Dismissing Scott's claims only on the evidence of men is tantamount to acquitting a defendant simply because he pleads innocence. Men had nothing to gain by concurring, but women had everything to gain by feigning detachment. Explicit affirmation would have demonstrated a woman's Fall and jeopardized her working relationships; explicit contradiction would have denied all women's reality and sanctioned widespread practices. When advising each other on career choices, women did not praise the stage. Established actresses who were appealed to by letter universally discouraged dairymaids, laundresses, factory girls, servants, and the pampered middle-classes from crowding the ranks still further and exchanging a quiet life for such a precarious one. In a book on women and the professions, Lena Ashwell observed that 'the unskilled, pleasure-loving, short-sighted but ambitious girl' entering the theatre had 'several shades of temptation . . . placed before her'.

> Not only the money, and the advantages which an outward show of prosperity may bring with it; not only amusements and luxuries; but a much more dangerous and difficult temptation, which is not possible in other trades . . . the offer of greater opportunities in her work, the opportunities which an 'understudy' may bring in its train; the opportunity of a small part; the gratification of ambition. There is no more immorality than in other trades, but there is an amount of humiliating and degrading philandering, a mauling sensuality which is more degrading than any violent abduction.[56]

This language is not precisely like Clement Scott's, for it provides concrete instances of temptations which all have to do with assiduous devotion to work, pursuit of advancement, and the womanly scourge of pleasing.

The vast majority of performers – and there were more women than men in 1897 – remained silent, saved their precious penny stamps, and let the matter slide. The conspicuous silent majority was female. It was this segment that Ashwell and Scott (who was a charitable man) would have preferred to steer into any other gainful, steady, uncrowded, respectable employment, or at any rate one that did not present the complicating risks of vagabondage, bohemianism, and co-sexual work to women who could not see through the game, who were not buffered by a theatrical family, and who played with an avocation rather than a vocation.

Between 1895 and 1897, actors advertised the knighthood of Henry Irving as proof of the profession's respectability, but as far as its women were concerned Scott pointed out the consequences of centuries of prejudice, licence, and hardship. It is no wonder that actresses tried to ignore the charges. It is no wonder that actresses kept their names out of the controversy, with the exception of two who were born into the profession (a circumstance that Scott specifically exempts from his conclusions). It is no wonder that the trio at the Garrick Club slunk away from the gentleman with the Elizabethan vocabulary, routed and confused. A whole year passed before the interview resulted in Scott's resignation from the *Telegraph*. The stroke was neither immediate nor terrible. The repudiation was neither complete nor unanimous. There was far too much to be accounted for.

THE QUINTESSENTIAL SEXUAL TERROR

According to Victorian lore 'once a prostitute, always a prostitute': the history of a 'woman-with-a-past' was never erased. Similarly, once a woman crossed the threshold of a stage door she was (gasp!) 'An Actress' for the rest of her days. Ellen Carol Dubois and Linda Gordon call Victorian prostitution 'the quintessential sexual terror,'[57] but for some families (particularly dissenting Protestants) the stage was almost worse. At least a prostitute-daughter was 'dead' to her family: actress-daughters lived on in full view of any member of the public who paid to see. Daughters who 'fell' from virtue or trod the boards alike found themselves penniless, disinherited, and unprotected by respectable families; though patronized by men, they were condemned by women and their natural circles. It was unthinkable to middle-class Victorians that any woman would freely, willingly choose to whore for a living, but it was undeniable that women did choose to enter the danger zone of artistic freedom and sexual opportunity in the theatre, however forced the decision may have been by economic circumstances and the limitations of alternatives. Except among evangelical social workers, prostitutes were not considered a suitable or desirable subject of conversation for middle-class ladies, but actresses (individually and collectively) were a conversationally acceptable substitute in almost every social group. The lessons that could be extracted (or the thrills that could be generated) were equatable. The press was obliged to reinforce stereotypes while gratifying voracious interest in sexuality, and to satiate prurient tastes with news of a substitute bohemian group.

The profession encouraged the respectable press to call attention to the fact that some theatrical women really were chaste, but the general public — accustomed to the transformative allure of theatrical illusion — distrusted what merely seemed to be. Many performers did step from the stage to the marriage altar, but matrimony was surely not the outcome of every affair. Despite the rise in the respectability of the profession, the attractive, boisterous actresses of the 1890s were still seen to attract men like bees to honey. Some even made choice alliances with peers, including Belle of the sisters Binton, a variety hall singer and dancer who became the Countess of Clancarty; Connie Gilchrist, a teenage burlesque dancer, later the Countess of Orkney; and Valerie Reece, another burlesque star, who became Lady Meux. The most successful and notorious of performers were the Gaiety Girls, of whom their manager, John Hollingshead, writes:

> The ballet-girl of 1894 differs in essentials very little from her sister (or mother?) of 1865. She has, of course, advanced with School Boards and the march of intellect. In 1865 she was satisfied with a holiday at Margate: in 1894 she likes to rub shoulders with royalty at Homburg, and to show herself in the winter at Monte Carlo. Who can blame her? Certainly not the advocates of education.[58]

Although the aspiration for Monte Carlo implies a rise in status, low wages were common to both generations. On wages of 30s. a week[59] with intermittent periods of unemployment, chorus girls could not afford to equip such ostentatious holidays. The inevitable conclusion is that some one else must have paid the bills.

As one Islington dancer explained: 'Perhaps no girl is subject to so many temptations as the ballet girl. Behind the scenes she is constantly being addressed by men of fortune and talent, and to a girl comparatively ignorant, the temptations are great, and the bright promises held out are many.'[60] The notion that ballet girls were unvirtuous was prevalent, but so were denials.[61] The Islington dancer's scenario of assignations, ignorance, and temptation is common in the theatre but not unique to it, and needs to be put in its proper context. Judgments about the waywardness of theatrical women reflect the social construction of gender as well as work. Sexual judgments about actresses are invariably at their expense: they, not their lovers in the privileged classes, stage door seducers, or employer-harassers are seen as guilty wrongdoers whose suffering is justified. In this sense, sexual judgements about actresses closely resemble the pattern for all Victorian women, but actresses confronted the consequences of this double standard daily, in public. They found no privacy in a work place, no anonymity in a thoroughfare, and no refuge in a new occupation. They were marked, and the very recognizability that ensured a livelihood also prohibited escape. Their challenge to the ideology of the domestic sphere and patriarchal supremacy in the public sphere account for their social ostracism and vilification.

Referring to the Maiden Tribute of Modern Babylon scandal, Gayle Rubin observes that 'sexuality in western cultures is so mystified, the wars over it are often fought at oblique angles, aimed at phony targets, conducted with misplaced passions, and are highly, intensely, symbolic'.[62] This seems to be borne out in the very attempt to define a prostitute. Dubois and Gordon observe that 'prostitution involves the separation of women into the good and the bad, a division with class implications',[63] in which case actresses (who were paid for their services as public objects of scrutiny and who were often blatantly displayed for sexual stimulation) fell on the bad side no matter what their private lives were like. The Victorian theatre and prostitution were alike in that they both traded on sensuality and pleasure, with women as the commodity.

Ruth Rosen and Judith Walkowitz observe that 'focusing exaggerated attention on prostitution was for many reformers a way of avoiding more complex and compromising socioeconomic issues.'[64] Like prostitutes, actresses were to a certain extent 'lawless'. As working mothers and wives (but not necessarily both), they threatened traditional family structures, the balance of economic power, and gender-based restrictions of association, movement, dress, education, and influence. In a society hostile to nocturnal womanhood, the actress was conspicuous. If she maintained her independence, guarded herself against assault, and insulated herself socially and financially, she was bound to create hostility. Her livelihood was also very fragile.

There is justification for the popular association of the trades: as described in the following chapter, sexual prurience and the disregard for vestimentary, kinesic, and genderized behavioural codes combined, in the living actress, to create a seemingly decorous dynamic that was blatantly false to anyone attuned to the violation of general ethical standards. Female performers, regarded as a single class by the dominant culture, received the stigma uniformly in spite of their professional specialties and socio-economic diversity. There are exceptions (a few exemptions and a few singled out for special approbation) but though the stigma endured, it was not deserved in most cases. Parallels and convergence between performers and prostitutes are demonstrable. Synonymity – the crux of the stigma – is not.

Despite the tendency for Victorian performers to be credited with increasing respectability and middle-class status and for actors to receive the highest official commendations, the popular association between actresses and prostitutes and belief in actresses' inappropriate sexual conduct endured throughout the nineteenth century. In the USA, religious fundamentalism accounts for much of the prejudice,[65] but in Great Britain, where puritanical views were not as influential on the theatre, other factors helped to preserve the derogatory view of actresses. In certain times and places actresses did have real links with the oldest of all 'women's professions',[66] but the notion that the dual identity of Roman dancers or the exploits of some Restoration performers justify the popular association between actresses and prostitutes in the Victorian era is patently insufficient. The notion persisted throughout the nineteenth century because Victorians recognized that acting and whoring were the occupations of self-sufficient women who plied their trades in public places, and because Victorians believed that actresses' male colleagues and patrons inevitably complicated women's transient life-styles, economic insecurity, and night hours with sexual activity. In the spirit of Gilbert and Gubar's axiom that experience generates metaphor and metaphor creates experience,[67] the actress and the prostitute were both objects of desire whose company was purchased through commercial exchange. While patrons bought the right to see them, to project their fantasies on them, and to denigrate and misrepresent their sexuality, both groups of women found it necessary to constantly sue for men's attention and tolerate the false imagery. Their similarities were reinforced by co-existence in neighbourhoods and work places where they excited and placated the playgoer's lust in an eternal loop, twisted like a Mobius strip into the appearance of a single surface.

Bert States regards performers' relation to dramatic texts as justification for the enduring association between actors and prostitutes, arguing that 'the actor is someone who consents to be used; one text is the same as another'.[68] This has phenomenological significance, but the performer is neither a chameleon nor a *tabula rasa*. If States means that a violation of personhood takes place – a textual rape – he does not account for the *actress's* particular stigma, and renders the strong prejudice against Victorian female dancers and supernumeraries (who spoke no text and assumed no characters) totally inexplicable. Without considering the interplay of theatre and community, the association cannot be explained.

1 Collage of pantomime scenes, *Days' Doings*, 24 December 1870. Reproduced by kind permission of the British Newspaper Library, Colindale.

Marie Lloyd

Jenn & Emma D'Auban
in the Indian Ballet

2 Drury Lane pantomime, *Robinson Crusoe*, 1881, *Illustrated London News*, January 1882. Reproduced by kind permission of Queen's University at Kingston.

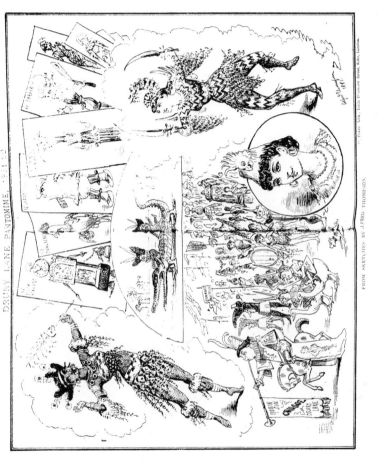

DRURY LANE PANTOMIME, 1881-2

FROM SKETCHES BY J.FRED. THOMPSON.

3 Drury Lane pantomime, *Robinson Crusoe*, 1881, *Theatre*, January 1882. Reproduced by kind permission of Queen's University at Kingston.

A FANCY SKETCH OF THE MYSTERY OF "MAKING UP" ON BOXING NIGHT.

4 A pantomime chorister, her attendants, dressers, and admirer, *Days' Doings*, 24 December 1870. Reproduced by kind permission of the British Newspaper Library, Colindale.

5 Nellie Farren in the burlesque *Ruy Blas*, Gaiety Theatre, 1889. Reproduced by kind permission of the British Library.

6 Fred Leslie in *Ruy Blas*, Gaiety Theatre, 1889. Reproduced by kind permission of the British Library.

7 Finette in a *volupté* pose, *carte-de-visite*, late 1860s. Reproduced by kind permission of the Kinsey Institute for Research in Sex, Gender, and Reproduction.

THE LAST NEW CAN-CAN.——MLLE. COLONNA AND HER PARISIAN TROUPE AT THE ALHAMBRA PALACE.

8 Colonna (on the right) and her troupe, *Days' Doings*, 8 October 1870. Reproduced by kind permission of the British Newspaper Library, Colindale.

9 Bouguereau, *Aurora*, realized in the first set of *tableaux
vivants* at the Palace Theatre, 1893. Reproduced by kind
permission of the British Museum, Department of Prints and
Drawings.

10 Solomon J. Solomon, *Cassandra*, realized in the first set of *tableaux vivants* at the Palace Theatre, 1893. Reproduced by kind permission of the British Museum, Department of Prints and Drawings.

11 Violet Vanbrugh as Rosalind, cabinet photo, *c.* 1888, in Sarah Thorne's company at Margate. Private collection.

"THE DESIRE OF THE MOTH FOR THE STAR."—*Mistress.* "And you dare to tell me, Belinda, that you have actually answered a *theatrical advertisement?* How *could* you be such *a wicked* girl?" *Belinda (whimpering).* "Well, mum,—*other* young lidies—gow on the—stige—why shouldn't *I* gow?"

12 Cartoon satirizing working-class women's theatrical aspirations. Reproduced by kind permission of *Punch.*

13 Song sheet cover for 'The Six Magnificent Bricks', 1866. Reproduced by kind permission of the British Library.

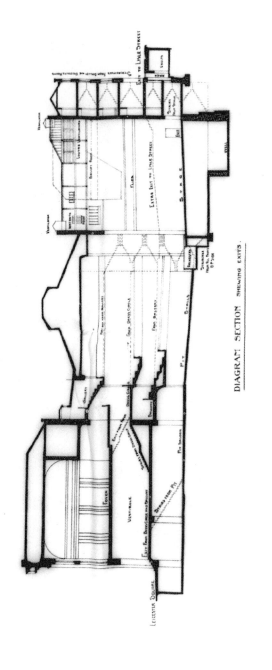

DIAGRAM SECTION SHEWING EXITS.

TWENTY ARCH's
by REGENT St SW

14 Empire Theatre showing gallery, dress circle, balcony, and pit and stalls levels contentious in LCC hearings in 1893. Reproduced by kind permission of the Greater London Public Record Office.

Part II

CONDITIONS OF WORK

4

ACTRESSES AND THE *MISE EN SCÈNE*

A series of paradoxes characterizes actresses' appearance on stage: while embodying the ideals of feminine beauty and setting the standards for female fashion, they were 'defeminized' by the very act of taking up a public career in the theatre. The same women who impersonated Dianas and Vestias also claimed a place in a competitive co-sexual world of work, spent their evenings away from home, and exhibited themselves before the public gaze. To complicate matters, femininity was the quality traditionally credited with making women the objects of male desire, yet actresses' 'defeminization' made them more desirable than ever in a sexual sense. On stage, femininity and sexual desirability co-existed, yet in order to accept the fiction of an idealized femininity in a stage persona, Victorians were required to separate the defeminized actress from her roles. They then had to decide which part of the individual would receive moral strictures.

In *Pendennis*, Thackeray explicitly depicts an actress separated into two parts. Miss Fotheringay, who is thoroughly charming as Ophelia, also has the at-home persona of Miss Costigan, the stage-player daughter of a *déclassé* Irish braggart. Only young and naive spectators are transfixed by her artificial half (Miss Fotheringay) and remain incapable of differentiating the public from the private woman; the wise and experienced majority of playgoers appreciate the artificial half while expressing unwavering repulsion for the real half (Miss Costigan). Thackeray's example demonstrates that despite Miss Costigan's chastity, dutifulness, and thrift, the private woman is believed to be unfeminine while the public chameleon (who plays characters and thus is not her real self) is femininity incarnate.[1] The same separation between the private and theatrical halves of an actress accounts for Ellen Terry's success on stage: she returned to the theatre, lauded, after she left her first husband G.F. Watts, and again after six years of being in a common-law relationship with Edward Godwin. Even with several ill-fated marriages, a succession of lovers, and two illegitimate children, Ellen Terry still evoked the consummation of 'womanliness' in her roles and could command universal respect and admiration in the practice of her art.

Actresses were subjectively judged, and separation of them as individuals from their roles could be complete. However, the private selves of women who did not specialize in conventionally feminine roles, or who performed in illegitimate lines of business that contravened gestural and vestimentary social norms, were particularly subject to unflattering social judgments. Since women's employment was concentrated in illegitimate lines of business it is essential to consider the circumstances of the majority by detailing the performance conventions that marked actresses' gender and had a bearing on the interpretation of their womanhood and social existence. The objective of this is not performance reconstruction, but rather an exercise in historical semiotics involving the playtext (the usual semiotic map in drama and theatre studies) when appropriate and available, but concentrating on the information provided by encodings in clothing, gesture, and pictorial composition which are major influences on interpretations of the visually transmitted text.

Many of the most enduring conventions of performance flagrantly violated standards that governed everyday life outside the theatre. Some playgoers sensed improprieties but were unsuccessful in having the conventions banned because they were unable to articulate precisely what and why conventions were improper. The conventions likely enjoyed long theatrical tenure because interpretation of the images could follow two distinct lines. The most common line interpreted performance simply as an entertaining spectacle intended to be read overtly and empirically only at its face value. Within this system, playgoers failed to recognize short hemlines or sexually referential gestures as anything other than exercises of theatrical licence. As long as conventions were observed, tolerance was guaranteed.

The other interpretive system recognized encodings borrowed from and supported by the contemporaneous language of sexuality. Recently, sexuality has been theorized as an assigned encoding (socially produced, not inherent), historically particular and heavily laden with the preoccupations of the time. Along with narrativity in the drama, sexuality exerts a strong influence on interpretation, and as Annette Kuhn notes 'meanings do not reside in images . . . they are circulated between representation, spectator and social forma-tion'.[2] Spectators' ability to read impropriety into the stage appearance of the actress – to scandalize the idealized femininity – required knowledge of the referential context of female erotic topography. Such encodings were intended to be perceived by only a limited portion of the audience attuned to the covert meanings and prone to enjoy sexuality that flagrantly violated general ethical standards. Without the full referential vocabulary, a spectator could not understand the covert meanings. This lexicon can be redis-covered, allowing the visual performance text to be read through its historical codes. This does not make the stigmatization of the actress or the defeminization of her stage persona 'true' or justifiable, but merely recognizes the imagistic gestalt in the minds of some spectators.

A logical place to start looking for the Victorian lexicography of sex is in pictorial and prose erotica that was available to men and functioned as the iconic sign of sexual fantasy and belief. Research in the two largest repositories of English erotica – the Private Case and associated collections of the British Library, and the archives of the Kinsey Institute for Research on Sex, Gender, and Reproduction – reveal some illuminating characteristics about the pornographic imagination and its relationship to the stage. Victorian erotica is somewhat haphazardly preserved, with elite rare editions retained out of proportion to their hold on the marketplace, but every effort has been made to study a cross-section of materials circulated in England between 1830 and 1910, from sumptuously bound and illustrated printed books to penny serials and cheap postcards.[3] In the extant material, the theatre in general and actresses in particular appear so frequently that acting is undoubtedly the most often specified occupational type of women characters. This observation is true of every format of erotica, suggesting that the referential codes derived from pornography were current among readers of every taste, that they were widely disseminated across the social and economic strata of male society, and that they are implicated in the viewing of every type of theatre for every class of audience.

Victorian erotica verified in a fictive (but for readers, a real) sense that the actress was inseparable from the whore and synonymous with sex. But unlike the generalized and anonymous 'schoolgirls', 'wives', 'maids', 'prostitutes', and 'ladies of fashion' that also populate erotica, the actress's identity could be specified. By naming Eliza Vestris, Mrs Honey, and Mrs Nisbett – all personally scandalous women who specialized in breeches roles – erotica of the 1840s seemed to verify the existence of the fantasized underworld of perpetually loose chemises, easily spread thighs, militarily erect penises, and double entendre. Just as importantly, it located this world in the theatre district of London's West End, lending geographic credibility.

Vestris's erotic cult spun spurious 'memoirs' until the 1890s,[4] demonstrating that sexual fantasy bore little relation to actresses' social conduct. Nevertheless, the stereotypes of actresses that evolved in such erotic 'biographies' created a tradition with its own rules of fiction and reality, readily extended by its readers to interpretation of living, breathing women. It is impossible to say whether the theatre supplied visions that became invested with eroticism in the context of pornography, or whether the theatre employed motifs already infused with sexuality, and it is unnecessary to resolve the question. What is important is that because of the existence of this large body of literature documenting, justifying, and enacting the erotic fictions associated with actresses it is impossible to claim that actresses were in control of all the signs they gave off. No matter how scrupulous their conduct was as private citizens, actresses had no authority or control over their public sign-making of bodily coverings, gestures, and spatial relationships lodged in a separate but symbiotically dependent source.

COSTUMING THE EROTIC TOPOGRAPHY

In the nineteenth century, biology rigidly determined education, employment, economic opportunities, reading material, and of course clothing. The historical meaning of sexuality is assimilated in clothing. On the street, fashion constantly fluctuated, reassigning focus from the bust in 1800 to the waistline in 1820, from the head and sleeves in 1830 to the shoulders in 1840, from the crinoline hoops of the 1850s to the bustle of the 1870s, and from the pencil silhouette of 1880 to the sweeping 'X' of the 1890s. Independent of this evolution, which took place in real time on the bodies of real women, the costumes of certain types of stage characters remained remarkably fixed, and the assignment of sexually 'innocent' and 'guilty' body parts saw very little change between the 1830s and the end of the century.

Before the movement for historical authenticity took hold, the cloth and decoration of theatrical costume alone signalled the dramatic role: black velvet and white satin dresses, point lace, and stomacher for the tragic line; pink, blue, and white satin dresses with feathers, fans, and veils for comedy; and scarlet or buff frocks with blue or green ribbons, crucifix pendant, and french head dress for melodrama.[5] Costuming for the illegitimate stage also had conventions of fabric and drapery signalling another range of parts. The uncorsetted below-the-knee diaphanous gown worn by Marie Taglioni in *La Sylphide* (1832) is credited with setting the standard for countless female roles that followed. The diaphanous fabrics and floating lines of ballet dresses in the 1830s were introduced to enhance the choreographic effect of Romantic plots, but it is clear from engravings and lithographs of *danseuses* that what was described as ethereality was seen as transparency, and that it was the bodies as much as the dances of naiads, shades, and water-nymphs that were prized. By associating a skirt's lightness, shortness, and looseness with the desirable qualities of femininity, ideal proportion, and grace, choreography and costuming worked together to please the ubiquitous voyeur. By freeing the torso from stiff boning, the costumes also signified a refusal to suffer and be still; the well-disciplined mind and well-regulated feelings that were associated with tight lacing gave way to connotations of loose morals and easy virtue, which also fuelled the misapprehensions of performers' accessibility and sexual availability favoured by men.[6]

Evidence abounds of how these costumes appeared on stage and in the imaginative fantasy of spectators. What could previously be displayed only through cross-dressing could now be revealed peek-a-boo in feminine roles. In a famous portrayal of Fanny Elssler (*La Volière*), the dancer alights from a jump in fifth position; her four layered skirt drifts down after her, the buildup of transparencies revealing the least at the hip, the most at the knee. In response to such spectacles, Sam Ward commented:

> [Elssler] is a charming dancer. The ideal of a fascinating mistress. . . . Her eyes charm the Pit and Boxes by a mightier spell than the boa constrictor's. He who yields to her influence must, for that moment, become a voluptuary. Her influence is sensual, her ensemble the incarnation of seductive attraction.[7]

Even a morally unblemished dancer such as Taglioni is depicted in a low *décolleté* off-the-shoulder gown, with transparent skirts clearly showing her entire leg and lower pelvis (*La Gitana*). Frequently, the feet of *danseuses* are depicted bare, though the choreography required heavily padded and darned shoes over the inevitable pink tights. In this highly conventionalized dance form, the defiance of gravity suggested unshod other-worldliness: if, in imagination, the feet were bare, so were the legs, and if the legs were bare the potential revelation of transparent skirts was unlimited. One visual message of the Romantic ballet was, therefore, that of highly contrived semi-nudity. Women did not actually perform barefoot or bare legged until the Trilby craze of 1895 paved the way for Maud Allan's 'classical' dances in the first decade of the twentieth century.[8]

Between the 1830s and 50s, dancers' hemlines slowly edged up from mid-calf to the classical length at the knee. By mid-century, this classical tutu had come to stand for beauty, vigour, suppleness, vivacity, and harmony in its own right. In repose as well as in motion, this costume carried over the message of sublimated eroticism that the fabula, casting, and choreography of Romantic dance had so ingeniously inscribed. In 1895, Wilhelm (William Charles Pitcher), a leading designer of ballets and pantomimes, explained just how long lived and entrenched the conventions of the old ballet were. *Danseuses* were particularly reluctant to part from vestimentary traditions, for as Wilhelm complained, their

> beau-idéal of costumes for all occasions is an abbreviated perversion of a modern *debutante's* ball-dress, shorn of two-thirds of its length and *décolletée* to exaggeration. This attire, which has been so graphically described as 'beginning too late and ending too soon,' is completed by a ribbon knotted round the throat, and by a corresponding bow in the hair (a favourite 'finishing touch'); and is insisted on, in spite of its glaring inappropriateness to the character say, of an evil temptress.[9]

The tenacity of this costume can be explained, in part, by its universal adoption by the corps de ballet of the music halls and the choruses of pantomime, burlesque, and extravaganza after the 1850s. In its new homes, the ballet skirt and its companion, pink tights, were the sign of the actress, marking a multitude of women who posed rather than danced in pageants of prettiness as objects of beauty and allure. It was as much the uniform of their work as a City man's derby or a jockey's coat: nonessential, but nonetheless irremovable.

Just as lines of business connoted degrees of dignity, the cut and fabric of costumes reflected the theatrical hierarchy. In the 1880s, one middle-class provincial actress who aspired to The Drama but was forced by economic circumstances to take a role in a pantomime expressed her degradation in terms of dress:

> Once I should have thought it dreadful to have to play in a pantomime. I never dreamed of anything less than Shakespeare and black velvet, and now I am very thankful and think myself fortunate to go on for a fairy queen in gauze and spangles.
> *December 28.* – The pantomime is still going on. I can only speak my lines and feel generally idiotic; there is no acting possible. I found my own dress, as [otherwise] I should have had to wear the abbreviated skirts of the ballet, and I should have felt more foolish than ever, walking on and off in such a costume. So I bought some silver tarlatan in High Street, and made a classical dress, which certainly looks more graceful. They say I am 'a lovely fairy queen'. Distance must indeed lend enchantment! I feel such a fool.[10]

For this woman, who scratched a living in leading and secondary parts in third rate companies, the step from legitimate business to the pantomime was momentous. Draping the fairy queen like Volumnia or Calphurnia instead of Odette or La Sylphide was a preferable compromise – despite the investment – to unveiling her legs according to the conventional cut and line of costumes adopted from the ballet. Without an impeccably chaste stage appearance this actress recognized that both her professional and private personae would be compromised. By going on the stage she had lost the good reputation of her private self, so she anxiously sought to retain the respectability of the half she could control through judicious image-making and co-optation of The Drama's vestimentary legitimacy.

While black velvet and white lace were the marks of artistry, gauze and spangles were the key to mass appeal and commercial success. As a cartoon in *The Days' Doings*, an erotic weekly of 1870–72, quipped: ' "Shakespeare" spells ruin, but "Legs" mean dividends: Instead of the revived drama, we have a galvanized corpse in spangled gauze, and a jumble of pink legs and costly accessories, under which the tragic and comic muse have been trampled and suffocated during the last twenty years and more.'[11] Like 'Jane Sampson' of the *Illustrated Times* Theatrical Types, successful candidates did not need to be highly skilled to earn a place nearest the footlights.[12] Physical attractiveness was extremely important. Female performers were commodified as the wearers of revealing costumes, but it was the revealed parts, not the costumes themselves, that were the real spectacle: the places where costumes were not took focus over where they were. A Tower division magistrate's description of ballet costumes in the Alhambra's *Babil and Bijou* proves where his eyes were drawn:

> Skirts were in most cases altogether abolished from the dresses of the Ballet or split apart & hollowed out in front, so that the legs encased in 'skin-tights' became visible right up to the body with nothing but what may be termed tight silk bathing drawers to conceal the fork. . . . I feel strongly that the object of such dressing can only be designed to excite the passions of the young & it must be very harmful for young people of both sexes to witness such exhibitions together.[13]

The exposure of legs has a long stage tradition, and the effect of this ploy on box office receipts suggests that its sexual power, first discovered in the reign of Charles II, did not wane under Victoria. Female legs have no inherent sexual meaning, but their referent is obvious when the custom is to obscure their existence. For the purposes of stage costume, the leg was divided into parts – foot, ankle, calf, knee, and thigh – though *pars pro toto* (the part for the whole) ruled. Many examples of cross-dressing in a knee-length tunic, tights, and boots exist from the early part of the century: Eliza Vestris as Don Felix and as Olivia (*John of Paris*), Marie Tree as Coelio (*Native Land*), Miss Woolgar as Rosalind, Mrs John Brougham (Annette Nelson) as Cherubino, and Lydia Foote as Moggy McGilpin (*Highland Reel*) provide a few examples of historical and theatrical types. This evolved into a burlesque cross-dressed costume consisting of a hip-length tunic over knickers (usually fringed); by the early 1870s, this costume eliminated the knickers and drew the bodice tightly around the uppermost part of the thighs, a silhouette (barely distinguishable from a 1940s bathing suit) which endured until the Edwardian era.[14] Another variation, just as daring in its way, is the tail coat and trousers pictured on Vestris singing 'My Heart's True Blue'; this was more common in the latter part of the century, evolving into the female lion comique. Trousers were not widely adopted by men until 1829, but by 1836 they were included in the basic wardrobe inventory of a female speciality: 'GENERAL BUSINESS AND ECCENTRICS: silk flesh-ings, frock coat and trousers and white waistcoat, gents shirt and false wristbands, black stock for neck, wellington boots.'[15] The pecuniary value of trousers is conveyed in correspondence between the Lord Chamberlain and W.J. Emden in 1869. A private warning was passed down about Mlle de la Ferte's ballet dress, resulting in the addition of a skirt to her costume. Emden's associate at the Olympic grumbled because the warning was not in the form of an official letter 'which he could publish with a notification that in consequence of the order the Ballet in future would appear in Trousers! which would be worth £10,000 to him'.[16]

Max Beerbohm tried to prove women's inferiority as artists by citing their inability to convincingly impersonate men, but the failing is not a deterministic inevitability. As Beerbohm acknowledges, the point of women's cross-dressing was to please, not deceive:

> In exact ratio as the man is more successful in a female character than *vice versa*, so is it, on the whole, more pleasant to see a woman in the character of a man than a man in the character of a woman. The greater the aesthetic illusion, the more strongly does our natural sense of fitness rebel against the travesty of nature.[17]

Usually, the purpose of men's cross-dressing was comic (from Charles Mathews's Mrs Tulip to Dan Leno's Queen of Hearts) while the *raison d'être* of women's cross-dressing was allure (from Vestris's Macheath to Nellie Power's Sindbad).[18] The male cross-dresser frequently negated the sexuality of characters by playing women that were either post-menopausal, extremely plain, or both. In such characters, sexuality was defunct or moot and the need to convey the 'unspeakable' was avoided. This pejorative character-making was a male prerogative; in the hands of mature actresses or even young 'old women' specialists the dominance, wit, and travesty of dame roles would have been sacrificed. In the Victorian theatre, but not in society, cross-dressers had a sanctioned role within a tightly delineated range: men could parody sexless women, and women could glorify what they could not suppress. In the latter case, neither convincing impersonation nor sexual ambiguity was possible. The female grotesque could only be comical when signified in ritual mockery by the other sex, which impersonated what did not exist.[19] (Charlotte Cushman is a rare exception to this principle.)

In complete contrast, the female cross-dresser impersonated young, vital, and often heroic men in the prime of life. Unlike straight female roles, this permitted an actress to *do* things and yet not play a villainess, harpie, or adventuress. She could take the romantic initiative in pantomime, comic liberties in burlesque, and satirize men and masculinity in the music halls. In drama, she could try some of the greatest acting roles. But instead of losing her identity in such characters, the actress's gender was highlighted. Her face, 'symmetry', and contoured silhouette marked her gender; prints and drawings of cross-dressed actresses from the 1830s to 50s usually show unmistakable anatomization, observing feminine curvature as faithfully as the camera later did in portrait photography. On the lyric stage, the actress's voice underlined the fraud. Kuhn hypothesizes that setting up the deliberate incongruity between clothes and gender serves as 'a quest to uncover the truth of the concealed body...precisely the desire that activates a narrative of sexual disguise'.[20] The offence to dramatic logic was substantial but inconsequential, for sexuality had its own narrative logic that distinguished Olivia from Viola, the pantomime boy from the *jeune premier*, Mazeppa from Godiva, and Menken from Maddocks.[21]

In the Victorian theatre, adult female performers were never sexless: sex was always apparent in gendered costume, whether through tights, breeches, skirts, corsetted silhouettes, hairstyles, or headgear. *Ruy Blas, or the Blasé Roué*, a burlesque performed at the Gaiety in 1889, provides an excellent example. In similar male characters (both romantic, rascally itinerants) costuming served to highlight a straight male's and cross-dressed female's sexual differences, despite their parallel activities in the plot.[22] As Don Caesar, Fred Leslie sported a rumpled shirt, tattered breeches, wrinkled patched tights, and practical though well worn boots, while the cross-dressed Nellie Farren as Ruy Blas was made up in an immaculate costume consisting of bolero jacket, lace cuffs, cinched waist, ornately trimmed knickers, the tightest of tights, and delicately buckled high heeled shoes. Farren's femininity was intractable and the point was to reveal it. Ruy Blas's various disguises as a court actor, lady-in-waiting, page, crossing sweeper, and matador repeatedly called attention to Farren's body as a feminine landscape.

While clothing functioned as the sign of gender and sexuality was the referent of revealing clothing, certain articles of costume were more heavily weighted by the erotic lexicography of male culture. The clothing inextricably associated with a 'guilty' body part became the indexical sign of the sexual part; in other words, it was fetishized. In the opinion of Anthony Storr, a sexologist, women use fetishized objects to attract men, so 'a fetish may, as it were, be a flag hung out by the woman to proclaim her sexual availability.'[23] But if this is so, how can one flag be distinguished from another in the Victorian theatre? Andrea Dworkin, a radical feminist, summarizes the problem:

> Since there is virtually no bodily part or piece of apparel or substance that is not fetishized by some men somewhere, it would be hard indeed for a woman not to hang out a flag without going naked, which would be construed as definitely hanging out a flag. From underwear to rubber boots and raincoats to leather belts to long hair to all varieties of shoes to feet in and of themselves: all these and more are fodder for male fetishists.[24]

The repetition of certain motifs must be accepted as a clue to identifying fetishes and correctly locating them in the historical past. Given the particularly strong stigma against ballet girls, it is not surprising that their line of business comes up again and again in erotic allusions or that their costumes were widely borrowed for other lines of business. As a type of woman performer they are not a fetish in and of themselves, but certain articles of clothing associated with dancers contributed to their fascination – particularly when combined with sexually inscribed movements.

GESTURE: 'EVERY LITTLE MOVEMENT HAS A MEANING OF ITS OWN'

Theatrical costume could and did inspire outrage when combined with genuine innovations in gesture. The cancan scandalized audiences that had become immune, by 1870, to the sight of ethereal *danseuses*, swaggering principal boys, female gymnasts, and 'nude' Mazeppas. William Green observed that economic crises in the precursors of the American strip show were successively avoided 'by tearing away another veil, inventing another gyration to woo new audiences',[25] but in the case of the cancan it was not the dance alone that was so scandalously appealing, and no disrobing occurred in the literal sense of the word. The first English

115

performance of the cancan, at the Princess's in 1866, was by four men. They attracted little notice. It was not until Finette, a woman dressed as a man, performed the cancan at the Lyceum in 1867 and Alhambra in 1868 that London really paid attention. Since the seventeenth century, female dance costume gradually shed its length, weight, and bulk to allow for elevation in jumps and kicks among ballerinas as well as *danseurs*. In the cancan, Finette marked the end of the shedding process, for she was cross-dressed in closed knickers and could kick higher than her head in a movement called *le presentez-armes*. The once classically graceful *ronds de jambe en l'air* dangled and elevated, again and again, taking on a new but entirely recognizable connotation.[26]

When Mlle Schneider performed the cancan in women's dress at the St James's in 1868, the gestural heresy was electrifying. A review of the opera, Offenbach's *Orphée aux Enfers* (*Eurydice*), summarizes the effect:

> When the curtain rose upon the last scene, the appearance of Mlle Schneider . . . in the costume of a Bacchante . . . reclined on the banquet-table . . . reminded the spectator of the superb beauties whom Rubens loved to paint. No wonder that when, after a comparatively stately minuet, this ripe-blooded maenad flung herself into all the fury of an irresistible *cancan*, the delight of the audience knew no bounds, and the reviled dance was repeated amid frantic applause.[27]

When the Colonna troupe of four women danced the cancan at the Alhambra in 1870, the shock was even more substantial and the erotic value the greatest, for two of the troupe dressed as women and two as men. In keeping with the cancan's reputed origin in the quadrille, the Colonna troupe paired two sets of dancers in short ballet skirts with two women in knickers and sailor blouses. While the 'women' wore tights that were coloured for invisibility, the 'men' teased the audience by wearing knickers that were highly visible and currently the centre of controversy about women's hygiene and modesty. The combination was extremely erotic. As one erotic magazine, *The Days' Doings*, proclaimed: 'A most energetic troupe they are . . . for "go", dash, and acrobatic convulsion [it] is unlike anything of the kind yet seen in London. An artist, in attempting to reproduce the movement of such a dance, lays himself open to the charge of exaggeration.'[28] It is no wonder that portraits of Colonna and Finette were both treasured commodities in erotic magazines.

Coinciding with the cancan craze in London, knickers (or drawers) were reclaimed after a long struggle from their origin as men's breeches; decorated with dainty tucks and lace, they were gradually being accepted by ordinary women as a properly feminine article of dress.[29] From 1860 to 1870 there was considerable interest in knickers, particularly their exotic fabrics and brilliant hues, though not all the lingering suspicions about them had been exorcised. Doctors recommended knickers as a safeguard against sexual violation, yet characters in *Rosa Fielding, or a Victim of Lust* (a novel of 1876) are adamant that these undergarments proved to be no impediment whatsoever. Though retailers promoted knickers as a mark of feminine gentility another novel, *The Mysteries of Verbena House*, portrays prostitutes as inveterate drawer-wearers: 'the bigger the whore – professional or otherwise – the nicer will be the drawers she wears, while the prude, or the cantankerous old maid will either wear the most hideous breeches imaginable, or none at all.'[30] Knickers' allusive purpose in the dance is obvious: cancan dancers like the Colonna troupe, Wiry Sal, and the 'Ta-ra-ra-BOOM-deay' Lottie Collins not only drew attention to their undergarments but also to what the undergarments thinly shielded. The predictable, repetitious, vertically thrusting movements of the dance recalled and invited a palpable response in male spectators. According to Frigga Haug, 'by drawing attention to the fact that they are not to be displayed, knickers function as a sign of the invisible. . . the effect on observers is to make them see that which is hidden as that which is most significant'.[31] The cancan enjoyed long popularity, and by the last decade of the century it had evolved a costume of its own – black stockings, garters, suspenders, frilly petticoats, and brightly coloured drawers – a vision of one stage of undress, suggestive of raucous foreplay and the ritualized outcome. *Photo Bits* insinuated that this interpretation of the cancan was still current in 1898; in this erotic magazine, a photograph of one woman doing the *ronds de jambe en l'air* and another seated with one leg extended alongside her head (*porte d'armes*) is accompanied by the caption 'Industrious and conscientious study is bound to push an actress forward', a heartless misquoting of Madge Kendal.[32]

The cancan created licensing trouble for music halls, so between 1870 and 1874 it was performed in theatres governed by the Lord Chamberlain (the Lyceum, Alhambra, Gaiety, and St James's). The Middlesex justices responsible for music halls dealt with the cancan by banishing it, probably recognizing that cleansing the salacious gestures of the dance was impossible. Judging by the Alhambra's defection to the Lord Chamberlain and jurisdictional transformation from a music hall to a theatre, the cancan reveals that the difference between the moral regulation of theatres and music halls was not so much a matter of audience standards, repertoire, or protection of the public good, but rather a question of the authorities' habit, ability, and inclination to recognize certain types of problems and repress certain aspects of performance. The Lord Chamberlain's criteria and experience of impropriety were rooted in the written text. Balletic plots were requested for a brief period following the Alhambra's Wigan vs Strange case of 1865, but no more than four plots were ever submitted, nothing was detectable in them, and the practice was discontinued.[33] For the Examiners of Plays, gestural infractions were anomalous and insuppressible without an accompanying text, whereas for the guardians of the music halls the suppression of texts was extremely problematic no matter how transparently objectionable the accompanying gestures were.

Bessie Bellwood's song 'What Cheer, 'Ria' (pronounced with selective elisions to sound like 'watch your rear') was far from subtle,[34] and Kate Harvey's 'You see I'm but a simple Country Maid' was a blatant untruth, but both songs were hugely enjoyed and tolerated in the halls. Marie Lloyd followed in their tradition, but was much more restrained. In 1896, she was summoned by the London County Council's (LCC) Theatres and Music Halls Committee (which succeeded the Middlesex justices in 1888) when Carina Reed, a follower of Laura Ormiston Chant, complained about Lloyd's song 'Johnny Jones'. Reed was deeply offended by a verse that roused laughter in the audience:

> I don't like boys, they are so rude,
> I would not like them if I could,
> Well Johnny Jones he's not so low,
> He tells me things what I don't know.
> One day a rude boy pulled my hair,
> And though I cried, he didn't care –
> He only laughed and went like so (*business*) –
> So I ran off to Ma to know –
> CHORUS What's that for, eh? Oh tell me Ma!
> If you won't tell me, I'll ask Pa!
> But Ma said, 'Oh, it's nothing, shut your row!'
> Well, I've asked Johnny Jones, see, so I know now.[35]

Lloyd sang the song absolutely straight for the Committee. No possible source of offence was found. Lloyd, who more than any of her contemporaries knew that 'Every little movement has a meaning of its own/ Every little movement tells a tale', then sang the parlour favourite 'Come Into the Garden, Maud', accompanying it with 'every possible lewd gesture, wink and innuendo', pawing the ground and drawing her pearls across her teeth.[36] This performance convinced the Committee that lewdness existed in their own minds, not in the lyrics, in which case nothing need or could be done; if their literacy of gestural referents was so comprehensive, the guilt rested on them, not the song. In Lloyd's own words:

> They don't pay their sixpences and shillings at a music hall to hear the Salvation Army. If I was to try to sing healthy moral songs they would fire ginger beer bottles and beer mugs at me. I can't help it if people want to turn and twist my meanings.[37]

Marie Lloyd's performance of 'The Naughty Continong [Continent]' demonstrates this principle. The song consists of a first person description of an Englishwoman's impressions of Parisian men. The third verse is about a ball and cancan dancing:

> A lovely sight to see, but the dance you would call
> Well a terribly 'leggy' show! yes, terribly warm, you know.
> For the mamzelles fair, throw their limbs about in a reckless way,
> And the young men there get a special seat for the grand display,
> At *these* little bits, I could give them fits,
> But I give 'em best, when they begin to do the splits.
> CHORUS Oh! you should see them – (*imitate splits*) no, I do it wrong!
> It's a terrible thing, but the regular thing,
> on the naughty Continong![39]

Moral reformers tried to raise objections to such questionable songs, but were almost always thwarted by their own verbal reticence and mimetic ineptitude when trying to convince licensing authorities of the affront. The Society for Prevention of Degradation of Women and Children's 1890 common law action against the

Folly Theatre, Manchester, is a case in point. Mr Hallifax's objection to one of Peggy Pryde's songs is described by an *Era* reporter:

> In the song Miss Pryde described herself as a servant [attending a couple on honeymoon]. In the first verse he [Hallifax] noticed nothing particular. The chorus, however, which was very frequently repeated, with the aid of every conceivable form of gesture, was as follows: –
>   'It would make you feel so funny to hear them go kiss, kiss;
>   It would make you feel so funny to see them go like this.'
> And then the artist made a squeezing gesture.
>   'It would make you feel so funny if you saw them –'
> And then there was a dead stop and a pause.
> Mr Costello [prosecuting barrister] – Did she do anything?
> Witness [Hallifax] – She made a gesture which I cannot describe just now... the chorus continued –
>   'It would make you feel so funny to see the things I see,
>   They think they're on the strict Q.T.,
>   They don't know I am peeping through the keyhole.'[39]

Peggy Pryde was requested to not sing the song again, but despite another performer's 'indecent manipulation' of part of his baggy trousers in a Nubian Orator act, and evidence of solicitation in the lounge, the magistrate took no action against the theatre.

The wide latitude given to lyrical performers – *honi soit qui mal y pense* – must have been extremely frustrating for moral reformers, who felt their charges of lewdness of mind ricochet back toward themselves. Campaigns against lascivious gestures theoretically stood a better chance of success when complaints could be supported by submissible visible evidence. Costume provided such opportunities, but there are very few instances of such complaints and they are invariably unsuccessful. Zaeo's exposed armpits were a *cause célèbre* in 1890 when featured on posters advertising the gymnast's performance at the Westminster Aquarium. The controversy led to the creation of the Bill Posters' Association as unofficial but effective censors of public hoardings, but the costume could not be legislated off the stage or public billboards. Years later, when a newspaper alleged that Zaeo's bare back threatened harm to public morals, she sued the publisher and was awarded considerable damages.[40]

Representations of nudity were well-established costuming conventions. In 1881, Emma D'Auban danced in what can only be described as the scantiest costume of a harem – the pretence was a tribal dance of American natives, and the pantomime was *Robinson Crusoe*. A picture from the *Illustrated London News* shows her midriff clearly visible through a thin layer of gauze. The costume was certainly an erotic sign, as variations appear on numerous postcards of would-be Salomes and Cleopatras,[41] but audiences must have been immured to such spectacles, for no objections were raised to *Robinson Crusoe*. Similar examples are found in Carlotta Grisi's costume for *La Péri* in which her torso is bare from the waist to just below the breasts (illustrated by Brandard, *c.* 1843) and Wilhelm's designs for the Bayadère Ballet in *The Golden Ring* (Alhambra, 1883). Fanny Cerrito took the dare further in *Ondine* by appearing in a bodice that was green on one side and pale pink on the other, with only a garland appearing to decorate her breast (illustrated by Numa Blanc, *c.* 1843). In 1898, the controversial La Belle Otero performed a matador act at the Alhambra dressed in a sleeveless, strapless brassiere, with tight pants that appeared to expose one leg in a curvaceous strip extending from the inside of the knee to the outside of the hip. Wilhelm's cupid design for *Rose d'Amour* (Empire, 1888) appears to be nude except for her wings, quiver, and a wrapping of transparent fabric around the hips and over one shoulder. Wilhelm knew, like Crissie 'The Pandora Palace of Varieties Prostitute' (prima ballerina in an erotic novel of 1899), 'that a little draping, flaunted about as she knew how, looks far more wickedly wanton than none at all'.[42] Perhaps indifference to such displays was a quirk of English (and French) prudery; Mrs Krum Hinderup would certainly have been appalled, for in Copenhagen in 1886 she performed Anitra's sultry dance dressed in a floor length evening gown, apparently relying on her elaborate low-slung girdle and ostrich plume fan to seduce Peer Gynt.

The LCC paid inspectors to write annual reports on music halls and to investigate *ad hoc* complaints about performances. A routine report on Gatti's Palace of Varieties blandly describes the step dance and striptease of the Irish vocalist W.P. Carey as 'somewhat suggestive':

> He dances a few steps, and then takes off his coat. Then a few more steps, and he removes his waistcoat. Finally he proceeds, in full sight of the audience, to divest himself of his trousers, unbuttoning them in front and letting them partly fall down. He however retires out of sight to take them completely off. On returning to the stage it is seen that he is attired in long

black drawers. I leave these facts to speak for themselves. This performance seems to give considerable satisfaction to the audience.[43]

This male striptease (rendered comic by Carey's failure to expose anything more at the end than the beginning of the routine) is in an entirely different spirit from Charmion's 'Disrobing Act' performed at the Alhambra:

> She appears on stage fully dressed in walking costume. Accidentally seeing the trapeze net she thinks she will try it. She does so & finds that her clothes are an impediment. After a little hesitation she disrobes on the trapeze.
>
> The difficulty that would arise under ordinary circumstances is dispensed with by the artist not wearing chemise or drawer[s].
>
> After the outer garments are removed, there is left a long white garment like a bodice & petticoat combined. She then hangs by her feet & this drops off over her head, leaving her in ordinary acrobatic costume. The whole performance is carried out as decorously as possible.[44]

In each case, the inspector's final sentence absolves the authorities from any need to pursue sanctions. In 1897, the Holborn Music Hall's program included a short kinematic projection of 'a picture of a woman who strips naked in front of the audience', as if the practice was perfectly mundane.[45] *Photo Bits* spoofed the vogue for disrobing acts in 1898 by suggesting that the scenery could be done away with so nothing should impede the audience's view of the tiers of dressing rooms.[46]

FIGURAL COMPOSITION IN THE *MISE EN SCÈNE*

In many cases, the sexual meaning encoded in costumes and gestures was further enhanced by sexual referents in the *mise en scène*. This seems to be especially true of acts of physical prowess – such as dancing and gymnastics – in which adults of both sexes performed together. In 1796, when Didelot first introduced simple lifts into a ballet at Drury Lane, the process of reduction of the *danseur* to a *porteur* and the reassignment of focus to the ballerina was initiated.[47] Lifts made *pas de deux* more athletic but also more erotic, if their presence on five of the first thirty issues of the pornographic weekly *The Exquisite* (published in London between

1840–42) is a reliable indicator. It seems likely that acrobatic teams could borrow the erotic encodings of the *pas de deux*, though three quarters of a century after *Zéphyr et Flore* the sight of an upside down man and a flying woman clasping each other's body, faces buried in torsos, may have been 'neutralized' by frequent repetition.

In an eye witness account of an act at the Oxford Music Hall in 1870, the ambulations of a female acrobat are admired for athletic and erotic reasons. Because of the nature of the gymnastic performance, acrobats were wise to wear close fitting garments. Mlle de Glorion's obliviousness to performing in such a costume along with a male partner horrified and fascinated the audience:

> The fair acrobat went down from the stage among the audience, alone, and walked, half nude as she was, through the crowd, to the other end of the long hall . . . and climbed the rope ladder that led up from the gallery to a small platform . . . which was suspended high up under the ceiling. There she stood, in sight of all the people; intent on preparing for her nightly peril, and taking no thought (nor did they, I think, just then) of the fact that she was almost utterly unclothed. . . . And she had to swing herself, high over the heads of the crowd, across that great space of eighty feet or so, and leap through the two discs and alight in his [her male partner's] inverted arms, which she could not even see. . . . She did it, of course; she leaped into the air, and in leaping, left the ropes that swung her, and dashed through the two hoops, and then was seen hanging in the arms of her mate, grasping his body, her face against his breast. . . . And, though it is not well to see a nude man fling a nude girl about as she is flung, or to see her grip his body in mid air between her seemingly bare thighs, I think that an unreflecting audience takes no note of these things and looks on him and her only as two performers. Still, the familiar interlacing of male and female bodies in sight of the public is gross and corrupting.[48]

In the course of the narration, Mlle de Glorion is successively denuded, from 'half nude' to 'barely clothed' to 'nude' to 'bare', though her costume (a close-fitting blue satin doublet, trunk hose, and tights) was in no way altered. Though her costume was morally objectionable, it was also integral to the male-female dynamic of the act and the erotic implications read by this particular male spectator. Whatever thoughts arose in the spectator's mind, no objections were voiced by the Oxford's audience, for Mlle de Glorion was a performer, dressed in the uniform of her work, doing what she was paid to do, and fulfilling one among many ritualized sequences in the evening's programme.

Solo acrobats could also provoke unease. As an equestrienne, trapeze artist, high wire performer, and daredevil,[49] the acrobat Zaeo embodied courage, athleticism, and vigour combined with Venusian beauty — all characteristics that women were not supposed to flaunt in public. The conclusion of her most famous act, a back somersault and fifty-four foot free fall from a flying trapeze,[50] further communicated her self-control and disturbed her critics. This was performed at numerous London music halls, but it only prompted objections at the Aquarium. There, the audience's perspective on the act was crucial: one LCC inspector remarked that the architecture of the hall necessitated that Zaeo perform her entire act directly over the heads of the audience. 'It is', he admitted, 'not altogether desirable to place a female in this indelicate position',[51] probably because it highlighted the whole female body in space from all possible angles of view. Her gestic pose of autonomous yet feminine physicality followed by the free fall marked Zaeo as the antithesis of the archetypal Good Woman: she was neither a specimen of clinging womanhood nor lighter than air. Furthermore, her fall — like the bold forays of New Women into the male world — marked her as a frightening predator of privilege, a virago, and an irresistible villainess who landed supine and proxemically accessible amidst the gaping titillated throng.

Movement was not a prerequisite for sexual inscription in the *mise en scène*. Stationary *tableaux vivants* (also known as living pictures and *poses plastiques*) usually reproduced well-known paintings or sculptures, or arranged bodies in imitation of a 'classical' style. Despite their honourable origins at the Comedie Italienne in 1761,[52] *tableaux vivants* had a circuitous and sordid route to the British stage. They were known in the pre-Victorian theatre, though only with male models: Astley's playbills announce Ducrow as the Living Model of Antiques (7 September 1829) and in *Raphael's Dream* (21 September 1830), and boast a Modern Alcides in Classical and Academick Poses supported by a team of gymnasts (7 September 1832).[53] Obviously, the sources for all-male compositions were finite and the taste for male muscles in *maillots* (one-piece body stockings) was limited. *The Swell's Night Guide Through the Metropolis* describes living wax works of naked and half clothed women in Windmill Street, Piccadilly, in the 1840s, as well as living picture exhibitions in what were probably taverns in the Waterloo district.[54] This staple of illegitimacy was a midnight ritual at the Coal Hole, though it severely disappointed James Greenwood:

> Amid the breathless silence of the auditory he [the Baron] peeped through the chink [in the back partition], rang the bell, and the curtain rose, and, behold! there were four ordinary and elderly females attired in fleshings and kilts, hand in hand, and revolving on a pedestal, as though the machinery that moved them were a roasting-jack.... Fancy a trio of bold-faced women, with noses snub, Roman, and shrewish, with wide mouths and eyes crowsfooted, having the impudence to represent the Graces!.... I came away with at least this comforting reflection for my shilling – that an inane and nasty, though old-fashioned, public exhibition was cutting its own throat with laudable expedition.[55]

The objective of living pictures such as *Diana Preparing for the Chase* (Parthenon Rooms, Liverpool, 1850) was to provide a narrative of ideal feminine beauty while the paradigmatic male erotic fantasy of voyeurism was legitimized by the pretense of classical mythology. Other pictures, such as *The Moorish Bath* (Palace, 1894) drew on the tradition of Orientalist painting which justified undress in a male voyeuristic fantasy of harem life. The naked female form was the ultimate classical ideal, persistently painted by Royal Academicians (especially William Etty, William Frost, Laura Herford, Albert Moore, Edward Poynter, and Lawrence Alma-Tadema).[56] Tableaux vivants borrowed the respect that neoclassical themes wielded in fine art. Passive, unaware, and sexually vulnerable women could be arranged on stage in perfect propriety because the 'fancy dress Classicism'[57] of the Royal Academy and Parisian Salon was the hegemonic artistic discourse on both sides of the English Channel.

The theatre borrowed more from fine art than just thematic legitimacy, and for more media than just the living pictures. The *volupté* or reclined female figure, which has a long tradition of voyeuristic representation dating back to the Renaissance, was kept current by Victorian painters such as Alfred Leighton. Giorgione's *Sleeping Venus* (*c.* 1510) is recalled by an actress identified only as Miss Moore in a photograph probably taken in the last years of the century. The most famous *volupté* prototype is Titian's *Venus of*

Urbino (*c.* 1538), which the 'British Blonde' Pauline Markham approximated in the 1860s, and Miss Fowler borrowed in the 1870s. This pose is reversed by Ingres in *La Grande Odalisque* (1814), which the cancan specialist Finette used in the 1860s. When actresses quoted the poses in their publicity photographs, they exploited the legitimation of the Royal Academy while relying on the sexual encodings and topicality of François Boucher and Edouard Manet to make the pictures sell.

Graham Ovenden and Peter Mendes describe Victorian photographic aesthetics in terms of a dialectic: the beautiful and pure are clothed, while the ugly and impure are unclothed.[58] Both are 'real,' but photography, unlike painting, gives no latitude for a more charitable interpretation. In actresses' publicity photos the clothed figure is, in a sense, unclothed by the habituation of the heterosexist male eye. Any pretence of purity is erased. The reading of the *volupté* is also affected by the inversion of the body along the horizontal plane, which organizes the picture around the pelvic area of weighted mass. Rudolf Arnheim explains the composition's dialectic in terms of the spiritual and animal impulses of the viewer which are embodied respectively in the head and pelvis areas of the subject:

> In a reclining figure . . . the head surrenders some of its prerogative; a transverse symmetry is created around the balancing center, which reduces the head to a counterpart of the feet. The oblique position of Goya's *Maja Desnuda* [similar to Markham's and Moore's poses] plays with the teasing ambiguity derived from the competition between the two centers. The lady's inviting eyes attract the viewer's attention while the balancing center of the whole painting supports the appeal of her sexuality.[59]

Whether or not the *volupté's* gaze is returned in invitation or invocation of sex, her susceptibility in repose certainly recalls a private rather than a public encounter.

In publicity photographs, as in the cancan, ballet prints, and *tableaux vivants*, clothed nudity was a carefully orchestrated spectacle. Visual artists could idealize the female form by painting out imperfections such as blemishes and disproportion. On stage, tights and *maillots* had a similar function to idealize nudity by smoothing over cellulite, monochromatizing hairiness, and encasing padding. Padding perfected form, enhancing the aesthetic effect but not the erotic desirability of women. In the erotic novel *Crissie*, the living statuaries in the scene of Cleopatra's garden are especially obscene and titillating because they do not wear any padding; the separate masses of their buttocks are clearly distinguishable, and belly, breasts, and pubis bulge naturally.[60] This is the kernel of erotic fantasies involving clothed nudity: the beauty must be real to be desirable. The greater the reality, the greater the effect. Live performance – though encouraging of imaginative fantasy – provided an arena for verification.

Like erotic zones of the body, physical proportions are transient fashions. In 1871, a cartoon stage manager displayed the new model leg to the opera bouffe chorus, explaining: 'The thin French leg is played out, ladies. Prussia has been victorious [in war], and we must have Dutch-built extremities. Make up your legs after this style in future. More robust, ladies, more robust!'[61] By 1904, the custom was disgraced: a cartoon in *Das Kleine Witzblatt* deconstructs the image of a gorgeous principal boy to its component parts (padded tights, padded corset, and wig), revealing the emaciated specimen in her dressing room.[62] Whereas the first example joins in the fun of artificiality, the later example reflects disbelief and distrust in stage illusion and the pretences of costume conventions. Aesthetic preferences were revised, and new standards of authenticity coinciding with the widespread introduction of electric light demanded changes in stage practice.

This is clearly reflected in the Palace Theatre of Varieties' 1893 innovation in the costuming conventions of *tableaux vivants*. The Palace was built after the formation of the LCC's Theatres and Music Halls Licensing Committee, and so it did not receive planning authority to build a promenade (the place where gorgeously dressed prostitutes traditionally strolled). When it was converted from the home of English opera to a high-class variety hall, shareholders and managers pressed again for a promenade, and were again refused. Recognizing that without a promenade the Palace would be uncompetitive with the nearby Alhambra, Empire, Oxford, and Tivoli, the management considered how it could attract a regular clientele while maintaining the pretence of clean 'family' entertainment. A solution was found in the costuming of the living picture models. Instead of covering women with 'classical' drapery or adding a short tutu around the midriff, they faithfully copied their nineteenth-century art sources even if it meant wearing only *maillots*. Customers were enticed in by hoardings showing 'nude and semi-nude females' and advertisements promising that 'the reproductions of these pictures by living persons to be seen inside are exact copies of the originals'.[63] Under this scheme, the Palace's balance sheet went from a operating deficit of £37,000 in its first year as an opera house to a profit of £6,000 in its first year as a music hall under Charles Morton's management.[64]

In response to a complaint about these living pictures, a LCC inspector was dispatched on 26 November 1893. He found that the dancers, singers, and eccentrics 'involved the usual display of limbs encased in tights', but the *tableaux vivants* 'are a new departure'.

> Some of them are very clever representations of pictures, and statuary to which the most severe could not object, but several are of a classical nature, represented by, apparently semi-nude, or nearly nude women. The last one, 'Aphrodite', [based on John Gibson's *Tinted Venus*] was apparently quite nude, except for a scarf over the loins. I say *apparently*, because in every case, I observed that the body, arms, and bosom were completely clothed in very delicate close fitting fleshings, which, when a warm light was thrown on them, appeared [from the vantage of the orchestra stalls] like nature.

The audience applauded in recognition of W.P. Dando's artistic sensibility and Alfred Glendenning's skill in reproducing these famous paintings of various European schools, interspersing the undraped figures with sentimental genre paintings like Luke Fildes' *The Doctor* and P.A. Cot's duo in *The Storm*. The *Tinted Venus*, Solomon J. Solomon's *Cassandra*, and Bouguereau's *Aurora* are typical of the undraped pictures: they display female bodies, nude except for a bolt of filmy cloth wound around one arm and loosely cast over the crotch. No one voiced objection, yet the inspector noted that some people would be adverse to 'such public and complete display of the female form, by living women. It is a matter of difficulty to fix the exact point where propriety ends, and impropriety begins. The borderland which divides the legitimate from the objectionable is not well defined.'[65] Over the ensuing months, the LCC was hounded to chart the borderland and suppress these exhibitions before other establishments, such as the Empire, copied the Palace's precedent setting undraped presentations.[66]

At the premiere of the Palace's second series on 26 February 1894, an inspector noted that 60 per cent of the pictures were 'either wholly or partially undraped'. A National Vigilance campaigner described the 'mere nudities' of the *tableau* based on Johann Dannecker's sculpture *Ariadne*:

'Ariadne' . . . so far as I can put it into language, represents a naked woman lying on the back of a lion. There were 4 or 5 wrinkles on the lower parts of the limb, distinguishing it from an ordinary picture. The left leg was placed under the lower part of the right leg, producing these wrinkles. She was lying in such a position that had it not been for the tights gross indecency would have been the result.

The model for Henrietta Ray's *Naiad* barely enhanced the decency of her tights by wearing a thin wisp of gauze over her loins:

The next picture to which I took exception was a picture called the 'Naiad,' & this picture represents a woman lying on a mound, slightly on the left side. The face is upturned, the neck, stomach, thighs & legs are fully exposed. Of course . . . . I believe there were tights. A very thin piece of gauze, mark you, is thrown slantingly across the person, but not sufficient to hide.

Although the gauze was 'such as would pass not only through a finger ring, but through a lace hole' the LCC Theatres and Music Halls Committee ruled that the provision of a thin scarf or spray of flowers across the pelvis was a sufficient compromise to decency. As long as the Palace realized works of fine art, it was up to the spectators to remind themselves of the presence of tights even though seeing them was 'a matter of inference & faith, not of observation & knowledge'.[67]

Objections were just as unsuccessful in 1881, when an individual complained to the Lord Chamberlain that Drury Lane's 'Statue Ballet' featured 'about 30 girls in tights from head to feet without a vestige of skirt & only a thin scarf for an apology to shield them'. Officials consulted various parties, including a clergyman, and concluded the plaintiff must be 'one of the overnice people who bring to the theatre the prurience which they see there'.[68] A similar device of costumed nudity was used in the Crystal Palace's pantomime of 1887–8. 'An English Mother' complained: 'A band of girls, about 30, I should think, from the ages of 10 to 16, naked to their waists, perform a dance [hand] in hand with just a little fringe of *net perfectly transparent* & which flies open as they dance.' She continued, 'whether they are incased [*sic*] in flesh elastics, makes no difference, it is *meant* to appear, & does appear, as if the girls were perfectly nude'. As the Crystal Palace's chairman insisted, however, a single complaint among over 50,000 visitors was not worth taking seriously.[69] In each of these cases movement was involved, and 'nudity' was incidental to the performance.

At the Palace, in contrast, 'nudity' was integral to stationary presentations. It was different in form and content. For the first time in mass entertainment for the middle classes, Palace *tableaux* employed the conventions of clothed nudity to create an illusion of actual nudity – not just a signification of it. When 'nudity' became thematic rather than incidental, the operation of the male hegemonic preference for female display became blatant, resulting in a public campaign to lobby for stricter controls. In the anti-liberal mood of the 1890s, *tableaux vivants* were singled out as an example of how representations of feminine beauty in stage performance overstepped the boundaries of acceptable immodesty. Maintenance of the conventional system of encoded nudity relied on limited access to pornography, the iconographic key to stage costume. By attracting attention to the conventions of costumed nudity, Palace *tableaux* aroused suspicions about other traditions of representation. It is probably not coincidental that the moral reformers who campaigned against the Palace were the same women and men who worked to destroy heaps of pornographic pictures and literature each year; it is possible that in the course of this work reformers such as William Coote and Laura Ormiston Chant acquired the key to erotic encodings in theatrical costumes, gestures, and *mise en scène*. It is possible that they learned to deconstruct the fantasy of the voyeur, and by knowing it they could attack it.

At the same time, scenes of explicit sex were becoming more readily and inexpensively available in the marketplace. For example, the tenor of naughty postcards featuring actresses and theatrical backdrops changed. In the 1870s, 6d. could purchase a series of Alhambra Palace postcards depicting the manager and conductor surrounded by the corps de ballet, or a set of stereotyped scenes behind the curtain, or poses by the transvestite acrobat Lulu; their competition consisted of dressed seaside postcards, windy weather shots, and Girls of the Period.[70] By the 1890s, postcard sets depicted a nude female gymnast on the swing and trapeze (thirty-six poses, 1s. 6d. per cabinet photo, or 15s. a dozen), and 'Behind the scenes at the Ballet, startling revelations' with fifteen 'highly erotical scene[s] between a well known abonnentand [and] the first star of the ballet' (in cabinet and *carte-de-visite* sizes); their competition consisted of scenes with naked prepubescent girls, interracial sex, and intergenerational lesbianism.[71]

In Windmill revue of the 1930s, the *mise en scènes* of Victorian *tableaux vivants* were copied wholesale, though because fine art prototypes were no longer required to lend legitimacy to realizations, the themes chosen by Vivian Van Damm ranged over a broader vista – one that reflects the unimportance of classical education and visual erudition in the twentieth century. In the 1890s, the thrill of *tableaux vivants* evolved from the knowledge that the models in the pictures were *living*. In the 1930s, the factor that protected the Windmill from prosecution was that the living *tableaux* were *pictures*, frozen in space. Marshall McLuhan would probably interpret this still frame as a 'cool' medium in the age of 'hot' cinema; by 1932, less anxiety was invested in the absence of clothes, whereas 'to the highly visual and lopsided sensibility of industrial societies, the sudden confrontation with tactile flesh is heady music, indeed'.[72]

The designer's materials – flesh and fabric – had not changed. By the 1930s, however, the 1893 costume of a Palace model had been sufficiently neutralized through repetition that it was as acceptable at the Windmill as at the Adelphi, where Oliver Messel's designs for *Helen* show that a curtain of chiffon over a *maillot* still served to represent the sexual beauty of Venus.[73] At the Windmill, the 'Very Naughty Nineties' were costumed traditionally in either tights and short breeches or cancan dresses, but artistic 'Inspiration' was allegorized as a nude woman, and a bolt of gauze still served to focus attention on the anatomy of an impersonalized chorus.[74] The wisp of fabric, like the Romantic ballet skirt and classical tutu, held an honoured place on the English stage because it was a fetishized object: not an instrument of concealment but rather a flag drawing attention to the site most sought after by the voyeuristic eye. Invested with powerful significations of male heterosexual eroticism, these items highlight the Victorian spectacle of absent costume and the paradoxes of propriety and immodesty, public and private vestimentary codes, and licit and illicit enjoyment of the female body.

EROTIC VERIFICATION

Pornography is not definitive of a society's view, but it is indicative of deep lying ideology. It is not in itself true, not believed, not universally reflexive, and not important in isolation, but like literature it bears truth insofar as it assumes to share and formulate readers' values, aims to foster belief in itself as a medium, and as long as its continued existence is dependent on success in the marketplace. Its various forms – books, periodicals, and photographs – are vital but neglected sources of information about popular culture and sexual lexicography. Its image system can be shown to be consistent with men's readings of stage performance; in Victorian Britain, pornography's referents did coincide with those of the theatrical *mise en scène*. Many aspects of Victorian *mise en scènes* become logically coherent when glossed with references to contemporaneous pornography. In the writing of theatre history, these glosses restore playgoers' subjective reading of performance. Everyone's semiotic history is uniquely personal, but given the distribution points and volume of Victorian pornography, it is reasonable to assert that Victorian males interpreted theatrical performance with reference to the staple motifs of sexual fantasy, pursuit, and pleasure from illicit literature.

It is no wonder, then, that the reputations of actresses in illegitimate genres were tarnished by the conditions of their work. As John Elsom observes, this is apparent in the social meanings of actresses' photographs:

> If we look back at those postcards of actresses . . . we are aware that they carried around with them the weight of their context. Because this girl had appeared at the Gaiety or the Alhambra, her photograph was fair game for our fantasies: and the significance of these photographs is that they subtly controlled the fantasies, hinting at possibilities in one direction or another. A haughty expression and a large hat, wild eyes and crinkled untidy hair, masculine neatness and a riding crop – when eroticism is assumed the deviations need not be stressed.[75]

The 'weight of their context' not only means that postcards were invested with a playgoer's emotional and physiological memory of watching the actress in the playhouse, but it also means that the actress's stage persona (her living presence amidst an audience) was invested with the playgoer's emotional and physiological memory of erotica (if any). A male playgoer's process of maturation and initiation into the masculine world increased his acuity of vision – as with Thackeray's character Pendennis – until he could recognize the artificiality of playacting, the degradation of the female by a public gaze, and the defeminization/de-idealization of actresses as working women.

Just as a large illegal sexual trade thrived in the streets and shop windows of Britain, the female body was commodified in the theatre into forms that were prominently displayed, socially hypocritical, and unsuppressed. The longevity of low necklines and high hemlines in the contour-hugging costumes of Victorian pantomime boys, burlesque stars, and Shakespearean heroines supersedes the whims of fashion, the wandering standards of discretion, and all the vestimentary codes of street, boudoir, and drawing-room. In any other public place, including masquerade balls, such costumes were unthinkable, yet on stage they were accepted. In the same sense that Louis Althusser sees ideological constructions 'neutralized' through representation,[76] the theatre flaunted its vestimentary, gestural, and figural heresies until they were taken for granted. Through frequent repetition, the heresies seemed natural, though their potency as sexual referents was intact.

Spectators who could not read the covert referents were unable to object to either the theatre or actresses on the deepest meaningful level; thus, those who most wanted to suppress or reform the theatre were least equipped to oppose it. The Examiners of Plays licensed written texts and had authority to regulate against certain gestures and costumes if offence was discovered in performance, but this official institution of censorship could not purge the unofficial messages carried by the female body – 'neutralized' as they were – and rarely tried to do so. Within the fictions of the dramatic world, the female body consistently and legally superseded the real world's governing principles.

Despite the ballet's volume-producing muslin petticoats, pornographically literate men saw straight through to the women beneath. The petticoats and skirts became fetishized as erotic signs of what they seemed to fail to conceal. *La Vie Parisienne*, a chic but not quite pornographic French magazine, played with the ballet skirt fetish in a passage alluding to the vogue for delicate underclothing in the 1880s; the implied reader is a bride, though the magazine was marketed and addressed to men.

> How pretty are these cloudy petticoats ... you will never be more seductive than when enveloped in their vapor. Your husband, always amorous, would like to put them on you himself, to see you in the form of a 'little dancer,' [in] a corset of white satin and multiple transparent skirts, from which your legs will emerge, rosy under their stockings. ... He will tell

you again that there is nothing comparable to you at the Opera . . . or in Eden![77]

Such *dishabille* may have been 'natural' in the Second Empire, but it was never 'moral' attire. After the 1830s, the negligée of Romantic fashion was improper, but the ballerina constantly recalled it in what became her uniform and remained as the sign of her occupation. The male reader of *La Vie Parisienne* is described as wanting to put the petticoats *on* a bride, not take them *off*, so like a true fetish they functioned as a surrogate for their referent and were stimulating in and of themselves.

In *Intrigues and Confession of a Ballet Girl*, an erotic novel dating from the early 1870s, the narrator describes her first rehearsal in the corps de ballet of Drury Lane Theatre:

> What a novel scene; here were girls of all ages, from ten to twenty . . . each dressed as their fancy pleased them; some with short skirts barely reaching to the knee, others with loose drawers, without skirt at all; most of them had light polka jackets made either of cotton or silk, and all with fleshings that reached from the waist downwards. By this style of dress their limbs were as free as when they appeared on the stage at night.[78]

These 'fleshings' are pink-coloured tights, the article most heavily invested with indexical signification of skin, eroticism, and sexual stimulation. *The Mysteries of Verbena House*, the pornographic novel of 1882 sometimes ascribed to the journalist and dramatist George Augustus Sala, graphically describes the effect of tights on the dancer, as well as their contiguity with earlier erotic cross-dressing:

> A lady, putting on her riding trousers becomes, consciously or unconsciously, akin to a hoyden assuming man's clothes, or nearer still, to a ballet girl drawing on her tights. She is subject to contact of the most perilous kind. The warm close substance that passes close to her flesh, that clasps her loins, and embraces her bum, and insinuates itself between her thighs, has, all senseless leather, cloth, or silk, as the case may be, something of the nature of a man's hand in it.
>
> Let the graces be stark naked, or vest them only with flowing drapery, and they may be as chaste as Susannah. Put them in drawers or tights and they become prostitutes.[79]

It is doubtful that science could verify tights' stimulating effect on those who wore them, but the excerpt clearly demonstrates the centrality of tights in fetishists' fantasies of pleasure.

Aside from their fetishistic effect, the skirts and tights of the ballet had an aesthetic function to simulate nudity. Tights were always worn, so there was no pretence in performance of actual flesh being exposed, yet while the optical trick provided steady encouragement to enjoy the pretended nudity, the possibility that the taut silken leggings might give way to their bulging contents provided steady titillation in hopeful anticipation of real nudity. The tendency to illustrate *danseuses* barefooted, as with Taglioni in *La Sylphide* (by Deveria) and the *Three Graces* (Taglioni, Elssler, and Cerrito, by Chalon) suggests that the artist's eye (and probably some spectators') routinely removed the ballet shoe and tights to reveal the foot and the leg as actually nude. It follows that if the foot and leg are 'read' as nude then the genitals must also be bare, since the missing garment – as erotic texts so often stress – would have extended all the way from toe to waist.

This convention of 'clothed nudity' in ballet was adopted wholesale into extravaganza, pantomime, opera bouffe, burlesque, and music hall acrobatics. The female leg, naked in tights, became synonymous with the female performer, with enjoyment, and with the theatre itself. In the 1870s, London's Oxford, Alhambra, Gaiety, Princess's, Canterbury, and Olympic all used leg motifs on the covers of programmes; in the 80s the Folly and Drury Lane adopted the same convention, and in the 90s the Empire continued what must, by then, have been a tradition. Provincial theatres followed suit.

The theme of clothed nudity giving way to actual nudity was articulated in music hall lyrics.[80] In 1896, Lady Mansel sang in the music halls about a dancer whose tights burst; the popular refrain 'and what I saw I mustn't tell you now' was presented as evidence against the Oxford when its licence came up for renewal before the LCC.[81] Erotica did not obscure the 'seen' with such coy double entendres, but described the consequence of bursting tights explicitly. In *Memoirs of a Russian Ballet Girl*, a sado-masochistic novel of 1901, the corps de ballet of a Grand Duke's dancing academy are deliberately fitted out with tights that will split at the rear when the dancers bend. These revealing, self-destructing costumes are indispensable foreplay to the sexual acts that follow every rehearsal and performance.[82] The effect of buttocks on the Englishman's libido is legendary, and fulsomely justified in

Victorian erotica which links the tights fetish with birching of 'the biggest, the most beautiful, the most richly furnished, and the most silkily smooth, and satin-like posterior' of Mariska the ballet girl.[83]

The linking of corporal punishment and the ballet may be due to the regimentation of the training and an association between dancing and other postural 'corrections' and controls agonizingly beloved by fetishists. It is probably not a sublimated punishment of ballerinas as deviant women, for in one episode in *My Secret Life* the rod is wielded by a woman dressed up as a dancer. Stephen Marcus identifies the confusion of sexual identities as a central theme in flagellant literature, and the ballet provides an excellent pretext for adventures. Infantilization, gender confusion through dress, exposure, role play, and bisexuality characterize flagellant literature, but also impinge on the burlesque plot, the casting of some ballets, and music hall lyrics. In flagellant erotica, 'the principal character in such scenes seems to be rehearsing some twisted recollection from early childhood',[84] which is not unlike the pretence of the late Victorian up-to-date pantomime plot, though a much sadder scenario in a dark nursery of topsy-turvydom.

Neutralization through repetition may have worked for some spectators, but for fetishists (and anyone aware of the fetishistic discourse) theatrical costume remained charged with powerful sexual meanings. Access to these meanings and to the literature articulating them was sufficiently controlled that the costumes could be displayed in forums as conservative and accessible to women as the *Illustrated London News*, and in entertainments as professedly family-oriented as pantomime. Whether the encodings were recognized as erotic or simply suspected of inconsistency with the propriety of normal society, the implications for the private reputation of female performers are clear.

5

THE GEOGRAPHY OF SEX IN
SOCIETY AND THEATRE

In July 1872, *Here and There*, a weekly erotic magazine published in
London, included the following story:

Recently in the Strand a tall dashing brunette, with the
unmistakable air which belongs to all members of the
theatrical profession, was hurrying along encumbered in no
slight degree by a somewhat bulky bundle... the speculations
which may have evolved themselves in the minds of passing
loungers as to its contents, soon had an opportunity of being
set at rest.... For the lady slipped and fell, and with her the
bundle, which, bursting open from the shock, scattered its
contents around... it took some time to restore the bundle,
which contained a number of theatrical odds and ends peculiar
to stage-angels and ballet-girls; amongst them, prominently
figuring, [were] a pair of wings such as the spectacular cherub
wears, and – a pair of tights.

The chronicler relishes all the subsequent details of this event: a
young swell picks up the tights and offers them with a bow, but the
woman is so embarrassed that she hesitates before snatching and
quickly stuffing them away. The account concludes: 'the scene was a
peculiarly suggestive one, there in the crowded Strand at noonday
– and everybody smiled at the tights – except the lady.'[1] This
anecdote succinctly summarizes the position of actresses in late-
nineteenth century English popular culture. The setting, the events,
the voyeuristic spectators' expectations and reception of the events,
and the medium in which the story appeared are all significant.

The woman's 'air' immediately identifies her as an actress,
therefore she is marked as a legitimate and rewarding target of the
public gaze. Knowing that she is an actress, the public's curiosity

about her parcel is stimulated. Actresses, after all, are one of the few types of women who change their clothes away from home and whose occupation necessitates the use of numerous fetishized garments. When the bundle bursts, the spectators note the significant objects: the wings that denote her as a ballet girl (suggesting low status and high sensuality) rather than a dramatic actress (inferring, by contrast, high status and high sensuality), and the tights that are worn by women in all genres of popular entertainment from music hall to pantomime, ballet, extravaganza, burlesque, opera bouffe, and Shakespeare.

When the swell picks up the ballet girl's tights he not only holds the symbol of her profession and the icon of her sexual appeal, but he also manipulates the indexical sign of her skin – of her actual self. Prostrate on the sidewalk, the hapless dancer is deprived of her pelvis and legs: the swell restores them to her. Though they are hers to have, they are his to hold. Her embarrassment in acknowledging this (and having to succumb obeisantly to it in the glaring midday sun) is understandable. The coherent system of sensual referents is played out in this episode at high noon, and not surprisingly culminates with the actress's hurried concealment of the tights from public view.

The story is set in a particular place – the Strand in Westminster (the West End) – which in the nineteenth century was as much a theatrical thoroughfare and the focus of London's dramatic life as New York's Broadway. The Strand was also the principal link between the leisured club land of Mayfair and the commercial square mile in the City of London. Aside from these official functions, the Strand sported a major nocturnal street market for prostitution all along its considerable length. Expectations of the dancer and her bundle were formed in part by the geography of sensual activity in the neighbourhood. Augmenting erotic associations of the theatres and street prostitution, Holywell Street (known throughout the British Empire as Booksellers' Row) stood at the eastern end of the Strand; the source of the anecdote, *Here and There*, was just the sort of serial sold for threepence or a penny in the shops of Booksellers' Row in every decade from the Regency period (when there were already at least ninety retailers of erotica on the street)[2] until it was cleared for the Aldwych reconstruction in 1899.

The inclusion of actresses and incidents within and around theatres in so much pornography throughout the Victorian period demonstrates the theatre's enduring erotic fascination. By specifying certain performers and setting stories in the West End where these stars and (in some cases) mere meteorite showers actually worked anchored the sexual fantasies to real women performing in real theatres and moving about on real thoroughfares. Consumers of erotica could seek out the real women at predictable times of day, follow them through the West End to and from their places of employment, pay fees to observe them at work, and follow them to their next destination. In this sense, the theatre was a viewing place that extended into the neighbourhood and interacted with it. Like prostitutes, actresses were public women; their livelihood depended on their attractiveness and recognizability. Even when the actresses in erotica were not real, they were a type that could be observed for a modest fee in hundreds of theatres and music halls — the most prestigious of both being in the West End.

In 1888, the *British Weekly* proclaimed that 'almost every Londoner knows the streets about the Strand where indecent books and pictures are sold'.[3] The actual volume of sales in pornography cannot be stated, and most of the evidence has disappeared forever, but one source gives the sales of erotic penny serials at 400,000 copies a week in 1902.[4] An enormous volume of erotic literature and prints circulated, and much of it was retailed through Holywell Street. In the theatre neighbourhood this material reproduced widespread fantasies about actresses, replicating the beliefs that eroticized them, and reinforcing their social stigma. The status of the theatre may have risen, and popular tolerance of performers may have increased, but actresses were still defined by what pornography and its marketplace relayed.

THE EROTIC NEIGHBOURHOOD OUTSIDE THE PLAYHOUSE

Westminster was not the only city with a theatrical zone. London's East End had its own concentration of entertainment venues in Whitechapel, with another zone extending in a narrow band from Bishopsgate through Shoreditch, northward past the National Standard Theatre and Alhambra Music Hall to the Britannia Theatre and Hoxton Hall. Glasgow's theatres, originally in the Saltmarket, were eventually concentrated along Cowcaddens and Sauciehall Streets. None of these were particularly salubrious environments. The proximity of many provincial patent theatres to either the ancient city core or railway terminus likewise delineates the character of their neighbourhoods. For the purposes of in-depth analysis (and in response to the generous provision of primary evidence and secondary urban history about the complex zone of Westminster), the following comments emphasize London's West End. No doubt the findings of this case study have some bearing elsewhere.

In a theatrical zone as compact and unified as the West End from the 1860s to the 1890s, a 'semiotic neighbourhood' may be postulated: a neighbourhood of all that is 'outside theatres' as well as 'all theatres' insides'. In Erving Goffman's terminology,[5] the West End was a residual zone *par excellence*. There, the 'front' of Mayfair and the shopping zones of St James's (along Piccadilly, Bond Street, Regent Street, and the Haymarket), St Giles North (Oxford Street), and St Pancras (Tottenham Court Road) provided sites of the formal social performances of the daytime while the zone's 'back' consisting of the Strand, Trafalgar Square, Leicester Square, Soho, and Covent Garden (in adjacent parishes) were the sites of the greater informality of evening. This informality deliberately confused the mixture of official and unofficial public spaces and behaviours. The West End was the sort of zone Gale Miller points to as a place 'where a variety of persons, actions, and relationships may be brought together into an unclear and potentially chaotic situation . . . characterized by unique patterns of action and interaction that are consciously directed toward the development of expectations about the setting and the communication of those expectations to others'.[6]

The concentration of Victorian theatres in the West End parishes of St Martin-in-the-Fields, St Anne (Soho), St Mary-le-Strand, St Clement Danes, and St Paul (Covent Garden) resulted from a number of factors. London's patented companies had tended to locate there ever since the late seventeenth century. It was well provided with public houses, dining establishments, private clubs, gambling houses, brothels, and other nocturnal resorts. As a growing network of roads, bridges, and railways converged on the Strand, ensuring vehicles and pedestrians easy access from every direction, successive entertainment innovations preserved pleasure-seekers' orientation toward this area. Following the relaxation of licensing in 1843, many new theatres located in this part of the West End because it was already an established neighbourhood for playgoing and other revelries. Catering was augmented with the transformation of night-cellars, saloons, and tavern concert rooms into music halls in the 1850s and 60s.

Licensing authorities were complicitous in creating the tightly packed theatre district. In 1860 Augustus Harris, who had recently spent £8,000 embellishing the Princess's Theatre, and Edward Weston, who invested £15,000 to turn the National Schoolrooms into a music hall, petitioned the Middlesex Justices to prevent Charles Morton from licensing the Boar and Castle as a music hall and further glutting the neighbourhood. Their case rested on the argument that five music halls and three theatres were already located within a half mile radius of the proposed site. They pleaded:

> That the Royal Princess's Theatre Oxford Street is within 532 yards of the said Boar and Castle, that the Soho Theatre Dean Street is only 544 yards therefrom, that the Queen's Theatre Tottenham Street is only 760 yards therefrom, that Weston's Grand Music Hall Holborn is only 952 yards therefrom, that the Raglan Music Hall Theobalds Road is only 1100 yards therefrom, that the Great Mogul [Drury Lane] is only 718 yards therefrom, that the National Assembly Rooms High Holborn are only 788 yards therefrom, and that Caldwells Assembly Rooms Dean Street are only 452 yards therefrom.[7]

The streets were clogged with traffic and the competition for patrons was ferocious, yet the licence was granted and six months later the Oxford Music Hall began a long and prosperous life. A similar case occurred in 1887, when the Alhambra Co. Ltd (Leicester Square) petitioned to prevent its neighbour the Empire from switching back to the Middlesex Justices' jurisdiction after several years as a 'theatre' licensed by the Lord Chamberlain. The petitioners complained that the immediate neighbourhood already sported eight music halls in addition to the Empire and Alhambra: the London Pavilion (Piccadilly Circus), Trocadero (Great Windmill Street), Gatti's (Villiers Street), Middlesex (Drury Lane), Royal Holborn Empire (High Holborn), Oxford (Oxford Street), Royal Aquarium (Tothill Street), and Royal Standard (Victoria Street).[8] If anything, the Alhambra understated its competition: even after St James's Hall and Charing Cross Music Hall are added, the list still comprises only 11.44 per cent of London's music hall market (approximately 18,082 of 158,013 seats).[9] The Empire's licence was granted, and the competition intensified further in 1890 with the completion of the Tivoli and in 1892 by re-designating D'Oyly Carte's new opera house (Cambridge Circus) as the Palace, a music hall.

The population of London continually grew, so notwithstanding fluctuations in the economy the industry's expansion is predictable. For the most part, the West End's theatres and music halls welcomed women and men alike, with a pricing level favouring the middle classes. Nevertheless, middle-class women's access to the full erotic life of theatres and streets in the West End was restricted by codes of propriety. In the same manner that closed carriages prevented women's blunt introduction to the squalor of thorough-fares, women were politely blinkered from contact with sordid activity inside theatres. Young women were expected to attend in the company of male or older female escorts, apparently because without anyone to navigate away from the sites and situations incompatible with innocence harm would inevitably occur. An accidental detour near a music hall's licensed bar, for example, would acquaint a woman with a host of prostitutes who marked that territory as their own every bit as distinctly as prostitutes in a doorway. Thus, middle-class men had access to the whole of theatres' public areas and full mobility as pedestrians in the streets surrounding theatres whereas women did not.

Among the middle class, the greater freedom of mobility accorded to men – even when in formal dress – determined that they, not women, were the targets of almost all the erotic and eroticized West End culture. The migration of the middle classes out of adjacent neighbourhoods such as St George Bloomsbury, St Giles, and parts of St Pancras into the deliberately pub-free and music hall-free new Victorian suburbs further away to the north resulted partly from the incompatibility of masculine leisure with family life.[10] One of Charles Cornell's songs epitomizes the syndrome: it relates the views of a man who keeps his bachelor exploits, hatred of his mother-in-law, attraction to a servant, and theatre-going habits secret from his wife:

> I'm a very strong admirer of the ballet and the play,
>   But I haven't told the missus up to now!
> And to watch the fairies dancing I pass may an hour away,
>   But I haven't told the missus up to now!
> When I see their graceful attitudes with love I'm burning hot,
> And when the angels flap their wings, they mash me on the
>   spot,
> And I feel as if I'd like to go at once and kiss the lot,
>   But I haven't told the missus up to now![11]

Isolation of women and children in the suburbs safeguarded traditions of masculine debauch, and as Jerome K. Jerome discovered on his first unauthorized foray to the Olympic, it reinforced the clubbiness of unexpected acquaintances and the conspiratorial air of the secret indulgers.[12]

The freer access of men to the pleasures of the West End implies three consequences:

1   The presence of various illegal, erotic, and gastronomic entertainments throughout the West End set up expectations about and within the zone, potentially effecting everything within it.

2   As the targets of erotic sales pitches, men's erotic awareness was heightened within the zone, and this includes theatre auditoria.

3   Accurate perception of the sexual referents in performance was restricted to one sex: the men for whom the whole erotic marketplace was geared. Actresses were turned into sexual commodities by both the conventions of their work and the ambiance of their work place.

Expectations were formed to a large extent by the sensual topography of the neighbourhood. Theatres were ideologically and geographically central to the zone, and standards of middle-class gentility increasingly dominated theatre aesthetics and auditorium behaviour, yet the principal routes leading to the West End retained their character as thoroughfares of vice. In the 1840s, the Strand and its courts were dotted with supper clubs; from the 1850s Piccadilly, Regent Street, and Oxford Street were all prominent daytime prostitution markets; in the 80s the axis streets from Tottenham Court Road to Portland Road sported a density of illegal gaming houses (often with dancing rooms attached) that was rivalled only in Soho; at the end of the century the mutoscope arcades clustered along Tottenham Court Road were very popular with the poor; and throughout the Victorian years, Holywell Street and the convergent Wych Street at the western end of Temple Bar were known throughout the Empire as the loca of the trade in erotic prints, drawings, books, magazines, photographs, slides, and apparatii of no equivocal purpose.

As Lord Sydney protested in the *Pall Mall Gazette* in 1869, theatres were integral to the depravity of West End night life. J. Ewing Ritchie endorsed this view:

The truth is, the evil of which he complains had become unbearable. If we are trying to purify the Haymarket, if the *pose plastique* is put down, if the infamous Judge and Jury Club [e.g. the Coal Hole, a precursor to music halls] is modified, if the abominations of Holywell-street exist no more, still less can it be permitted that fashionable vice should mainly usurp the boxes of the theatres, and indecency and indecorum shamelessly run riot on the stage.[13]

None of these enterprises are unique to the West End, but unlike The Cut in Lambeth, the City Road through Islington, and the Ratcliffe Highway through Wapping, the entertainments of the West End were simultaneously perceived and grandly pardoned as integral parts of the squalor, petty larceny, and sexual markets that surrounded them. The penny theatres in Whitechapel, in contrast, were cleared out entirely once the neighbourhood became a focus for sectarian reformers: there, nothing inimical to middle-class purity, once detected, was free from missionary interference.[14] Clerics in Knightsbridge also felt their philanthropic work was counteracted by the greater attractions offered in cheap theatres, and tried to replicate the East End missionaries' success.[15] But in the West End, the customary rounds of men's evenings included a veritably sacrosanct combination of actresses and, in its most innocent conclusion, a late supper.

Few, if any, areas of London were free of prostitutes. The West End's trade was nominally divided between the theatre district, and Chelsea and Hanover Square further west (Kings Road, Sloane Square, and Victoria).[16] Daytime prostitution centred on the principal middle-class shopping streets, but at night the market shifted to accommodate the main pedestrian and vehicular routes of theatre-goers. From 7.00 p.m. when traffic flowed between Mayfair, the City, and Charing Cross Station until 2.00 a.m. when most pleasure-seekers had turned homeward, prostitutes were said to keep the Strand 'literally impassable'.[17] Pimped prostitutes strolled Covent Garden, Duke's Court (off Drury Lane), Russell Court (off Bow Street), and all of the Strand from Holywell Street to Trafalgar Square – precisely following the course of theatres and two-a-night music halls. Haymarket prostitutes were more specialized, engaging in their trade between 11.00 p.m. and 1.00 a.m.; in other words, between the closing of Her Majesty's, the Comedy, Pavilion, and Haymarket Theatres and the opening of Evans's, Dubourg's, the

Hotel de Paris, the Cafe de l'Europe, the St James's and other eating/ entertainment houses in the Leicester Square and Piccadilly Circus area.[18] The St James's Restaurant was closely associated with the scandalously open prostitution trade in Piccadilly Circus, and the police freely admitted that it harboured prostitutes. In testimony before the LCC's Theatres and Music Halls Licensing Committee, D. Wilton Collin of the West London Mission claimed to see some of the same prostitutes in St James's Restaurant as in the Alhambra and Empire music halls on a given evening.[19] Most fashionable West End restaurants and music halls considered the presence of appropriately dressed prostitutes to be an asset in advertising the establishment, drawing male clients, and increasing legitimate revenues. In both types of venue, the coincidence of prostitutes, alcoholic drink, and entertainment symbiotically improved profits. Recognizing this, reformers' strategy in obstructing the business of St James's Restaurant was not to press for greater vigilance against prostitution (a ploy that the Metropolitan Police could not be trusted to enforce) but to oppose renewal of its drinking licence and insist on architectural separation of the restaurant premises from the adjacent halls where entertainments by the Moore and Burgess minstrels and comparable groups were featured.[20]

The theatre not only enhanced arousal generated in the neighbourhood, but also stimulated men in preparation for subsequent forays in the West End. As one gentleman in *The Confessions of Nemesis Hunt*, an enormously popular erotic novel of 1902, pointed out to his theatre companion after a burlesque:

> You *may think* it trash, though I know you've been at least a dozen times, but the public love it, and the public deserve to be catered for. Take the men in tonight's audience. They had worked hard during the day, and they had dined heavily when their work was over. They did not want to *think*, their tummies were much too full. They wanted to laugh easily, and, above all, to see lots of pretty girls, and feel their old jocks stiffen.[21]

In erotic prose, the theatre did not function as a blank backdrop, but was a very particular milieu wherein illusion enhanced attractiveness and provided a ready-made imaginative context for erotic fantasy. The repetition of motifs in pornography demonstrates that the social environment for sexual adventure was significant and indeed crucial to enjoyment. The pornography was, therefore, doubly a social site of the ideology and practices of its consumers. Serio-comic songs from the music halls confirm the same idea. As Marie Lloyd sang, her dear Uncle Sam, 'a jolly old cock', was attuned to the choice locations for beginning erotic escapades: the seaside, third class railway carriages, and theatres:

> He once saw an up-to-date play in the West,
> And sweet chorus ladies so scantily dressed;
> Round to the stage door later on he did roam,
> And found 'something choice' coming out, going home.
> CHORUS: Then he stood it a supper at Scott's,
> And bought it a bottle to please it;
> For it's dear little waist
> Seemed to tickle his taste —
> And he knows a good thing when he sees it![22]

On another occasion Uncle Sam resorted to Regent Street, where he encountered a prostitute bedecked with make-up and a wig from Clarkson's, the theatrical supplier.

No matter how decorous the West End theatre became, or representative an audience it attracted (including women, families, and a cross section of social classes), the erotic ambiance of the West End and the pre-eminence of actresses in pornography created a potential effect on men within theatre auditoria. Male spectators who were literate in the pornographic codes observed performance and performers in the light of the erotic jokes, cartoons, short stories, and illustrations that 'document' social judgements about actresses in pornography. Given the preoccupation in the masculine literature of pornography, the street market in sex, and the presence of the referent, the marketplace in sensuality unavoidably extended beyond the doorsteps of theatres and music halls and into their auditoria, promenades, bars, lounges, and backstage areas.

EROTIC ZONES WITHIN THE PLAYHOUSE

In pornography, the playhouse is sometimes a place that draws women away to work (to the great interruption of delightful intercourse that would otherwise continue around the clock), and is sometimes a haven of rest to which people may retire without diminishing their arousal in-between athletically taxing debaucheries. Some theatres generated expectations from their thresholds. For example, sidewalk posters alerted attention to the innovative nude *tableaux* at the Palace. Middlesex Music Hall displayed violent images outside its doors: 'one man cutting another ones [*sic*] throat (standing behind with a knife across his victim's throat), the other picture representing a fight with glass wine bottles & firetongs on a staircase, both combatants smothered in blood.'[23] In the Zaeo scandal at the Aquarium, the sexual enticement of the acrobat's larger than life form extended from the theatre's immediate area to hoardings throughout the whole of metropolitan London. A more modest case demonstrating the same principle occurred at a penny theatre in Shoreditch, where announcements of 'Vidco's Beauty Show' were emblazoned across a shop front:

> It was a suggestive title; it aroused curiosity in the breasts of the Shoreditchers, and lured sundry pennies from their pockets.... It exhibited its warning to the public from the shop-window also, in juxtaposition with a French print of a young lady taking off her slippers before retiring to rest – a print that seemed struggling hard to draw the line between propriety and impropriety without shocking the suscept-ibilities of the police – and the warning was to the following effect: '*Boys and girls under fourteen not admitted*'.... A beauty show where boys and girls under fifteen were not admitted, was too much for the masses, and they flocked in, their eyes gleaming with eagerness for the display.[24]

Within playhouses the sexual enticement could be expunged or drawn out by an internal geography of erogenous zones. This geography was individuated by customs of social behaviour that varied in different establishments and historical periods. For example, sexual activity was widely assumed to be practised in the curtained boxes of Regency theatres, but decades later the auditoria of music halls were decorous while at establishments like the Empire the long 'American' bar, stalls promenade, and dress circle lobby were the infamous assignation points for prostitutes and clients. This pattern is typical of late-Victorian music halls, and there is no doubt that prostitutes attended the halls for other people's entertainment, not their own. The Empire was the most notorious because its prostitutes were the most gorgeously dressed, but each house attracted women bedecked in proportion to the entrance fee.

Moralists charged that at the Oxford Music Hall 'the promenades and drinking bars thereof are permitted to be used largely and habitually as a resort of common prostitutes for purposes of solicitation and immoral bargaining and that excessive drinking indecent conversation and disorderly conduct take place therein'.[25] Prostitutes' objective in the promenades was obvious: many of them sat all night at tables by the bar where they could not even see the show.[26] Most moral reformers believed that the danger of the promenades lay in the ready supply of women and strong liquors together in the same place. Thus, James Greenwood writes in 1869:

> It is at the refreshment-bars of these palatial shams and impostures, as midnight and closing time approaches, that profligacy may be seen reigning rampant. Generally at one end of the hall is a long strip of metal counter, behind which superbly-attired barmaids vend strong liquors... the un-blushing immodesty of the place concentrates at this long bar. Any night may here be found *dozens* of prostitutes enticing simpletons to drink... her main undisguised object being to induce him to prolong the companionship after the glaring gaslight of the liquor-bar is lowered.[27]

Soliciting zones within music halls varied from one to another. At Collins' on Islington Green, an inspector found the gallery free of prostitutes, though the stalls level was less praiseworthy:

> This part is besieged by a goodly number of unfortunates of the better-class sort. The bar, which is at the back, is supplied with side lounges and these are the hunting grounds of these women. I observed no importuning but it is not required with such conveniences. A tipsy young man will invariably drop down beside one of these females.

The skirt dance of Alice Leamar, in which 'the high pitching of the legs and the continual twirling, with the hands, of the muslin petticoats' was judged 'very suggestive' so as to give the audience 'unbounded satisfaction' is mentioned in the same report, as if to verify that the patrons of the stalls had some stimulus to be patrons of another kind.[28]

Activity in the Empire Theatre's gallery may have been more lively than Collins'. An unsigned letter in the Greater London Record Office describes how the theatre's front-of-house manager, Robert William Ahern, was seen dragging, kicking, and punching a pacific man from the gallery. He is cited as explaining that 'this man was a *sodomite*, & that more than half the audience in the shilling promenade were of that class & that he often turned out half a dozen a night & gave them a good kicking'. This is surely not what Oscar Wilde had in mind when he quipped a scant few months later in *The Importance of Being Earnest* that Jack and Algy should go round to the Empire at ten, but if the report is accurate it is highly likely that Wilde knew about the Empire gallery, for the source paraphrases Ahern saying 'it was the only place in London where this class of people congregated . . . he could lay his hands on 200 sods every night in the week if he liked'.[29] This suggests that the famous Boulton and Park transvestite case twenty-five years earlier at the nearby Strand Theatre may not have been an isolated incident.[30] Ahern does not speculate on the reasons homosexual men selected the Empire as a rendezvous, nor does he make it clear that he evicted transvestites. Whether the Empire's bill of fare provided stimulation for homosexual desire is a matter beyond speculation. But in retrospect it seems tremendously significant that the intense homophobia shown around Wilde's ordeal (which culminated, after two trials, with his sentencing on 25 May 1895) played no part in the Empire controversy in October 1894. This draws attention to the likelihood that apart from selecting an area of the metropolis and a class of music halls in which to concentrate licence objections, moral reformers also chose their campaign precisely and carefully. Instead of trying to close the Empire because it harboured male homosexuals in the lowest priced area, reformers cited the indecency of women's bodies – revealingly shown in cross-dressed and feminine characters – and linked this to immorality among the highest paying customers engaging in heterosexual solicitation at the stalls and dress circle levels.

The stages on which women performed were almost always highly charged erogenous zones. Audience enthusiasm and profits were closely related, and revelation of the female form had a lot to do with the equation's success. Madame Vestris, for example, made a fortune by exhibiting her sexual attractiveness in breeches parts. Later in her career she achieved artistic notoriety by setting performances within box sets, making herself seem less approachable within a domestic scenic framework. By enhancing the physical and existential distance between the stage and the auditorium, she fundamentally altered the playhouse dynamics. Within the closed domestic scenic interior, Vestris seemed to restore the 'proper' demarcation of public and private realms, or at least achieved a partial illusion of having done so. She also declared bankruptcy twice. Marie and Squire Bancroft completed the boxed enclosure,

locking it in a proscenium frame; in addition they also eliminated
farces and afterpieces from their bills, for without a sexual ambiance
the salacious interludes were pointless. When the Bancrofts moved
to the larger Haymarket they attacked the pit (a prized vantage for
connoisseurs of the female leg); they flourished, but by 1880' there
were other venues for anatomical display.

A reputation for excellent entertainments – on stage and in the
promenades – made the Alhambra the most popular tourist
attraction in mid-Victorian London. By the latter decades of the
century, most West End managers vehemently claimed to prohibit
unauthorized access backstage, implying that despite popular belief
to the contrary influential spectators could not approach actresses in
the wings, dressing rooms, or green rooms. If this prohibition was
enforced, the powerfully erogenous backstage would be neutralized, but evidence relating to the Alhambra suggests that the
practice endured. A letter in the Greater London Record Office
pseudonymously signed by a 'Comic Singer with daughters in the
profession' inquired: 'why are the men well known for their
seductive ways (the military officers as a rule), encouraged and
brought behind the scenes to solicit and entice young girls to
partake of supper, drives, &c. which means indirectly for an immoral
purpose[?]' Distance loaned enchantment, but proximity was better.
The reason these men wanted to be backstage was clearly related to
the performance conventions. The 'Comic Singer' continues:

> Who is answerable for the studied indecency of the costumes
> exhibited in 'Enchantment and Antiope'[?] In the latter ballet a
> number of young girls appear in fleshing tights *only* to
> represent the nude figure ... a small gauze hung round the
> waist which could be plainly seen through thus making things
> more suggestive [than if there was] no extra covering round the
> loins[,] abdomen[,] or posterior... the dresses were not worn
> to facilitate art as the girls only moved to a slow movement.
>
> The thing was only introduced to please the men fre-
> quenters of the stalls, a class of men who use the place nightly
> and do more mischief than the prostitutes.[31]

Instead of barring men's access backstage, managers may have
compliantly facilitated it. The 'Comic Singer' clinched his argument
by asking a damning supplementary question: 'Why can paper and
envelopes be obtained in the stalls and letters sent behind & taken
by one of the attendants making appointments with the girls?' It is

not surprising that men wanted to meet the lightly dressed performers, and if the management conveniently provided station- ery and messengers this is tantamount to sanctioned solicitation. His concluding point, 'let us have a little propriety... or is the Alhambra too powerful to be interfered with!'[32] is important: the Alhambra's shareholders reaped generous dividends during this period, and the profiteers had no reason to give up a winning formula. Evidently they did not give up the formula, for ten years later N.S. Parker – ungrammatical in his indignation – noted that backstage visits still persisted at the Alhambra:

> In one case I know of, a young girl of 16 – who had only been at the theatre a week – was spoken to by two men who came from a box in front whom she was afraid not to speak to & who made her an improper proposal.... It is by no means an isolated case.[33]

FORESTALLING THE EROTIC

In the mid-Victorian period, commentators like Greenwood were mainly concerned about moral turpitude effecting what he termed 'young swells of the "commercial" and shopman type'. In later decades concern broadened to include middle-class men, yet during the 1870s and 80s the people who were predisposed to complain about performance organized into groups concentrating on re- claiming souls and cleaning up leisure in working-class neighbour- hoods. Under the auspices of Methodist, Wesleyan, and Baptist congregations, the YMCA, total abstinence federations, vigilance and watch committees, and Women's Rescue Missions, lobbying groups brought increasing attention to the issue of impure leisure. A common moral sense drew them together into an ideological bloc focusing on theatres' disregard for propriety. They were never able to rally the cooperation of the Lord Chamberlain, who was apathetic, or local magistrates, who almost always sided with managers' commercial interests. In frustration, they themselves became managers of what were considered some of the most degenerate establishments in the East End, such as Wilton's Music Hall. An anecdotal history of the East London Wesleyan and Methodist Mission suggests the naive attraction of such projects:

> Mrs. Reginald Radcliffe and Miss Macpherson were passing through Grace's Alley into Wellclose Square as the evening

performances in the music-hall were proceeding. The dreadful hubbub that came from the hall startled them. They paused to listen, and were so impressed that they paid the admission fee and went in to see really what could be going on. The sights on the stage and the entire condition of things became so awful to them, that they fell down on their knees together, in the centre of the hall, and in view of the stage and crowd of onlookers, prayed that God would break the power of the devil in the place, and bring the premises into the use of Christian people.[34]

The East London Mission disliked this so much it bought the company. Religious sectarians repeatedly targeted the East End in this way: before the Mission took over Wilton's, the Salvation Army bought the notorious Grecian Theatre in the City Road. Other branches of the leisure reform effort attempted to attract young people away from 'low' theatrical entertainments and into schemes like the Working Lads Institute, the girls' Evening Home, Toynbee Hall, and the Peoples' Palace.[35] Across the river, the housing reformer Emma Cons converted the Old Vic to a temperance hall under the auspices of Morley College.

In 1891, Robert Buchanan asked how far 'the moral sense of majorities' would be allowed to dictate public access to art;[36] in contemporary usage, the term 'moral majority' retains Buchanan's original implication of Christian pressure groups attempting to exert leverage in community control and secular politics. In 1888, when the power to licence music halls was transferred from local magistrates to the new LCC's subcommittee on Theatres and Music Halls, reformers jumped at the chance to influence the new body, pinning their hopes on Frederick Charrington (a member of the National Vigilance Committee's General Council) who was elected to represent Mile End. When Augustus Harris (manager of Drury Lane Theatre and councillor for the Strand electoral division) was disqualified from membership in the LCC's Theatres and Music Halls Licensing Committee due to conflict of interest, the scales seemed to be weighted in favour of reform. Charrington immediately attacked world-famous high class music halls in the West End, far from his constituency.

The first contentious case to come before the Theatres and Music Halls Committee concerned the Trocadero music hall (Great Windmill Street). Accusations centred on some sexual byplay in an acrobatic sketch and on a seriocomic singer, Maud Hilton, who insisted and subsequently demonstrated that her legs were not bowed but merely bandied. The Committee recommended that the licence not be renewed, but the Council as a whole overturned the recommendation.[37] The reformers were equally disappointed when the Council did not heed the Dean of Westminster's complaint that the Royal Aquarium (Tothill Street, Whitehall) was the resort of prostitutes.[38] They had also hoped that combined charges of immoral performance and prostitution would close the Empire Theatre (Leicester Square), but the evidence was so badly presented that nothing could be done. (When asked how he recognized prostitutes, Charrington's witness, a grocer, explained 'by their manner of going so about — the manner of passing by people and looking out with their eyes', and when asked to justify his objection to costumes the most specific remark he could make was 'I thought the dresses were exposing the shapes of the performers very much'.[39] That was precisely the point, of course.) Apart from the *naïveté* of witnesses, the major impediment to reformers' success was the lack of precise legal nomenclature for infractions. The root of moralists' objection was that performance conventions and the ambiance of music halls were sexually exciting to men, but this was difficult to prove empirically under the quasi-legalistic procedures of the LCC. To their credit, Committee members did not confuse assertions with evidence, and would not accept moralists' ascription of all women well-dressed and on their own as prostitutes. In testimony, male and female reformers alike resorted to euphemisms, verbal accounts of fleeting gestural nuances, and blatantly subjective interpretations, relying far too much on their own bourgeois bearing to make vague statements authoritative. Routed by the failure of these initial attempts on West End music halls, the moral majority returned its attention to working-class neighbourhoods and there perfected the rhetorical flourishes needed before trying again to persuade councillors of corruption in their own beloved middle-class haunts.

Like the magistrates who targeted song saloons in Islington and Clerkenwell in 1863, the reformers' attention turned in 1891 to halls in a tightly delineated area: the East End's Tower district. On the basis of testimony from a ship's cook, banker's clerk, workers with the Hope Mission for Fallen Women, and pastor of the Wesleyan East End Mission, renewals of the dancing licences for the Rose and Crown and the Angel and Crown public houses in Wapping were denied, despite the fact that neither the police nor the vestry ever lodged complaints against the premises or their proprietors. Reviewing the case, the LCC accepted the comments of its Inspector as equally indicative of both houses:

> I am of the opinion that not only is prostitution tolerated, but that it is even fostered by the management, at all events in the person of the elderly woman behind the bar [wife of the proprietor]. . . . I can find no other name for such a place than a hell.[40]

The women, he alleged, were all common prostitutes, the men were all foreign sailors, and the combination had an inevitable result. Evidence both from the LCC hearings and resultant litigation strongly suggests that the authorities took advantage of the proprietors' low status as East End immigrants in order to financially cripple these popular centres of audience-generated entertainment, and that this was undertaken at the request of evangelists active in the neighbourhood.[41] Other local residents testified that the Rose and Crown was well-conducted, there was no drunkenness, and that working-class people of both sexes were as liable to attend as sailors and prostitutes,[42] yet neither the Rose and Crown nor the Angel and Crown were ever re-licensed for music or dancing.

Through a combination of economic buy-outs, political pressure, and partisan officials, the moralists were successful in suppressing and controlling working-class entertainment in Whitechapel and Wapping. Buoyed by these victories, the middle-class reformers once again turned attention to their own institutions. The new campaign was ambitious: they deliberately targeted the halls that had particularly high local and international profiles, and particularly prestigious clienteles. Vindicated by small successes in the East End, the National Vigilance Association and Laura Ormiston Chant (founding editor of its paper the *Vigilance Record*) led a crusade by the middle class upon the middle class.

It is clear from the testimony before the LCC in 1894 that Chant recognized that the threat of promenades not only lay in the coincidence of liquor and prostitutes, but also in simultaneous viewing of the scantily-dressed female stage performers and the gorgeously outfitted prostitutes. It is probably no coincidence that members of the National Vigilance Association pinpointed this as a problem at this phase of the campaign, for in 1891 the Association subsumed the Society for the Suppression of Vice,[43] an organization that had busied itself seizing 'obscene' material since 1834.[44] The knowledge required to carry on the work of the Society for the Suppression of Vice may have been indispensable in finally recognizing the erotic semiotics of performance. Observing the effect of performance on men who were husbands, brothers, and sons of the middle class while comprehending its pornographic referents was too much for the reformers to endure. At the same session of the LCC that Lady Henry Somerset initiated objections to the Palace's exhibition of *tableaux vivants*, Chant objected to the renewal of the Empire's licence. Whereas the LCC refused to interfere with the artistic content of performance (actually, it failed to recognize why it should interfere with Palace *tableaux* despite their content), it was able to act on Chant's argument regarding the costumes and gesturing of actresses in the midst of the Empire's sexual marketplace.

The Empire, the focal point of Leicester Square, was considered a vital nexus of West End immorality involving prostitutes, alcohol, variety theatres, supper clubs, dancing halls, and gambling houses. At the height of the Empire controversy, a *Daily Telegraph* correspondent irately summed up the neighbourhood as follows:

Within a radius of one hundred yards of the Empire Theatre at the present moment there exist at least a dozen of these night hells [dancing clubs opening after 12.30 a.m.]. . . . Here you can dance with the best and the finest of the demi-monde to the strains of a more or less efficient orchestra, with vitriolised drink supplied to you at fabulous prices. . . . Here, if you are in that way inclined, you can have a music-hall song-and-dance turn supplied to you between the waltzes, if you are of a 'variety' loving turn of mind, and from here you can be taken home to some of the souteneur robbing dens of Soho if you are not careful. . . . It was at one of these places that I, with my own eyes, saw another poor creature well soaked in drink persuaded to divest herself of every vestige of her clothing and dance to an applauding crowd of shameless cardsharpers and well-dressed rogues and vagabonds. It is at these dens that the licensing laws are openly defied, that the lowest form of human scum is allowed to gather under the legalising [*sic*] aegis of a club and the purity policy of a goody-goody Council.[45]

Targeting the Empire theatre was a small but manageable goal in attacking this neighbourhood of interconnected vice. The profits reaped by its shareholders were notoriously high, and reformers longed to disrupt this extremely lucrative exploitation of men's arousal.

In separate studies of the Empire scandal, Penelope Summerfield and Joseph Donohue both note the importance of the promenades to reformers' arguments, focusing on the issue of prostitution.[46] By all reports, the visual codes of prostitution were pretty clear: prostitutes were sublimely well-dressed and invited conversation by looking men directly in the eyes or by casually bumping against their legs. As long as a woman understood and obeyed the subtle limitations on English public behaviour and vestimentary decorum the nature of her character could be easily discerned; an isolated error by the acting manager, Charles Dundas Slater, who once mistook a wealthy American woman in an opera cloak for a prostitute, demonstrates the point.[47] Voluminous verbatim testimony from the LCC hearings reveals, however, that it was not prostitution alone that brought about the action against the Empire: it was the contiguity of behaviour in the promenades to the performance on stage that preoccupied the witnesses. Laura Ormiston Chant's testimony clearly shows how the complainants focused on the effect that balletic costumes and gestures had on the audience.

> To begin with, there was one dancer in flesh coloured tights, & I used no opera glasses at first, but at last I had to use them to see whether she even had tights on or not, so nearly was the colour of the flesh imitated. She had nothing on but a very short skirt — which when she danced & pirouetted flew right up to her head, & left the rest of the body with the waist exposed except for a very slight white gauze between the limbs. . . . Also there is one central figure . . . in flesh coloured tights, who wears a light gauzy lacy kind of dress, & when she comes to the stage, it is as though the body of a naked woman were simply disguised with a film of lace. There is also a dancer who dances in black silk tights with a black lace dress, and . . . she gathers up all her clothing in the face of the man before whom she is dancing, and stretches up her leg, & kicks him upon the crown of his head. I noticed that the audience took these peculiarly objectionable parts very quietly.[48]

The moral majority found the ballets in dubious taste, but the crux of the problem was that other patrons found the dances and costumes indecent and thus provocative of sexual desire. With desire so inflamed regularly each evening at ten o'clock, the women of the promenades had a guaranteed clientele. After years of campaigning, the moral majority finally succeeded in convincing the LCC that provocative performance and solicitation had a causal relationship in a West End music hall.

In order to disassociate performance's instigation of desire from the outlet in the promenades, the LCC ruled that the Empire must install barriers between the back of the seating at the levels of the dress circle and upper circle so that strolling men in the promenades could not watch the performance, drink, and circulate among prostitutes at the same time.[49] As the reformers discovered, neither the civic authorities nor the managers would take steps to ban prostitutes from the premises, so this represents a calculated attempt to inhibit the sexual consequences of performance.

Following the Empire campaign, the moral majority relaxed its watch on music halls. Occasional complaints were registered with the LCC in the ensuing years, but little more was done in London in the way of organized opposition to licensing.[50] The *Vigilance Record*, formerly a reflection of the Association's excellent organization and widespread activities, was published irregularly after 1894.[51] Installation of the Empire barricades marks the culmination of the reformers' efforts but it was ultimately a hollow victory, for the neighbourhood's vice was too pervasive for this to be a pernicious blow. As one promenade prostitute remarked during the height of the controversy, interference with the Empire's architecture would neither ruin her business nor propel her to a reformed life-style: she and her colleagues would simply switch to the Alhambra, Palace, or Pavilion, saying 'We can give them all a turn.'[52] It took George Edwardes, the lessee, six lackadaisical months to fully complete the architectural renovations,[53] and at the licensing sessions in October 1895, a year after the Vigilance Association's victory, the Committee leniently allowed the barricades' removal despite a plurality of Moderate Party members (Conservatives) on the newly elected Council.[54] Neither the audience nor the performances had noticeably changed. They were swayed by Edwardes' plea that it was unfair to impose the condition solely on his music hall, which since the alterations began had reaped £30,000 less than in the previous fiscal year, lowering shareholders' dividends from 75 per cent to 30 or 40 per cent on old stock. His promise of good conduct satisfied the authorities.[55]

Reformers regarded the erotic contiguity of the neighbourhood and theatres every bit as objectionable as music halls, but for practical reasons eschewed the Lord Chamberlain's office (which only responded receptively to complaints based on text or safety hazards) and targeted the institutions licensed through the new metropolitan county councils. At the instigation of the anti-music hall campaign, reformers explicitly stated their intention of extending the campaign to theatres once they were successful with the halls. A leader in the *Vigilance Record* in 1889 claimed:

> After the music-halls will come the theatres. The Lord Chamberlain's shadowy jurisdiction, which is exercised with such timidity, will have to be reinforced before long by the more vigorous authority of a Licensing Committee which will simply crush by its veto every theatre where the acting, the dresses, or the plays are an offence to public decency.[56]

But a concerted anti-theatre campaign never materialized. Theatre managers effectively countered by pointing out the absurdity of the licensing system that required every dramatic script to undergo official scrutiny while music hall programmes were officially checked only once a year in anticipation of the Committee sessions.[57] Theatre managers knew enough about the Examiner of Plays' criteria to predict which plays would not pass the inspection, and either withheld them entirely or commissioned alterations before submitting texts for licensing. The famous blue pencil sought passages likely to cause religious controversy, political embarrassment, or moral indignation. Several scripts from the 1890s, in the musical comedy genre William Archer called 'the real New Drama',[58] demonstrate how far the Examiner of Plays could be pushed, and how blind his office was to scenarios that reinforced notions about theatre as a sexual marketplace.

Internal memoranda from E.F. Pigott (Examiner of Plays) to his supervisor Sir Spencer Ponsonby-Fane (Vice-Lord Chamberlain) regarding a licence for *A Gaiety Girl* in 1893 focus on the compromising depiction of the character of a divorce court judge.[59] What remains in the amended script is a study of Society's changing mores, centering on musical comedy actresses' irresistibility for men and their challenge to 'respectable' women's values. The Gaiety Girls' first words proclaim that they circulate in the highest circles and behave according to the reigning moral code:

> Here come the ladies who dazzle Society,
> Leaders of etiquette, pinks of propriety,
> *Crème de la crème* of the latest variety
>   End of the century girls!
> Strictest observers of social formalities
> Wearers of modern modistes' specialities
> Only residing in tip-top localities
>   Flocking where fashion unfurls.[60]

Nevertheless, they are snubbed by prudish women like Lady Virginia Forest, a divorcée who relentlessly prowls for a second husband. An early comment underlines the gentry's hypocritical self-righteousness:

> Lady Virginia: (Coldly) My idea of entertainment is frivolity without degradation.
> Reverend Montague Brierly [Honorary Chaplain to the 9th Life Guards]: (Aside) She ought to be on the County Council!

Society women's hypocrisy is contrasted to Gaiety Girls' compassion, a superiority that is literally embodied in the actresses' undeniable physical attractiveness. Demonstration of the Gaiety Girls' moral superiority centres on the society women's false accusation that Alma Somerset, a Gaiety Girl, stole a diamond comb (damning evidence in Lady Virginia's divorce case), though it was actually planted on her by Lady Virginia's maid. This does not lessen the actresses' attractiveness in the eyes of men whom the society girls dearly want to ensnare. The Gaiety Girls are pragmatic, not haughty, when one quips:

> Cissy: I wonder how gentlemen can associate with Society girls when they can get actresses.
> Haydee [another Gaiety Girl]: They seldom do!

The implication is that elite women are the last to recognize actresses' rightful claim to social respect, and that they are consequently suffering in the marriage market.

In Act II, on the coast of the Riviera, the society women proclaim their superior modesty by calling attention to their fashionable afternoon dresses in contrast to the Gaiety Girls' smart bathing costumes.

> Lady Edytha Aldwyn: That ladies cannot bathe — if they so please —

Without encountering creatures such as these,
Is really most annoying!

The Gaiety Girls' choral retort is biting:

Cissy, Haydee, and Ethel: You ladies by birth are a curious lot!
Though ev'ry advantage you've seemingly got,
    Yet, if we may take you as a sample,
    You're exceedingly anxious to trample
    With the pride of position superior
    On the girl who's your social inferior.
You hunt for a husband – you plot and intrigue,
And never exhibit a sign of fatigue,
    And a fellow with money you rush at
    In a way that an actress would blush at.
    We would rather be ladies by nature
    Than mere Upper Ten-nomenclature!

Ironically, the situation is sorted out in a fancy dress carnival. The disguised young society women manage to break free from their chaperone, Lady Virginia, and trade dominoes with the Gaiety Girls. The 'right' couples are united, including the Chaplain's daughter and the Judge's nephew, and the Gaiety Girl Alma Somerset and an upstanding Life Guards Captain.

In Town, another popular early musical comedy, also uses masquerading as a means to level the position of society women and actresses, and to institute marital pairs in accordance with the new social order. Although the Duke of Duffshire remarks 'It is harder to get into a green room than to get into parliament,' the entire dramatis personae manages to wind up backstage at the Ambiguity Theatre, including the Duke's chaplain, The Rev. Samuel Hopkins. The theatre's role in changing moral standards is clear:

Duke: It's very wrong, my reverend sir,
    For a clergyman or a minister
    To go behind the scenes at nights
    And talk to naughty girls in tights!
    For should your Bishop chance to hear,
    He must suspend you, so I fear,
    But if in such disgrace you fall,
    I shall not mind at all – not at all!

In Town and other musical pieces delighted in pointing out clerics' appreciation of the most questionable aspects of erotic byplay, implicating even the most puritanical sects. One of Kate James' music hall songs, for example, celebrates the *joie de vivre* still apparent in a Salvation Army lass, formerly a Gaiety Girl:

> Just to show what a wicked girl I used to be
> And how I carried on at the naughty Gaiety;
> > The General of our Army will tell me to advance,
> > And show our happy soldiers the PAS-DE-QUATRE dance
> > [the cancan].
> But they look so shocked, when I twist about and twirl
> > And illustrate a Gaiety naughty girl;
> > > But one old soldier begged of me to do it twice,
> > > And said it was very naughty but devilish nice.[61]

Thus, lyrics assert universal masculine complicity in enjoying theatrical delights. As the *In Town* chaplain points out, the real sticking point in accepting actresses into a reformed social order was the elite of female Society.

> Hopkins: It's very sad, indeed, your Grace,
> > For a Duke to come to a wicked place,
> > For all the world knows what it means
> > When nobles go behind the scenes!
> > And if the Duchess hears of this,
> > Your life will *not* be one of bliss;
> > But though the row may not be small,
> > *I* shall not mind it — not at all.

But even the Duchess of Duffshire is found in a green room, a situation that she is resigned to accept as 'very wrong but very true'. Ultimately, the gorgeous actresses overturn the hegemony of false feminine propriety. The chorus simultaneously refers to itself as private citizens and actresses in the triumphant verses:

> We are the fair Ambiguity Girls,
> Worshipped by bankers and brokers and earls,
> Gorgeous in genuine diamonds and pearls,
> > Daintiest mantle and hat!
> Though we are terribly modest and coy,
> Nice little lunches we rather enjoy,
> Chicken and quails, with a glass of 'the Boy,' [champagne]
> > Surely there's nothing in that!

We are so beautiful, dancing in tights,
Mashers adore us for hundreds of nights,
Sending us bracelets and little invites,
    Waiting outside on the mat![62]

The Shop Girl also asserts the appropriateness of a modern 'dancing girl, burlesque or operatic' to be 'mother of a race aristocratic / Who will have their noble rights to ancestress in tights', in this case reinforcing the notion of actresses' challenge to class rigidity by revealing that a charming shop attendant is the lost heiress to £5 million. This enables the foundling to marry her beau, son of a knighted solicitor, overturning his mother's objections.

All of these scripts assert that women from the formerly despised classes really provide the more appropriate genetic material for aristocratic regeneration. The teleology of their social position, as the Frivolity Theatre actress Miss Plantagenet ('Andantino Spagnoletti') asserts in *The Shop Girl*, closely resembles the upper crust's. They both, for example, are the subjects of photographs and the focus of the masses' and gentlemen's fascination in the fashionable West End:

I'm a lady not unknown to fame
Critics call me by my Christian name
And you see my photograph on show
Just wherever you may care to go!
I've been taken in my dinner gown
Looking modestly and shyly down,
Or kicking high with petticoats that fly,
    The smartest girl in town!

Her transformation to Duchess is, therefore, an easy matter, for social success is a matter of acting correctly:

Ah, dear boys you won't be very glad,
When I'm married to a noble lad.
I shall turn most singularly prim,
And I reckon I'll look after him!
Oh, I'll be a very proper sort,
Quite propriety itself in short,
And all the peers will vote me a success,
    The grandest dame at Court![63]

In some regards, the elevation of choristers to duchesses in musical comedy plots represents relaxing attitudes about actresses' impropriety. The remaining point of social resistance to their acceptance into genteel society is highlighted as severe friction with reigning matrons of inscrutable 'respectability'. Their wholesale acceptance by men, for moral and sexual reasons, was chronicled in the wedding announcements of society columns. Although this seemed to raise the profile of the mass of female performers, it is just as elitist as 'ennobling' actresses for their artistry.

Beneath the ranks of the theatrical peerage remained thousands of utterly obscure performers living with and like the working classes. *The Shop Girl* attempts to equate store clerks and the 'Frivolity Girls', but most people still saw a clear difference. Though performers were better organized politically, the un-hygienic conditions of their work places, the financial insecurity of touring companies, and the opportunities and inducements for sexual coercion — which is different from social opportunity — endured. As the *Great Thoughts* controversy of 1897 to 1898 showed, actresses still walked precariously on extremely unstable ground. Actresses still suffered the indignity of prejudice and disrespect from people inside and outside the profession, and the reasons for this were inscribed in their work and work places. Traditions of performance were inscrutable, but moral reformers broke the code and demonstrated how female performers functioned at the centre of an erotically-bonded neighbourhood. With their recognition of this system came the realization that numerous powerful social institutions — including the Lord Chamberlain's Office, county magistrates, local government, and the police — would not cooperate to challenge or change performance. The task of reform was truly enormous: indeed, it was impossible without the assistance of at least some of these institutions. Theatrical impropriety was symptomatic of a complex network of Victorian attitudes and practices. The consequence for actresses was a social identity saturated with moral equivocacy. The work, not the individual, made this an inevitability. This marked their social identity in the culture.

NOTES

INTRODUCTION

1 Linda J. Nicholson, *Gender and History: The Limits of Social Theory in the Age of the Family*, New York, Columbia University Press, 1986, p. 40.
2 Lawrence Stone, *The Past and the Present Revisited*, revised edn, London and New York, Routledge & Kegan Paul, 1987, pp. 87–8.
3 Griselda Pollock, *Vision and Difference: Femininity, Feminism and the Histories of Art*, London and New York, Routledge, 1988, pp. 31–2.
4 Stone, op. cit., p. 89.
5 Martin Meisel, *Realizations*, New York, Columbia University Press, 1983.

1 THE SOCIOECONOMIC ORGANIZATION OF THE THEATRE

1 For background on Victorian employment, see: M. Mostyn Bird, *Woman at Work: A Study of the Different Ways of Earning a Living Open to Women*, London, Chapman and Hall, 1911; Edith J. Morley (ed.) *Women Workers in Seven Professions: A Survey of their Economic Conditions and Prospects*, London, Routledge, 1914; Wanda Fraiken Neff, *Victorian Working Women: An Historical and Literary Study of Women in British Industries and Professions, 1832–1850*, 1929, reprinted London, Allen & Unwin, 1966; Ivy Pinchbeck, *Women Workers and the Industrial Revolution 1750–1850*, 1930, reprinted London, Virago, 1981; and H. Byerley Thomson, *The Choice of a Profession: A Concise Account and Comparative Review of the English Professions*, London, Chapman and Hall, 1857.
2 Janet Murray's collection of primary readings gives a good impression of Victorian ideas about proper feminine behaviour: *Strong-Minded Women and Other Lost Voices from Nineteenth-Century England*, New York, Pantheon, 1982. Secondary studies include: Leonore Davidoff, *The Best Circles: Society, Etiquette and the Season*, London, Croom Helm, 1973; Carol Dyhouse, *Girls Growing up in Late Victorian and Edwardian England*, London, Routledge & Kegan Paul, 1981; and Deborah Gorham, *The Victorian Girl and the Feminine Ideal*, London and Canberra, Croom Helm, 1982. Christopher Kent's essay 'Image and Reality: The Actress and Society' is in a useful collection on gender stereotyping, sexuality, and social fragmentation, in Martha Vicinus (ed.) *A Widening Sphere: Changing*

Roles of Victorian Women, London, Methuen, 1977.

3   Michael Baker, _The Rise of the Victorian Actor_, London, Croom Helm, 1978.

4   Neither Augustus Harris's knighthood (1891) nor May Whitty's D.B.E. (1918) were for service to the theatre.

5   Other D.B.E.s were conferred on Madge Kendal in 1926, Mary Susan Tempest in 1937, and Irene Vanbrugh in 1941.

6   See Charles Kean's letters to Col. C.B. Phipps, 10 September 1856, and 16 March 1867, in the University of Rochester Library.

7   Horace Wyndham, _Chorus to Coronet_, London, British Technical and General Press, 1951.

8   See Derek R. Layder, 'Occupational Careers in Britain with Reference to the Acting Profession', 2 vols, Ph.D. dissertation, University of London, 1976.

9   This came to a head in the _Great Thoughts_ controversy. See Chapter 3.

10 Edward Higgs, 'Women, Occupations and Work in the Nineteenth Century Censuses', _History Workshop Journal_, 1987, vol. 23, pp. 59–80.

11 Cyril Ehrlich, _The Music Profession in Britain Since the Eighteenth Century: A Social History_, Oxford, Oxford University Press, 1985, pp. 156–61.

12 Clara Morris writes of her American experience, but the situation was identical in the United Kingdom. See 'A Word of Warning to Young Actresses', _Century Magazine_, 1900, vol. 60, p. 41. The latter figure is from Michael Bennett Leavitt, _Fifty Years in Theatrical Management (1859–1909)_, New York, Broadway Publishing Co., 1912, p. 592.

13 Havelock Ellis, _Man and Woman: A Study of Human Secondary Sexual Characters_, London, Walter Scott, 1894, pp. 324–5.

14 Lena Ashwell, _The Stage_, London, Geoffrey Bliss, 1929, p. 73.

15 George Rowell, _The Victorian Theatre 1792–1914_, 2nd edn, Cambridge, Cambridge University Press, 1978, pp. 22–9, 81–2.

16 Rudolf Dircks, _Players of To-Day_, London, Simpkin, Marshall, Hamilton, Kent, [1892], pp. xx–xxi.

17 Michael Sanderson, _From Irving to Olivier: A Social History of the Acting Profession in England 1880–1983_, London, Athlone, 1984, p. 331. Sanderson misplaces the decimal in the bracketed figure.

18 Similar problems plague Benjamin McArthur's study of American actors. His table of players' paternal occupation is drawn from the _Dictionary of American Biography, National Cyclopedia of American Biography, and Notable American Women 1607–1950_ and includes 115 actors and 83 actresses for a statistically insignificant sample of 198 performers representing a 40 year period. He does not attempt to show change over time. _Actors and American Culture, 1880–1920_, Philadelphia, Temple University Press, 1984, p. 31.

19 'A Fact to be Faced', _Stage_, 23 February 1893.

20 Joan N. Burstyn, _Victorian Education and the Ideal of Womanhood_, New Brunswick, N.J., Rutgers University Press, 1984, p. 13.

21 Madge Kendal, _The Drama: A paper read at the Congress of the National Association for the Promotion of Social Science, Birmingham, Sept. 1884_, London, David Brogue, 1884, p. 10.

22 Mrs E.J. Burbury, _Florence Sackville, or Self-Dependence_, 3 vols, London, Smith, Elder, 1851.

23 Simone de Beauvoir, *The Second Sex*, 1952, reprinted New York, Vintage, 1974, p. 782.

24 See the *Stage* articles (1883–4) reprinted in Michael R. Booth (ed.) *Victorian Theatrical Trades*, London, Society for Theatre Research, 1981. Only the variety stage (loosely definable as music hall, a succession of unconnected 'turns' on a stage, and circus, primarily physical and visual rather than verbal with unconnected acts performed in a ring) had interchangeable categories, with music hall borrowing the physical acts such as Blondins, Leotards, and their facsimiles.

25 Fit-ups and booth theatres are analogous, emerging out of statute and charter fair traditions in the seventeenth century and continuing after the 1843 Act. See Josephine Harrop, *Victorian Portable Theatres*, London, Society for Theatre Research, 1989. For the sharing of duties, see Cecil Price, 'Regulations of a 19th Century Theatrical Booth', *Theatre Notebook*, 1949/50, vol. 4, pp. 8–9. For background on the organization of English companies, see James C. Burge, *Lines of Business, Casting Practice and Policy in the American Theatre 1752–1899*, New York, Peter Lang, 1986.

26 Gareth Stedman Jones, *Outcast London: A Study of the Relationship Between Classes in Victorian Society*, Oxford, Clarendon Press, 1971, reprinted Harmondsworth, Penguin, 1984, p. 27.

27 Genres of legitimate theatre, in contrast to the variety stage, are all characterized by a unifying story line. The distinctive forms of drama, comedy, farce, extravaganza, and pantomime are described by Michael R. Booth in *Prefaces to English Nineteenth-Century Theatre*, Manchester, Manchester University Press, 1980. Pantomime (exclusive of the harlequinade), extravaganza (burletta), and ballet used many of the same scenic features as well as a corp of female dancers, though ballet was a non-verbal form. Nineteenth-century burlesque was satirical, but unlike topical farce (à la Toole) it used song and a corp of female dancers. The origins and constant evolution of genres had a distinct bearing on employment traditions and careers.

28 Stedman Jones, op. cit., p. 27.

29 E.T. Smith, 'A Plea for the Theatre', supplement to *Era*, 4 December 1860, p. 3.

30 Michael R. Booth, *Victorian Spectacular Theatre 1850–1910*, London, Routledge & Kegan Paul, 1981, p. 85.

31 Greater London Record Office, Inspector's Report, 5 December 1891, LCC/MIN/10,769.

32 Documented cases include Helen Taylor, Mary Stafford (Flora Mayor), and the anonymous author [Alma Ellerslie?] of *The Diary of an Actress or Realities of Stage Life*, ed. H.C. Shuttleworth, London, Briffith, Farran, Okeden & Welsh, 1885.

33 T.W. Robertson, 'Theatrical Types. No. IV. – Leading Ladies, Walking Ladies, and Heavy Women', *Illustrated Times*, 13 February 1864, p. 107.

34 At the Britannia Theatre (Hoxton), 'super' appears to have been a male appellation, while 'ballet girls' served as walk-ons in dramatic pieces.

35 Leman Thomas Rede, *The Road to the Stage*, London, J. Onwhyn, 1836, p. 15.

36 T.W. Robertson, 'Theatrical Types. No. VIII – Chambermaids, Soubrettes, and Burlesque Actresses', *Illustrated Times*, 23 April 1864, p. 267.

37 Davenport Adams, 'Neglected Lines. III. – The Light Comedian and the Singing Soubrette', *Stage*, 2 April 1896, p. 8.
38 Derek and Julia Parker, *The Natural History of the Chorus Girl*, London, David & Charles, 1975, p. 22.
39 See Sanderson's chapter on 'Financial Rewards and Safeguards 1890–1914', op. cit., pp. 79–94.
40 Mrs Mathews, 'Ennobled Actresses', *Bentley's Miscellany*, 1845, vol. 17, p. 600; Noel B. Gerson, *Because I Loved Him: The Life and Loves of Lillie Langtry*, New York, William Morrow, 1971, p. 84–7; Christopher Thomson, *Autobiography of an Artisan*, 1847, p. 259; and Joseph Knight, 'Who is the Greatest Living English Actress – and Why?', *The Idler*, November 1885, vol. 8, p. 393.
41 Ehrlich, op. cit., p. 44.
42 H.G. Hibbert, *Fifty Years a Londoner's Life*, London, Grant Richards, 1916, pp. 211–12; 'The Electric Dance', *Era* 1 April 1893, p. 15.
43 George Foster, *The Spice of Life: Sixty-five Years in the Glamour World*, London, Hurst & Blackett, [1939], p. 102.
44 Charles Booth, 'On the Economics of Music Hall,' *Theatre Quarterly*, October-December 1971, vol. 1, p. 46.
45 John Ebers, *Seven Years of the King's Theatre*, London, William Harrison Ainsworth, 1828, p. 395.
46 J.H. Anderson, Letter, *Stage*, 7 August 1885, p. 18.
47 'The Theatrical Business – I', *St James's Gazette*, 10 January 1885, p. 6.
48 'What a Ballet Costs: A Peep Behind the Scenes', *Sketch*, 12 February 1896, p. 114.
49 Ann Catherine Holbrook, *The Dramatist: or, Memoirs of the Stage*, Birmingham, Martin & Hunter, 1809, p. 38.
50 Rede, op. cit., pp. 5–9.
51 [Adelaide] Mrs Charles Calvert, *Sixty-Eight Years on the Stage*, London, Mills & Boon [1911], p. 14.
52 Letter, *Era*, 4 December 1853, p. 10.
53 Henry Mayhew, *London Labour and the London Poor*, vol. III, London, Charles Griffin [1856], p. 150. This may be an improvement on Thomson's experience, probably acquired in the 1820s: the combined efforts of Thomson, his wife, and their young son often earned more than 1s. a night (and on two occasions they earned 4s. each) but they did not play every night. (Thomson, op. cit. p. 195).
54 Letter, *Stage*, 26 October 1893, p. 14.
55 Squire Bancroft and Marie Wilton, *The Bancrofts: Recollections of Sixty Years*, London, John Murray, 1909.
56 Foster, op. cit., p. 96.
57 Leading Article, 'Actors' Salaries', *Era*, 26 October 1907, p. 21.
58 Fitzroy Gardner, 'Does Acting Pay? A Warning', *Daily Mail*, 18 October 1907, p. 6.
59 ibid., p. 6.
60 'A Chat with Kate Phillips', *Era*, 5 May 1894, p. 11.
61 A. Bulley and Margaret Whitley, *Women's Work*, London, Methuen, 1894, pp. 33–4.
62 *Stage*, 2 December 1895, p. 11.

63   Stedman Jones, op. cit., pp. 30–1.
64   Cicely Hamilton, *Life Errant*, London, J.M. Dent, 1935, p. 43.
65   C.H. d'E. Leppington, 'The Gibeonites of the Stage: Work and Wages Behind the Scenes', *National Review*, 1891, vol. 17, p. 261.
66   'A Chorus Lady's Claim [Morris v. Edwardes]', *Era*, 7 March 1896, p. 10.
67   Hamilton, op. cit., p. 44.
68   Barbara Drake, *Women in Trade Unions*, 1920, reprinted London, Virago, 1984, pp. 44–5.
69   Holbrook, op. cit., pp. 36–7.
70   Daisy Halling and Charles Lister, 'A Minimum Wage for Actors', *Socialist Review*, August 1908, p. 443.
71   'An Actress's Breach of Promise Suit', *Era*, 21 January 1893, p. 10.
72   'Actress's Breach of Promise', *Era*, 15 February 1893, p. 14.
73   'A Theatrical Breach of Promise Case', *Era*, 6 May 1893, p. 8.
74   Hibbert, op. cit., p. 209.
75   Leppington, op. cit., p. 261.
76   Bird, op. cit., p. 94; and Clementina Black, *Married Women's Work*, 1915, reprinted London, Virago, 1983, Appendix I.
77   Black, op. cit., Appendix I.
78   'The Theatrical Business – I', *St. James's Gazette*, 10 January 1885, p. 6; Leppington, op. cit.; and *Stage*, 26 October 1893, p. 14.
79   Lena Ashwell, 'Acting as a Profession for Women', Edith J. Morley (ed.) op. cit., p. 300.
80   Based on weekly wage statistics of textile workers in the North of England in Clara Collet, *Report on the Statistics of Employment of Women and Girls*, pt. 2, 1894, pp. 972, 991, 1000; and wages of working class women and girls in a variety of industries and occupations reported in George H. Wood's Appendix to B.L. Hutchins and A. Harrison *A History of Factory Legislation*, London, P.S. King, 1907, pp. 261, 279.
81   Burstyn, op. cit., p. 13.
82   From annual reports of the Fund in the *Stage*: 17 January 1890, p. 11; 29 January 1891, p. 9; 28 January 1892, p. 14; 2 March 1893, p. 16; 31 January 1895, p. 14; 25 January 1894, p. 14; and 23 January 1896, p. 14. The percentage of beneficiaries is based on the 1891 published Census of England and Wales.
83   *Report from the Select Committee on Theatrical Licensing and Regulations with Proceedings, Minutes of Evidence, Appendix and Index*, p. 56, 1866; and Letter, *Daily Telegraph*, 19 October 1894, p. 3.
84   Leading article, 'Unpaid Rehearsals', *Stage*, 23 November 1883, p. 12.
85   Gardner, op. cit., p. 6.
86   'Chit Chat', *Stage*, 10 May 1889, p. 9.
87   Leppington, op. cit., p. 251.
88   Ashwell, op. cit., p. 303.
89   A. Maude Royden, *Downward Paths: An Inquiry into the Causes which Contribute to the Making of the Prostitute*, London, G. Bell, 1916, p. 161.
90   Halling and Lister, op. cit., p. 442.
91   Bird, op. cit., p. 18.
92   Edith F. Hogg, 'School Children as Wage Earners', *Nineteenth Century*, August 1897, vol. 42, pp. 235–44.

93 Jerome K. Jerome, *On the Stage – and Off: the Brief Career of a Would-be Actor*, London, Leadenhall Press, [1885]; and 'Theatrical Gossip', *Era*, 10 August 1899, p. 8.

94 See 'Children in Pantomimes', *Stage*, 7 December 1883, pp. 12–13; 'The Fairies of the Stage', *Pall Mall Gazette*, 9 February 1885; *Times*, 11 July 1889, p. 3; and *National Review*, 1891, vol. 17, p. 261.

95 Letter from John Tebbutt, *Stage*, 26 July 1889, p. 7.

96 Rudolph De Cordova, 'The Stage as a Career: an Actor's Experience', *Forum*, July 1894, p. 622.

97 Gardner, op. cit., p. 6; see also *The Confessions of a Dancing Girl by Herself*, London, Heath, Cranton & Ouseley, [1913], p. 59.

98 Gardner, op. cit., p. 6.

99 Bird, op. cit., p. 19.

100 'How a London Work-Girl Lives on Ten Shillings a Week,' *British Weekly*, 21 December 1888, p. 118.

2 SEX, GENDER, AND SOCIAL DEMOGRAPHY

1 *Stage*, 20 January 1888, p. 13.

2 *Stage*, 5 December 1895, p. 11.

3 Traian Stoianovich, *French Historical Method: The Annales Paradigm*, Ithaca and London, Cornell University Press, 1976; Lawrence Stone, *The Past and the Present Revisited*, revised edn, London and New York, Routledge & Kegan Paul, 1987.

4 Stone, op. cit., p. 42.

5 ibid., pp. 45–56.

6 ibid., p. 36.

7 The West End parishes are St Clement Dane's, St Paul (Covent Garden), St Anne (Soho), St Mary-le-Strand, and St Martin-in-the-Fields. Lambeth incorporates a considerable area, including Waterloo, Newington, Stockwell, and Clapham. Prominent Surreyside theatres include the Old Vic, Canterbury Hall, Surrey Theatre, and Astley's Amphitheatre. Public Record Office (London) Classes RG–9 and RG–11.

8 Including the Glaswegian parishes of Tradeston, Clyde, Blythswood, and Central in 1861, and Milton and Blackfriars/City in 1881 (the closest approximation of the original districts following boundary redivision), comprising General Register Office (Edinburgh) Class 644.

9 Surveyed Liverpool parishes consist of Islington, Lime Street, and Dale Street on both censuses.

10 George Foster, *The Spice of Life: Sixty-five Years in the Glamour World*, London, Hurst & Blackett, [1939], p. 46.

11 The numbers of foreign-born performers dropped in Westminster and Liverpool whereas Lambeth shows slight increases, possibly because its circus and music halls continued to use foreign talent as a drawing card.

12 John Arthur Jackson, *The Irish in Britain*, London, Routledge & Kegan Paul, 1967, pp. 83–4; and Janet Roebuck, *Urban Development in Nineteenth-Century London: Lambeth, Battersea and Wandsworth, 1838–88*, Chichester, Phillinne, 1979, p. 132.

13 Andrew Gibb, *Glasgow: The Making of a City*, London, Croom Helm, 1983, p. 127.

14 Michael Booth, 'East End and West End: Class and Audience in Victorian London', *Theatre Research International*, 1977, vol. 2, pp. 98–103; and Clive Barker, 'The Chartists, Theatre Reform, and Research', *Theatre Quarterly*, 1971, vol. 1, pp. 3–10.
15 'The Employment of Women', *Meliora*, January 1860, vol. 2, pp. 312–13.
16 'The Vocations of Women', *Sixpenny Magazine*, March 1866, vol. 12, pp. 60–4.
17 Tracy C. Davis, 'Victorian Charity and Self-help for Women Performers', *Theatre Notebook*, 1987, vol. 41, pp. 114–28.
18 Gareth Stedman Jones, *Outcast London: A Study in the Relationship Between Classes in Victorian Society*, 1971, reprinted Harmondsworth, Penguin, 1984, pp. 281–314.
19 *Stage*, 16 March 1888, p. 17.
20 Greater London Record Office, LCC/MIN/10,920, 4 October 1891.
21 Philip H. Highfill, Kalman A. Burnim, and Edward A. Langhans, *A Biographical Dictionary of Actors . . . in London, 1660–1800*, Carbondale, Southern Illinois University Press, 1973, vol. 9, pp. 228–9, and vol. 10, pp. 409–10. Elizabeth Barry and Anne Bracegirdle also co-managed patent companies with Thomas Betterton during this period. The Wakelins were active later in the century (op. cit., vol. 1, pp. 318–19, vol. 5, pp. 228–9).
22 Sybil Rosenfeld, *The Georgian Theatre of Richmond Yorkshire and its Circuit*, London, Society for Theatre Research, 1984, p. 2.
23 For records of their licensing, see Diana Howard, *London Theatres and Music Halls, 1850–1950*, London, Library Association, 1970.
24 J.S. Bratton (ed.) *Music Hall: Performance and Style*, Milton Keynes, Open University Press, 1986, pp. 101–2.
25 *Stage*, 6 May 1887, p. 16.
26 Letter, *Stage*, 11 March 1887, p. 10.
27 Carolyn G. Heilbrun, *Writing a Woman's Life*, London, Women's Press, 1989, p. 25.
28 Clive Swift, *The Job of Acting: A Guide to Working in Theatre*, London, Harrap, 1976, pp. 126–7.
29 [Adelaide] Mrs Charles Calvert, *Sixty-Eight Years on the Stage*, London, Mills & Boon, [1911].
30 Naomi Royde-Smith, *The Private Life of Mrs. Siddons: A Psychological Investigation*, London, Victor Gollancz, 1933.
31 Bampton Hunt (ed.) *The Green Room Book or Who's Who on the Stage: An Annual Biographical Record of the Dramatic Musical and Variety World*, London, T. Sealey Clark, 1906, pp. 375–6.
32 Ann Catherine Holbrook, *Memoirs of an Actress*, Manchester, J. Harrop, 1807.
33 Letter, *Stage*, 28 November 1890, p. 11.
34 John Coleman, 'Decline and Fall of the Old Circuits', *Stage*, 4 September 1885, p. 10.
35 Heilbrun, op. cit., p. 46.
36 ibid., p. 42.
37 Leslie Hannah, *Inventing Retirement: The Development of Occupational Pensions in Britain*, Cambridge, Cambridge University Press, 1986, pp. 6–13.
38 Leader, *Stage*, 26 February 1890, pp. 10–11.

39 *Rules and Regulations of the General Theatrical Fund Association (adopted 22 January 1839)*, London, S.G. Fairbrother, 1848, pp. viii–ix.
40 *Era*, 2 April 1891, p. 15.
41 *Stage*, 19 November 1891, p. 14.
42 *Stage*, 18 April 1894, p. 11.
43 *Stage*, 16 February 1893, p. 14; and 'The Royal Maternity Charity', *English Woman's Journal*, July 1862, pp. 268–9.
44 *Stage*, 26 November 1896, p. 11.
45 *Stage*, 27 October 1892, p. 11.
46 *Stage*, 5 July 1894, p. 11.
47 *Stage*, 20 April 1888, p. 13.
48 Letter, *Stage*, 22 June 1888, p. 13.
49 *Stage*, 6 July 1888, p. 8.
50 *Stage*, 29 April 1887, p. 10.
51 *Stage*, 12 March 1896, p. 11.
52 *The Three Arts Club [rules and list of members]*, London, 1912.
53 The Theatrical Mission, *'Stars', a Year's Work in the Theatrical Mission*, 1892.
54 *Charities Register and Digest*, London, 1890, p. 491.
55 *Era*, 15 March 1890, p. 17.
56 *Stage*, 2 March 1893, p. 18.
57 *Stage*, 2 February 1893, p. 13.
58 From reports in *Stage* and *Era*, 1892–96.
59 *Pall Mall Budget*, 27 January 1887, p. 11; Leopold Wagner, *How to Get on Stage and How to Succeed There*, London, Chatto & Windus, 1899; and Selwyn Tillett, 'Each in His Accustomed Place', *'Ruddygore' Commemorative Booklet*, Saffron Walden, Arthur Sullivan Society, 1987, pp. 4–17.
60 Foster, op. cit., p. 27; Sullivan quoted in Arthur Jacobs, *Arthur Sullivan. A Victorian Musician*, Oxford, Oxford University Press, 1984, p. 316.

3 THE SOCIAL DYNAMIC AND 'RESPECTABILITY'

1 Copelman, Dina M., 'Masculine Faculty, Women's Temperament: Victorian Women's Quest for Work and Personal Fulfillment', *Women's Studies*, Spring 1987, vol. 13, pp. 185–201.
2 Henry F. Chorley, *Pomfret; or, Public Opinion and Private Judgment*, 3 vols, London, Henry Colburn, 1845, vol. 3, pp. 43–4.
3 ibid., vol. 3, p. 239.
4 ibid., vol. 3, p. 240.
5 'Genuine Gossip. By an Old Actress. Chapter I. The Shakesperians', *Era*, 23 January 1853, pp. 9–10.
6 See Helen Taylor's correspondence and diaries in the Mill Collection at the London School of Economics.
7 [Alma Ellerslie?], *The Diary of an Actress or Realities of Stage Life* (ed.) H.C. Shuttleworth, London, Griffith, Farran, Okeden & Welsh, 1885, p. 53.
8 ibid., pp. 50–1.
9 Sybil Oldfield, *Spinsters of this Parish: The Life and Times of F.M. Mayor and Mary Sheepshanks*, London, Virago, 1984, p. 90.
10 Anonymous, *The Actress of the Present Day*, 3 vols, London, James Harper, 1817, vol. 1, pp. 20–1.

11 Geraldine Jewsbury, *The Half Sisters*, 2 vols, London, Chapman and Hall, 1848, vol. 2, pp. 251–2

12 ibid., vol. 2, pp. 73–4.

13 Annie Edwards, *The Morals of May Fair*, 3 vols, London, Hurst & Blackett, 1858.

14 Joanna Richardson, *The Courtesans. The Demi-monde in Nineteenth-century France*, London, Weidenfeld & Nicolson, 1967, p. 225.

15 Henry Mayhew, *London Labour and the London Poor*, extra vol., London, Charles Griffin, 1862, p. 255.

16 County totals are from the published censuses of England and Wales. Parish figures are calculated from the manuscript censuses in the Public Record Office.

17 'The Greatest Social Evil', *Tait's Edinburgh Magazine*, 1857, vol. 24, pp. 748–9.

18 Mayhew, op. cit., pp. 262–3.

19 From Middlesex court records in the Greater London Record Office. Records of 108 summary convictions for riotous behaviour among common prostitutes (in violation of the Vagrant Act, 5 George IV) survive for 1860–2, and though there is no reason to suspect that there are omissions the findings are curious. There is no justification for why Westminster police court heard such cases when neither Bow Street nor Marlborough Street police courts heard a single one (all Middlesex police courts' summary convictions are interfiled). Both Kensington and Chelsea had low actress populations (0.0215 per cent and 0.0235 per cent of women), and none of the prostitutes' names coincide with occupational self-declarations of any theatrical occupation on the hand enumerated census of 1861 in St Martin's, St Mary-le-Strand, St Paul (Covent Garden), St Anne (Soho), St Clement Dane, St Pancras (south and west sections), or Lambeth, so evidently actresses were not travelling outside their residential and work areas to carry out prostitution. Many of the convicted prostitutes came before the courts again and again, clearly returning to the streets and their full-time occupation at the end of each prison term.

20 Revd G.P. Merrick, *Work Among the Fallen as seen in the Prison Cells*, London, Ward, Lock & Co., 1890, pp. 25–6; and A. Maude Royden, *Downward Paths: An Inquiry into the Causes which contribute to the Making of the Prostitute*, London, G. Bell, 1916, pp. 194–5. Royden's figures are based on a field of 830, of whom 257 were subjects in the 1908 Royal Commission on the Feeble-Minded, 552 were referred through charities, and twenty-one were interviewed in West End restaurants and music halls where they sought their clientele. Eight of the 573 mentally normal subjects gave their previous occupation as 'The Stage, etc.'

21 Ivor Guest, *Victorian Ballet-Girl: The Tragic Story of Clara Webster*, London, Adam and Charles Black, 1957, p. 28.

22 William W. Sanger, *The History of Prostitution: Its Extent, Causes, and Effects Throughout the World*, 1897, reprinted New York, Eugenics Publishing Co., 1939, p. 330; and William Acton, *Prostitution*, ed. Peter Fryer, New York, Frederick A. Praeger, 1969, pp. 140–2.

23 *Report from the Select Committee on Public Houses. 1854. Minutes of Evidence*, p. 70.

24 ibid., p. 281.
25 'Report from the Select Committee on Dramatic Literature (1832),' *Westminster Review*, January 1833, pp. 41–2.
26 *Report on the Select Committee on Theatrical Licensing and Regulations with Proceedings. 1866. Minutes of Evidence*, p. 57.
27 Advertisement, *Era*, 5 July 1868, p. 8. This exceeds the totals for South Kensington Museum (1,402,591) and the Zoological Gardens (1,083,563). The Alhambra netted annual receipts of about £150,000, which yielded shareholders 17 per cent.
28 'Empire Theatre. Scene at the Re-Opening', *Daily Telegraph*, 5 November 1894, p. 3.
29 E.S. Turner, *Roads to Ruin: The Shocking History of Social Reform*, London, Michael Joseph, 1950, pp. 229–31; Eric Trudgill, *Madonnas and Magdalens*, London, Heinemann, 1976, p. 127; Ivor Guest, *The Empire Ballet*, London, Society for Theatre Research, 1962, p. 82.
30 'The Greatest Social Evil', op. cit., p. 748.
31 Robert D. Storch, 'Police Control of Street Prostitution in Victorian London: A Study in the Contexts of Police Action', *Police and Society*, ed. David H. Bayley, Beverly Hills, Sage, 1977, pp. 51–2, 65.
32 *Paul Pry*, 22 January 1849, p. 4.
33 Prologue at the Opening of the Theatre in Drury Lane, 1747.
34 [William Rathbone Greg], *Westminster Review*, 1850, vol. 53, pp. 547–8.
35 From an original study of women's statements on their lives prior to conviction and imprisonment in the only prison for women in metropolitan London, serving Middlesex, Surrey, southern Essex to Southend, and northern Kent to Gravesend, Merrick op. cit., pp. 20–7; cited in Judith R. Walkowitz, *Prostitution and Victorian Society*, Cambridge, Cambridge University Press, 1980, p. 21.
36 Greg, op. cit., p. 458. See also Sanger, op. cit., p. 331.
37 Winifred Emery, 'The Stage as a Profession. IV – Something About Success', *Woman*, 8 January 1891, p. 3.
38 Ouida, 'The Woman Problem', *Lippincott's Monthly Magazine*, June 1909, vol. 83, p. 714.
39 John Styles, *An Essay on the Character, Immoral, and Antichristian Tendency of the Stage*, Newport, Isle of Wight, Medina Press, 1806, p. 34.
40 Greg, op. cit., pp. 458–61; Mayhew, op. cit., p. 257.
41 'A Chat with Marie Lloyd', *Era*, 28 October 1893, p. 16.
42 'The Alleged Frauds', *Stage*, 9 June 1892, p. 7.
43 'A Music Hall Agent', *Era*, 25 June 1892, p. 7.
44 'Alleged Theatrical Fraud', *Stage*, 11 January 1894, p. 19; and 18 January 1894, p. 14.
45 'Chit Chat', *Stage*, 22 February 1894, p. 11.
46 National Vigilance Association, *Thirteenth Annual Report*, London, 1898, p. 10.
47 *Era*, 18 June 1892, p. 15; and 25 June 1892, p. 14.
48 Alfred L. Crauford, *Sam and Sallie: A Romance of the Stage*, London, Cranley & Day, 1933, p. 212.
49 ibid., pp. 215–16.
50 H.B. Hibbert, *Fifty Years a Londoner's Life*, London, Grant Richards, 1916, p. 76.

51 Leopold Wagner, *How to Get on the Stage and How to Succeed There*, London, Chatto & Windus, 1899, p. 179.

52 From the penny reprint: Raymond Blathwayt, ' "Does the Theatre Make for Good"? An Interview with Mr. Clement Scott,' London, A.W. Hall, 1898, pp. 3–4.

53 *Ibid.*, p. 4.

54 Guy Boas, *The Garrick Club 1831–1947*, London, Garrick Club, 1948, pp. 77–8.

55 Blathwayt, op. cit., p. 5.

56 Lena Ashwell, 'Acting as Profession for Women', *Women Workers in Seven Professions*, ed. Edith J. Morley, London, George Routledge, 1914, p. 307.

57 Ellen Carol Dubois and Linda Gordon, 'Seeking Ecstasy on the Battlefield: Danger and Pleasure in Nineteenth-century Feminist Sexual Thought', *Pleasure and Danger: Exploring Female Sexuality*, ed. Carole S. Vance, Boston, Routledge & Kegan Paul, 1984, p. 32.

58 John Hollingshead, *My Lifetime*, 2 vols, London, Sampson Low, Marston, 1895, vol. 1, p. 231.

59 C.H. d'E. Leppington, 'The Gibeonites of the Stage: Work and Wages Behind the Scenes', *National Review*, 1891, vol. 17, p. 261.

60 Letter, *Era*, 25 January 1852, p. 12.

61 See 'Theatrical Types. No. XI. – The Corps de Ballet', *Illustrated Times*, 16 July 1864; Anna Cora Mowatt, *Autobiography of An Actress*, Boston, Ticknor, Reed & Fields, 1854, pp. 314–17; and 'The Moral Ministry of the Ballet,' *Stage*, 16 July 1886, pp. 17–18.

62 Gayle Rubin, unpublished essay (1981) quoted by Judith R. Walkowitz in 'Male Vice and Female Virtue: Feminism and the Politics of Prostitution in Nineteenth-Century Britain', *Powers of Desire*, ed. Ann Snitow, Christine Stansell, and Sharon Thompson, New York, *Monthly Review*, 1983, p. 426.

63 Dubois and Gordon, op. cit., p. 33.

64 Ruth Rosen cited Walkowitz in *The Lost Sisterhood: Prostitution in America, 1900–1918*, Baltimore and London, Johns Hopkins University Press, 1982, p. 46.

65 Claudia D. Johnson, *American Actress: Perspective on the Nineteenth Century*, Chicago, Nelson-Hall, 1984, pp. 3–36.

66 For more information on actress/prostitutes of the Restoration see: Sanger, op. cit.; or Antonia Fraser, *The Weaker Vessel: Woman's Lot in Seventeenth-Century England*, London, Methuen, 1984, pp. 473–93.

67 Sandra M. Gilbert and Susan Gubar, *The Madwoman in the Attic: The Woman Writer and the Nineteenth-Century Literary Imagination*, New Haven, Yale University Press, 1979, p. xiii.

68 Bert O. States, *Great Reckonings in Little Rooms. On the Phenomenology of Theater*, Berkeley, University of California Press, 1985, p. 127.

4 ACTRESSES AND THE *MISE EN SCÈNE*

1 William Makepeace Thackeray, *The History of Pendennis*, London, B. Davies, [1848–50].

2 Annette Kuhn, *The Power of the Image: Essays on Representation and Sexuality*,

London, Routledge & Kegan Paul, 1985, p. 6.

3   This literature is fully discussed in Tracy C. Davis, 'The Actress in Victorian Pornography', *Theatre Journal*, October 1989, vol. 41, pp. 294–315.

4   *Memoirs of the Life of Madame Vestris of the Theatres Royal Drury lane and Covent Garden. Illustrated with Numerous Curious Anecdotes*, privately printed, 1830 [*c*. 1840]; *Confessions of Madame Vestris; in a series of letters to Handsome Jack*, n.p., New Villon Society, 1891.

5   The sartorial equipment of each female speciality is listed in Leman Thomas Rede, *The Road to the Stage*, London, J. Onwhyn, 1836, pp. 25–8.

6   Helene R. Roberts, 'The Exquisite Slave: The Role of Clothes in the Making of Victorian Woman', *Signs*, Spring 1977, vol. 2, pp. 554–69.

7   Cited in Ivor Guest, *Fanny Elssler*, London, Adam and Charles Black, 1970, p. 146.

8   This was strictly observed in late Victorian England, though widely disbelieved. When Charles Reed and Edith Mary Reed publicly accused Madge Ellis of appearing bare legged, Ellis threatened to sue. She settled out of court for £300 and a signed apology. 'London Purity Crusade', *Daily Mail*, 27 January 1897. The bare-legged dances of Lola Montez belong principally to the American stage of the mid-century.

9   C. Wilhelm, 'Art in the Ballet', *Magazine of Art*, 1895, p. 14.

10 [Alma Ellerslie?], *The Diary of an Actress or Realities of Stage Life*, ed. H.C. Shuttleworth, London, Griffith, Farran, Okeden & Welsh, 1885, p. 155.

11 *The Days' Doings*, 1870.

12 'Theatrical Types. No. XI. – The Corps de Ballet,' *Illustrated Times*, 16 July 1864, p. 43.

13 Public Record Office (London), letter from A.J. Crowder to the Lord Chamberlain, 30 June 1882, LC1/399.143.

14 The consistency of line from the 1880s to 1900s is demonstrated in the comprehensive collection of designs for pantomime, ballet, and extravaganza by Wilhelm in the Victoria and Albert Museum, Department of Prints and Drawings.

15 Rede, op. cit., p. 28.

16 Public Record Office (London), letters 8 and 9 February 1869, LC1/222.

17 Max Beerbohm, 'Max, Mr Archer, and Others', *Saturday Review*, 15 October 1898, pp. 498–9.

18 Sources of comedy in male theatrical cross-dressing are outlined in Corinne Holt Sawyer, 'Men in Skirts and Women in Trousers, from Achilles to Victoria Grant: One Explanation of a Comedic Paradox', *Journal of Popular Culture*, Fall 1987, vol. 21, pp. 1–16.

19 Critical traditions concerned with the negative connotations of women as spectacles are discussed in Mary Russo, 'Female Grotesques: Carnival and Theory,' *Feminist Studies/Critical Studies*, ed. Teresa de Lauretis, Bloomington, Indiana University Press, 1986, pp. 213–29. According to Natalie Zemon Davis, cross-dressing reveals the misogyny harboured towards strong women in pretended power reversals. Alternately, Jacques Lacan theorizes women's sexuality as the attempt to hide what is not there (a phallus), and male virility as paradoxically feminine; the consequences for men's cross-dressing could be the negation of 'the phallic mark of desire'

(the feminine) and the signification of a basic, stable male identity.

20 Kuhn, op. cit., p. 49.

21 Mr Maddocks appeared as Mazeppa at Astley's on 8 March 1853. A playbill illustration depicts him tied face up on the wild horse; he is bare chested and wearing only tight shorts extending part way down his thighs (British Library, Playbills). Menken, who appeared to be naked, actually wore a pale gymnastic suit of blouse and short pantaloons (Kinsey Institute, Photographs).

22 Playtext by A.C. Torr (Fred Leslie) and Herbert F. Clark, Lord Chamberlain's Plays, 53434, lic. 172(F), British Library Department of Manuscripts. Multiple costume illustrations from British Library Playbills, vol. 475.

23 Anthony Storr, *Sexual Deviation*, Harmondsworth, Penguin, 1964, p. 56.

24 Andrea Dworkin, *Pornography: Men Possessing Women*, London, Women's Press, 1981, p. 124.

25 William Green, 'Strippers and Coochers – the Quintessence of American Burlesque,' *Western Popular Theatre*, ed. David Mayer and Kenneth Richards, London, Methuen, 1977, p. 157.

26 Peter Fryer, *Mrs. Grundy: Studies in English Prudery*, London, Dennis Dobson, 1963, p. 230.

27 'French Plays', *Daily Telegraph*, 15 July 1869, p. 3.

28 'The Alhambra Company and the "Days' Doings"', *The Days' Doings*, 22 October 1870, p. 2.

29 C. Willett and Phillis Cunnington, *The History of Underclothes*, London, Michael Joseph, 1951, p. 176.

30 Cited in Ronald Pearsall, *Public Purity, Private Shame: Victorian Sexual Hypocrisy Exposed*, London, Weidenfeld & Nicolson, 1976, p. 71.

31 Frigga Haug *et al.*, *Female Sexualization: A Collective Work of Memory*, trans. Erica Carter, London, Verso, 1987, p. 137.

32 *Photo Bits*, 24 December 1898, p. 27.

33 Public Record Office (London), letter from W.B. Donne to The Viscount Sydney, 10 November 1870, LC1/232.

34 'What Cheer 'Ria' plays on Cockney pronunciation: an effusive greeting to a woman named Maria takes on the double entendre 'watch your rear'. It celebrates a woman 'in the weagetable line' who spends her savings on a fancy dress, goes to the music hall, and sits by the chairman. Her friends in the gallery spot her and shout
CHORUS   What cheer Ria! Ria's on the job,
          What cheer Ria! did you speculate a bob?
          Oh Ria she's a toff and she looks immensikoff,
          And they all shouted 'What cheer Ria!'
The hoax is up when she trips over a man's wooden leg, insists it isn't her fault, and justifies her friends' greeting/warning when she is chucked out of the hall. Words by Will Herbert, music written and performed by Bessie Bellwood, London, Hopwood & Crew, 1887.

35 'What's That For, Eh? or I Know Now', words by W.T. Lytton, Music by George Le Brun, 1895, reprinted *Marie Lloyd*, London, EMI Music Publishing, 1977.

36 John Elsom, *Erotic Theatre*, London, Secker & Warburg, 1973, p. 23.

37 *New York Telegraph*, 14 November 1897, cited in *Lloyd*, op. cit., p. 3.
38 Words by J.P. Harrington, Music by George Le Brun, 'The Naughty Continong', London, Howard & Co., n.d.
39 'Alleged Music Hall Impropriety', *Era*, 1 March 1890, p. 17.
40 Tracy C. Davis, 'Sex in Public Places: The Zaeo Aquarium Scandal and the Victorian Moral Majority,' *Theatre History Studies*, 1990; National Vigilance Association Annual Reports, [London], 1895 and 1896; and Maurice Rickards, *Banned Posters*, Park Ridge N.J., Noyes Press, 1972.
41 Several examples (probably French) can be found in the postcard collection of the Kinsey Institute, and in Erik Norgaard, *With Love: the Erotic Postcard*, London, Macgibbon & Kee, 1972, pp. 80–1.
42 *Crissie: A Music-Hall Sketch of To-Day*, [London], The Alhambra, 1899, p. 152.
43 Greater London Record Office, Inspector's Report, 15 August 1890, LCC/MIN/10,816.
44 Greater London Record Office, Inspector's Report, 6 October 1898, LCC/MIN/10,769.
45 Greater London Record Office, complaint received in January 1897, LCC/MIN/10,828.
46 *Photo Bits*, 23 December 1898, p. 23.
47 Joan Lawson, *A History of Ballet and its Makers*, London, Dance Books, 1973, p. 46.
48 From a manuscript in the Munby Collection of Trinity College, Cambridge, reprinted in Michael Hiley, *Victorian Working Women: Portraits from Life*, London, Gordon Fraser, 1979, pp. 117–19.
49 Roy Busby, *British Music Hall: An Illustrated Who's Who from 1850 to the Present Day*, London, Paul Elek, 1976, p. 190.
50 Antony Hippisley Coxe, *A Seat at the Circus*, revised edn, Hamden CT, Archon Books, 1981, p. 110.
51 Greater London Record Office, Report of Inspector, 16 August 1890 LCC/MIN/10,891.
52 Jack W. McCullough, 'Edward Kilanyi and American Tableaux Vivants', *Theatre Survey*, May 1975, vol. 16, pp. 25–6.
53 Playbills, British Library.
54 The Hon. F.L.G., *The Swell's Night Guide Through the Metropolis*, London, c. 1840; see also Peter Webb, *The Erotic Arts*, revised edn, London, Secker & Warburg, 1983.
55 James Greenwood, *The Wilds of London*, London, Chatto & Windus, 1876, pp. 105–6.
56 Jeremy Maas, 'Victorian Nudes', *Saturday Book*, 1971, vol. 31, pp. 183–99.
57 Webb, op. cit., p. 192.
58 Graham Ovenden and Peter Mendes, *Victorian Erotic Photography*, London, Academy Editions, 1973, p. 7.
59 Rudolf Arnheim, *The Power of the Center: A Study of Composition in the Visual Arts*, revised edn, Berkeley, University of California Press, 1983, p. 99.
60 *Crissie*, op. cit., pp. 136–9.
61 *The Days' Doings*, 29 April 1871, p. 212.
62 *Das Kleine Witzblatt*, 22 January 1904, p. 9.
63 Greater London Record Office, 1894, LCC/MIN/10,870.

64   Greater London Record Office, 1895, LCC/MIN/10,870.
65   Greater London Record Office, 1893, LCC/MIN/10,870.
66   *Entr-acte*, 3 March 1894.
67   Greater London Record Office, from W.A. Coote's verbal submissions to the licensing hearings, LCC/MIN/10,870.
68   Public Record Office (London), letter from C. Hewitt, 8 January 1891, and Lord Chamberlain's office memo to Ponsonby Fane, 21 January 1891, LC1/383.6.
69   Public Record Office (London), letters 13 and 17 January 1888, LC1/507.
70   From *The Days' Doings*, and reproduced in Peter Fryer, compiler, *The Man of Pleasure's Companion: A Nineteenth Century Anthology of Amorous Entertainment*, London, Arthur Baker, 1968, p. 57.
71   From advertisements in the *Catalogue of Curiosa and Erotica* (1892), British Library. Typical examples are reproduced in Jean-Pierre Bourgeron (ed.) *Nude 1900*, New York, Morgan & Morgan, 1980; Paul Hammond, *French Undressing: Naughty Postcards from 1900 to 1925*, New York, Pyramid, 1975, p. 102; and Webb, op. cit.
72   Marshall McLuhan, *Understanding Media: The Extensions of Man*, New York, Mentor, 1964, p. 116.
73   *Sketch*, 10 February 1932, p. 1.
74   Windmill Revuedevilles numbers 148 and 113. Souvenir programmes, Mander and Mitchenson Theatre Collection.
75   Elsom, op. cit., pp. 26–7.
76   Kuhn, op. cit., p. 4.
77   'The Wedding Presents', *La Vie Parisienne*, 17 May 1884, p. 270; quoted in Valerie Steele, *Fashion and Eroticism: the Ideals of Feminine Beauty from the Victorian Era to the Jazz Age*, New York, Oxford University Press, 1985, p. 196.
78   *Intrigues and Confession of a Ballet Girl; disclosing startling and voluptuous scenes before and behind the curtain, enacted by well-known personages in the theatrical, military, medical and other professions; with kisses at Vauxhall, Greenwich, &c., &c., and a full disclosure of the secret and amatory doings in the dressing room, under and upon the stage, in the light and the dark, by one who has had her share*, [London, Rozez and Co., c. 1870], p. 8.
79   Quoted in Peter Fryer, *Forbidden Books of the Victorians*, London, Odyssey Press, 1970, p. 134.
80   According to the Goncourt brothers, it was also articulated by Dumas père: ' "What do you wish . . . when you can only make money in the theatre by making girls' tights rip. These constantly ripping tights made the fortune of Directeur Holstein. He ordered his dancers to wear tights that had a ripped seam, always on the same spot. Those were the days for opera glass." ' Diary entry 14 February 1866, quoted in Henry L. Marchand, *The French Pornographers: Including a History of French Erotic Literature*, 1933, reprinted New York, Book Awards, 1965, p. 230.
81   Greater London Record Office, Inspector's Report, 8 October 1896, LCC/MIN/10,868; and Susan Pennybacker, ' "It was not what she said but the way in which she said it": The London County Council and the Music Halls', *Music Hall: the Business of Pleasure*, ed. Peter Bailey, Milton Keynes, Open University Press, 1986, p. 131.

82 [Edward Dumoulin], *Memoirs of a Russian Ballet Girl*, 2 vols in 1, Monte Carlo, [Charles Carrington], 1901. Although, like many erotic books, this was published abroad it was intended for the English market.

83 From a flysheet advertising *Memoirs of a Russian Ballet Girl* inserted in the *Biblioteca Carringtoniensis*, Kinsey Institute.

84 Stephen Marcus, *The Other Victorians: A Study of Sexuality and Pornography in Mid-Nineteenth-Century England*, New York, Basic Books, 1964, p. 127.

5 THE GEOGRAPHY OF SEX IN SOCIETY AND THEATRE

1 *Here and There*, 20 July 1872, p. 346.

2 Edward J. Bristow, *Vice and Vigilance: The Purity Movement in Britain since 1700*, Dublin, Gill & Macmillan, 1977, p. 45.

3 *British Weekly*, 16 March 1888, pp. 365–6.

4 Bristow, op. cit., p. 218.

5 Erving Goffman, *The Presentation of Self in Everyday Life*, Garden City, Doubleday, 1959, pp. 134–5.

6 Gale Miller, 'Entertainment as Deviant Work', in *Odd Jobs, the World of Deviant Work*, New York, Prentice-Hall, 1978, p. 159.

7 Greater London Record Office, 27 September 1860, MR/LMD 11/7 and MR/LMD 11/8.

8 Greater London Record Office, 21 September 1887, MR/LMD 24/3.

9 *Report from the Select Committee on Theatrical Licensing and Regulations with Proceedings. Minutes of Evidence, Appendix, and Index*, 1892, pp. 450–1.

10 Donald J. Olsen, *The Growth of Victorian London*, Harmondsworth, Penguin, 1976, p. 25.

11 Words and Music by Charles Cornell, 'I Haven't Told the Missus up to Now,' London, Francis Brothers and Day, [1887].

12 Jerome K. Jerome, 'Variety Patter', *The Idler*, March 1892, pp. 121–35.

13 J. Ewing Ritchie, *The Night Side of London*, London, Tinsley Brothers, 1869, p. 95.

14 See F.W. Robinson, 'A Round of Penny Shows', *Black and White*, 28 November 1891. Compare James Greenwood, *The Wilds of London*, London, Chatto & Windus, 1876.

15 Public Record Office, letter from Revd J. Villiers, Vicar of St Paul's Knightsbridge, 26 October 1891, LC1/547. He complained of a show in an iron building in the part of the neighbourhood called The Potteries. It 'consists of acting dancing and singing of the most *blackguard* and *degrading* nature. It concerns me because 2 or 3 men with myself are working a ragged boys club in the district, and of course it is awfully up-hill work trying to compete with the attractions of a girl dancing in tights at the other end of the street.'

16 Greater London Record Office, Middlesex Police Court Records.

17 *Paul Pry*, 22 January 1849, p. 4.

18 George Augustus Sala, *Twice Around the Clock, or the Hours of the Day and Night in London*, London, Houlston & Wright, 1859.

19 Greater London Record Office, 10 October 1894, LCC/MIN/10,899.

20 Greater London Record Office, LCC/MIN/10,899. They were not successful in opposing the liquor licence before the Middlesex Licensing

Bench at St James's Vestry Hall. The success of the second objective was, however, upheld on appeal.

21 [George Reginald Bacchus?], *The Confessions of Nemesis Hunt*, 3 vols, London, privately printed, 1902–6, vol. 2, p. 4.

22 Words by J. P. Harrington, Music by George Le Brunn, 'He Knows a Good Thing When he Sees It', London, Francis, Day, & Hunter, 1895.

23 Greater London Record Office, letter from a correspondent signed Barnett, 2 February 1902, LCC/MIN/10,855.

24 Robinson, op. cit.

25 Greater London Record Office, testimony of Carina Reed, 29 September 1896, LCC/MIN/10,868.

26 Greater London Record Office, testimony of C.C. Reed, 14 October 1896, LCC/MIN/10,868.

27 James Greenwood, *The Seven Curses of London*, 1869, reprinted Oxford, Basil Blackwell, 1981, pp. 201–2.

28 Greater London Record Office, Inspector's report, 25 August 1890, LCC/MIN/10,790.

29 Greater London Record Office, letter, 15 October 1894, LCC/MIN/10,803.

30 Peter Ackroyd, *Transvestism and Drag: The History of an Obsession*, New York, Simon & Schuster, 1979, pp. 83–5. The Boulton and Park case also implicated Lord Arthur Pelham Clinton, Martin Luther Cumming, Louis Charles Hurt, and C.H. Thomas as cross-dressers. The Strand's popularity as a crossing-dressing venue is likely. See *Times*, 7 December 1870, p. 9.

31 Greater London Record Office, letter, 14 October 1889, LCC/MIN/10,769.

32 ibid.

33 Greater London Record Office, letter, 5 January 1899, LCC/MIN/10,769.

34 Henry Walker, *East London: Sketches of Christian Work and Workers*, London, Religious Tract Society, 1896, reprinted High Wycombe, Peter Marcan, 1984, pp. 165–6.

35 W.J. Fishman, *East End 1888: A Year in a London Borough Among the Labouring Poor*, London, Duckworth, 1988, pp. 303–24; Deborah E.B. Weiner, 'The People's Palace: an Image for East London in the 1880s', *Metropolis London: Histories and Representations Since 1800*, ed. David Feldman and Gareth Stedman Jones, London and New York, Routledge, 1989, pp. 40–55.

36 Robert Buchanan, *Daily Telegraph*, 28 May 1891.

37 Greater London Record Office, 1889, LCC/MIN/10,920.

38 Greater London Record Office, 1889, LCC/MIN/10,891.

39 Greater London Record Office, 1889, LCC/MIN/10,803.

40 Greater London Record Office, 30 December 1890, LCC/MIN/10,885.

41 This is consistent with closures earlier in the century. Penelope Summerfield notes that 'half of the proprietors refused licences between 1860 and 1864 had foreign surnames'. Immigrant communities posed problems for the police, and this was one way of controlling their members. See 'The Effingham Arms and the Empire: Deliberate Selection in the Evolution of Music Hall in London', *Popular Culture and Class Conflict: Explorations in the History of Labour and Leisure*, ed. Eileen and Stephen Yeo, Brighton, Harvester, 1981, p. 214.

42 Greater London Record Office, 13 October 1892, LCC/MIN/10,885.

43 *Vigilance Record*, 15 July 1891, p. 64.

44 Bristow (op. cit., p. 49) cites figures indicating the scale of the Society's operations: between 1834 and 1880 it seized 385,000 obscene prints and photos, 80,000 books and pamphlets, and 28,000 sheets of obscene songs, circulars, stereotypes, and copper plates.

45 Letter from 'M.F.', *Daily Telegraph*, 17 October 1894, p. 3.

46 Summerfield, op. cit.; Joseph Donohue, 'The Empire Theatre of Varieties Licensing Controversy of 1894: Testimony of Laura Ormiston Chant before the Theatres and Musical Halls Licensing Committee', *Nineteenth Century Theatre*, Summer 1987, vol. 15, pp. 50–60.

47 Greater London Record Office, Verbatim testimony, 10 October 1894, LCC/MIN/10,803.

48 ibid.

49 Edwardes complied after he got a legal ruling from the Queen's Bench on the LCC's right to annex conditions to licensing. His complaints of conflict of interest among Councillors were discharged. (Greater London Record Office, LCC/MIN/10,803.)

50 The National Vigilance Association successfully opposed nine music and dancing licences in Pontypool, and there were other isolated provincial campaigns on matters such as naughty postcards (see *Vigilance Record*, December 1895, p. 9, and 1902 passim).

51 Nevertheless, the *Vigilance Record* continued until 1932.

52 *Daily Telegraph*, 18 October 1894, p. 3.

53 Greater London Record Office, 6 May 1895, LCC/MIN/10,803.

54 See Sir Gwilym Gibbon and Reginald W. Bell, *History of the London County Council 1889–1939*, London, Macmillan, 1939.

55 Greater London Record Office, Testimony, 2 October 1895, LCC/MIN/10,803.

56 Leader, 'The County Council and Public Morals', *Vigilance Record*, 15 April 1889, p. 30.

57 See, for example, John Hollingshead's letter to *The Times*, 8 October 1898.

58 Cited in *The Cambridge Guide to World Theatre*, ed., Martin Banham, Cambridge, Cambridge University Press, 1988, p. 698.

59 Public Record Office, 6 and 8 October 1893, LC/1/601.(116).

60 British Library, Lord Chamberlain's Plays, 53535 (I). Libretto by Owen Hall, lyrics by Harry Greenbank, music by Sidney Jones, *The Gaiety Girl*, first produced at the Prince of Wales's 14 October 1893.

61 This song has no connection with the musical *The Gaiety Girl*. Words by T.S. Lonsdale, Music by W.G. Eaton, 'A Gaiety Girl', London, Francis, Day, & Hunter, [1894].

62 British Library, Lord Chamberlain's Plays, 53509 (L). Libretto by Adrian Ross and James Leader [J.C. Tanner], music by F. Osmond Carr, *In Town*, first produced at the Prince of Wales's 15 October 1892.

63 British Library, Lord Chamberlain's Plays, 53562 (B). Libretto by H.J.W. Dam, Music by Ivan Caryll, Adrian Ross, and Lionel Monkton, *The Shop Girl*, first produced at the Gaiety Theatre 24 November 1894.

BIBLIOGRAPHY

UNPUBLISHED DOCUMENTS

British Library, London, Department of Manuscripts, Lord Chamberlain's Plays.
British Library, London, Playbills.
General Register Office, Edinburgh, Census of Scotland, Document Class 644.
Greater London Record Office, London, London County Council Theatres and
    Music Halls Licensing Committee, Document Class LCC/MIN.
Greater London Record Office, London, Middlesex Court Records, Licences for
    Music and Dancing. Document Class MR/LMD.
Greater London Record Office, London, Middlesex Court Records, Summary
    Convictions. 1860–62.
London School of Economics, London, British Library of Political and Economic
    Science, John Stuart Mill Collection.
Public Record Office, London, Censuses of England and Wales, Document Class
    RG-9 (1861) and RG-11 (1881).
Public Record Office, London, Lord Chamberlain's Papers, Document Class LC1.
University of Rochester Archives, Rochester, New York, Clement Scott Papers
    and other Miscellaneous Letters.
Victoria and Albert Museum, London, Department of Prints and Drawings,
    Wilhelm tracings books and original designs.

MUSICAL ARCHIVES

British Library, Department of Music
Harvard Theatre Collection

PICTORIAL ARCHIVES

British Museum Department of Prints and Drawings
Harvard Theatre Collection
Kinsey Institute for Research in Sex, Gender, and Reproduction
Mander and Mitcheson Theatre Collection
New York Public Library at Lincoln Centre
Royal Opera House Archives at Covent Garden
Theatre Museum, London
Yale Center for British Art

CONTEMPORANEOUS PUBLISHED DOCUMENTATION

(1) Journals and Newspapers Extensively Consulted

Black and White
British Weekly
The Daily Telegraph
Days' Doings
Entr-acte
Era
Exquisite
Graphic
Here and There
Illustrated London News
Illustrated Times
Pall Mall Gazette
Paul Pry
Photo Bits
Sketch
St James's Gazette
Stage
The Times (London)
Vigilance Record

(2) Statutes

Theatre Regulation Act, 6 & 7 Victoria (1843).

(3) Books, Reports, Articles, and Official Publications

The Actress of the Present Day, 3 vols, London, James Harper, 1817.

Ashwell, Lena, 'Acting as a Profession for Women', *Women Workers in Seven Professions*, ed. Edith J. Morley, London, George Routledge, 1914.

[Bacchus, George Reginald?], *The Confessions of Nemesis Hunt*, 3 vols, London, privately printed, 1902–6.

Bancroft, Squire and Wilton, Marie, *The Bancrofts. Recollections of Sixty Years*, London, John Murray, 1909.

Beerbohm, Max, 'Max, Mr Archer, and Others', *Saturday Review*, 15 October 1898.

Biblioteca Carringtoniensis (Kinsey Institute).

Bird, M. Mostyn, *Woman at Work: A Study of the Different Ways of Earning a Living Open to Women*, London, Chapman and Hall, 1911.

Blathwayt, Raymond, ' "Does the Theatre Make for Good?" An Interview with Mr. Clement Scott', London, A.W. Hall, 1898.

Bulley, A., and Whitley, Margaret, *Women's Work*, London, Methuen, 1894.

Burbury, Mrs E.J., *Florence Sackville, or Self-Dependence*, 3 vols, London, Smith, Elder, 1851.

Calvert, [Adelaide] Mrs Charles, *Sixty-Eight Years on the Stage*, London, Mills & Boon, [1911].

Catalogue of Curiosa and Erotica, 1892 (British Library).

Charities Register and Digest, London, 1890.

Chorley, Henry F., *Pomfret; or, Public Opinion and Private Judgment*, 3 vols, London, Henry Colburn, 1845.

Collet, Clara, *Report on the Statistics of Employment of Women and Girls*, pt. 2, 1894.

The Confessions of a Dancing Girl by Herself, London, Heath, Cranton & Ouseley, [1913].

Confessions of Madame Vestris; in a series of letters to Handsome Jack, n.p., New Villon Society, 1891.

Crissie: A Music-Hall Sketch of To-Day, [London], The Alhambra, 1899.

De Cordova, Rudolph, 'The Stage as a Career: an Actor's Experience,' *Forum*, July 1894.

Dircks, Rudolf, *Players of To-Day*, London, Simpkin, Marshall, Hamilton, Kent, [1892].

[Dumoulin, Edward], *Memoirs of a Russian Ballet Girl*, 2 vols in 1, Monte Carlo, [Charles Carrington], 1901.

Ebers, John, *Seven Years of the King's Theatre*, London, William Harrison Ainsworth, 1828.

Edwards, Annie, *The Morals of May Fair*, 3 vols, London, Hurst & Blackett, 1858.

[Ellerslie, Alma?], *The Diary of an Actress or Realities of Stage Life*, ed. H.C. Shuttleworth, London, Griffith, Farran, Okeden & Welsh, 1885.

Ellis, Havelock, *Man and Woman: A Study of Human Secondary Sexual Characters*, London, Walter Scott, 1894.

Emery, Winifred, 'The Stage as a Profession. IV – Something About Success', *Woman*, 8 January 1891.

'The Employment of Women', *Meliora*, January 1860, vol. 2.

Gardner, Fitzroy, 'Does Acting Pay? A Warning', *Daily Mail*, 18 October 1907.

'The Greatest Social Evil', *Tait's Edinburgh Magazine*, 1857, vol. 24.

Greenwood, James, *The Seven Curses of London*, 1869, reprinted Oxford, Basil Blackwell, 1981.

——, *The Wilds of London*, London, Chatto & Windus, 1876.

[Greg, William Rathbone], *Westminster Review*, 1850, vol. 53.

Halling, Daisy, and Lister, Charles, 'A Minimum Wage for Actors', *Socialist Review*, August 1908.

Hogg, Edith F., 'School Children as Wage Earners', *Nineteenth Century*, August 1897, vol. 42.

Holbrook, Ann Catherine, *Memoirs of an Actress*, Manchester, J. Harrop, 1807.

——, *The Dramatist: or, Memoirs of the Stage*, Birmingham, Martin & Hunter, 1809.

Hollingshead, John, *My Lifetime*, 2 vols, London, Sampson Low, Marston, 1895.

Hon. F.L.G., The, *The Swell's Night Guide Through the Metropolis*, London, c. 1840.

'How a London Work-Girl Lives on Ten Shillings a Week', *British Weekly*, 21 December 1888.

Hunt, Bampton (ed.) *The Green Room Book or Who's Who on the Stage: An*

Annual Biographical Record of the Dramatic Musical and Variety World, London, T. Sealey Clark, 1906.

Hutchins, B.L. and Harrison, A., *A History of Factory Legislation*, London, P.S. King, 1907.

Intrigues and Confession of a Ballet Girl; disclosing startling and voluptuous scenes before and behind the curtain, enacted by well-known personages in the theatrical, military, medical and other professions; with kisses at Vauxhall, Greenwich, &c., &c., and a full disclosure of the secret and amatory doings in the dressing room, under and upon the stage, in the light and the dark, by one who has had her share, [London, Rozez and Co., c. 1870].

Jerome, Jerome K., 'Variety Patter', *The Idler*, March 1892.

——, *On the Stage — and Off: the Brief Career of a Would-be Actor*, London, Leadenhall Press, [1885].

Jewsbury, Geraldine, *The Half Sisters*, 2 vols, London, Chapman and Hall, 1848.

Kendal, Madge, *The Drama: A paper read at the Congress of the National Association for the Promotion of Social Science, Birmingham, Sept. 1884*, London, David Brogue, 1884.

Knight, Joseph, 'Who is the Greatest Living English Actress — and Why?', *The Idler*, November 1885, vol. 8.

Leavitt, Michael Bennett, *Fifty Years in Theatrical Management (1859–1909)*, New York, Broadway Publishing Co., 1912.

Leppington, C.H. d'E., 'The Gibeonites of the Stage: Work and Wages Behind the Scenes', *National Review*, 1891, vol. 17.

'London Purity Crusade', *Daily Mail*, 27 January 1897.

Mathews, Mrs., 'Ennobled Actresses,' *Bentley's Miscellany*, 1845, vol. 17.

Mayhew, Henry, *London Labour and the London Poor*, London, Charles Griffin, 1856–62.

Memoirs of the Life of Madame Vestris of the Theatres Royal Drury Lane and Covent Garden. Illustrated with Numerous Curious Anecdotes, privately printed, [c. 1840].

Merrick, Revd G.P., *Work Among the Fallen as seen in the Prison Cells*, London, Ward, Lock & Co., 1890.

Morley, Edith J. (ed.) *Women Workers in Seven Professions: A Survey of their Economic Conditions and Prospects*, London, Routledge, 1914.

Morris, Clara, 'A Word of Warning to Young Actresses', *Century Magazine*, 1900, vol. 60.

Mowatt, Anna Cora, *Autobiography of An Actress*, Boston, Ticknor, Reed & Fields, 1854.

National Vigilance Association, *Annual Reports*, London.

Ouida, 'The Woman Problem', *Lippincott's Monthly Magazine*, June 1909, vol. 83.

Parliamentary Accounts and Papers. Censuses of England and Wales, 1841–1911.

Parliamentary Accounts and Papers. Censuses of Scotland, 1861–1911.

Rede, Leman Thomas, *The Road to the Stage*, London, J. Onwhyn, 1836.

'Report from the Select Committee on Dramatic Literature (1832)', *Westminster Review*, January 1833.

Report from the Select Committee on Dramatic Literature with Minutes of Evidence, 1832.

Report from the Select Committee on Public Houses. 1854. Minutes of Evidence.

Report from the Select Committee on Theatres and Places of Entertainment, 1892.

Report from the Select Committee on Theatrical Licensing and Regulations with Proceedings, Minutes of Evidence, Appendix, and Index, 1866.

Ritchie, J. Ewing, The Night Side of London, London, Tinsley Brothers, 1869.

'The Royal Maternity Charity', English Woman's Journal, July 1862.

Royden, A. Maude, Downward Paths: An Inquiry into the Causes which Contribute to the Making of the Prostitute, London, G. Bell, 1916.

Rules and Regulations of the General Theatrical Fund Association (adopted 22 January 1839), London, S.G. Fairbrother, 1848.

Sala, George Augustus, Twice Around the Clock, or the Hours of the Day and Night in London, London, Houlston & Wright, 1859.

Sanger, William W., The History of Prostitution: Its Extent, Causes, and Effects Throughout the World, 1897, reprinted New York, Eugenics Publishing Co., 1939.

Styles, John, An Essay on the Character, Immoral, and Antichristian Tendency of the Stage, Newport, Isle of Wight, Medina Press, 1806.

Thackeray, William Makepeace, The History of Pendennis, London, B. Davies, [1848–50].

The Theatrical Mission, 'Stars,' a Year's Work in the Theatrical Mission, [London], 1892.

Thomson, Christopher, Autobiography of an Artisan, n.p., 1847.

Thomson, H. Byerley, The Choice of a Profession. A Concise Account and Comparative Review of the English Professions, London, Chapman and Hall, 1857.

The Three Arts Club [rules and list of members], London, 1912.

'The Vocations of Women', Sixpenny Magazine, March 1866, vol. 12.

Wagner, Leopold, How to Get on Stage and How to Succeed There, London, Chatto & Windus, 1899.

Henry Walker, East London: Sketches of Christian Work and Workers, London, Religious Tract Society, 1896, reprinted High Wycombe, Peter Marcan, 1984.

Wilhelm, C., 'Art in the Ballet', Magazine of Art, 1895.

SECONDARY PUBLISHED DOCUMENTATION

Ackroyd, Peter, Transvestism and Drag: the History of an Obsession, New York, Simon & Schuster, 1979.

Acton, William, Prostitution, ed. Peter Fryer, New York, Frederick A. Praeger, 1969.

Arnheim, Rudolf, The Power of the Center: A Study of Composition in the Visual Arts, revised edition, Berkeley, University of California Press, 1983.

Ashwell, Lena, The Stage, London, Geoffrey Bliss, 1929.

Bailey, Peter (ed.) Music Hall: the Business of Pleasure, Milton Keynes, Open University Press, 1986.

Baker, Michael, The Rise of the Victorian Actor, London, Croom Helm, 1978.

Banham, Martin (ed.) The Cambridge Guide to World Theatre, Cambridge, Cambridge University Press, 1988.

Barker, Clive, 'The Chartists, Theatre Reform, and Research', Theatre Quarterly, 1971, vol. 1.

Black, Clementina, *Married Women's Work*, 1915, reprinted London, Virago, 1983.

Boas, Guy, *The Garrick Club 1831–1947*, London, Garrick Club, 1948.

Booth, Charles, 'On the Economics of Music Hall', *Theatre Quarterly*, October–December 1971, vol. 1.

Booth, Michael R., 'East End and West End: Class and Audience in Victorian London', *Theatre Research International*, 1977, vol. 2.

——, *Prefaces to English Nineteenth-Century Theatre*, Manchester, Manchester University Press, 1980.

——, *Victorian Spectacular Theatre 1850–1910*, London, Routledge & Kegan Paul, 1981.

——, (ed.), *Victorian Theatrical Trades*, London, Society for Theatre Research, 1981.

Bourgeron, Jean-Pierre (ed.) *Nude 1900*, New York, Morgan & Morgan, 1980.

Bratton, J.S., ed., *Music Hall: Performance and Style*, Milton Keynes, Open University Press, 1986.

Bristow, Edward J., *Vice and Vigilance: The Purity Movement in Britain since 1700*, Dublin, Gill & Macmillan, 1977.

Burge, James C., *Lines of Business, Casting Practice and Policy in the American Theatre 1752–1899*, New York, Peter Lang, 1986.

Burstyn, Joan N., *Victorian Education and the Ideal of Womanhood*, New Brunswick, NJ, Rutgers University Press, 1984.

Busby, Roy, *British Music Hall. An Illustrated Who's Who from 1850 to the Present Day*, London, Paul Elek, 1976.

Copelman, Dina M., 'Masculine Faculty, Women's Temperament: Victorian Women's Quest for Work and Personal Fulfillment', *Women's Studies*, Spring 1987, vol. 13.

Coxe, Antony Hippisley, *A Seat at the Circus*, revised edn, Hamden CT, Archon Books, 1981.

Crauford, Alfred L., *Sam and Sallie: A Romance of the Stage*, London, Cranley & Day, 1933.

Davidoff, Leonore, *The Best Circles: Society, Etiquette and the Season*, London, Croom Helm, 1973.

Davis, Tracy C. 'Victorian Charity and Self-help for Women Performers', *Theatre Notebook*, 1987, vol. 41.

——, 'The Actress in Victorian Pornography', *Theatre Journal*, October 1989, vol. 41.

——, 'Sex in Public Places: The Zaeo Aquarium Scandal and the Victorian Moral Majority', *Theatre History Studies*, 1990.

de Beauvoir, Simone, *The Second Sex*, 1952, reprinted New York, Vintage, 1974.

de Lauretis, Teresa (ed.) *Feminist Studies/Critical Studies*, Bloomington, Indiana University Press, 1986.

Donohue, Joseph, 'The Empire Theatre of Varieties Licensing Controversy of 1894: Testimony of Laura Ormiston Chant before the Theatres and Musical Halls Licensing Committee', *Nineteenth Century Theatre*, Summer 1987, vol. 15.

Drake, Barbara, *Women in Trade Unions*, 1920, reprinted London, Virago, 1984.

Dubois, Ellen Carol and Gordon, Linda, 'Seeking Ecstasy on the Battlefield: Danger and Pleasure in Nineteenth-century Feminist Sexual Thought',

Pleasure and Danger: Exploring Female Sexuality, ed. Carole S. Vance, Boston, Routledge & Kegan Paul, 1984.

Dworkin, Andrea, *Pornography: Men Possessing Women*, London, Women's Press, 1981.

Dyhouse, Carol, *Girls Growing up in Late Victorian and Edwardian England*, London, Routledge & Kegan Paul, 1981.

Ehrlich, Cyril, *The Music Profession in Britain Since the Eighteenth Century. A Social History*, Oxford, Oxford University Press, 1985.

Elsom, John, *Erotic Theatre*, London, Secker & Warburg, 1973.

Fishman, W.J., *East End 1888: A Year in a London Borough Among the Labouring Poor*, London, Duckworth, 1988.

Foster, George, *The Spice of Life: Sixty-five Years in the Glamour World*, London, Hurst & Blackett, [1939].

Fraser, Antonia, *The Weaker Vessel: Woman's Lot in Seventeenth-Century England*, London, Methuen, 1984.

Fryer, Peter, *Mrs. Grundy: Studies in English Prudery*, London, Dennis Dobson, 1963.

——, (compiler), *The Man of Pleasure's Companion: A Nineteenth Century Anthology of Amorous Entertainment*, London, Arthur Baker, 1968.

——, *Forbidden Books of the Victorians*, London, Odyssey Press, 1970.

——, (ed.) *Prostitution*, New York, Frederick A. Praeger, 1969.

Gerson, Noel B., *Because I Loved Him: The Life and Loves of Lillie Langtry*, New York, William Morrow, 1971.

Gibb, Andrew, *Glasgow: The Making of a City*, London, Croom Helm, 1983.

Gibbon, Sir Gwilym and Bell, Reginald W., *History of the London County Council 1889–1939*, London, Macmillan, 1939.

Gilbert, Sandra M. and Gubar, Susan, *The Madwoman in the Attic: The Woman Writer and the Nineteenth-Century Literary Imagination*, New Haven, Yale University Press, 1979.

Goffman, Erving, *The Presentation of Self in Everyday Life*, Garden City, Doubleday, 1959.

Gorham, Deborah, *The Victorian Girl and the Feminine Ideal*, London and Canberra, Croom Helm, 1982.

Green, William, 'Strippers and Couchers – the Quintessence of American Burlesque', *Western Popular Theatre*, David Mayer and Kenneth Richards (eds), London, Methuen, 1977.

Guest, Ivor, *Victorian Ballet-Girl: The Tragic Story of Clara Webster*, London, Adam and Charles Black, 1957.

——, *The Empire Ballet*, London, Society for Theatre Research, 1962.

——, *Fanny Elssler*, London, Adam and Charles Black, 1970.

Hamilton, Cicely, *Life Errant*, London, J.M. Dent, 1935.

Hammond, Paul, *French Undressing: Naughty Postcards from 1900 to 1925*, New York, Pyramid, 1975.

Hannah, Leslie, *Inventing Retirement: The Development of Occupational Pensions in Britain*, Cambridge, Cambridge University Press, 1986.

Harrop, Josephine, *Victorian Portable Theatres*, London, Society for Theatre Research, 1989.

Haug, Frigga, *et al.*, *Female Sexualization: A Collective Work of Memory*, trans. Erica Carter, London, Verso, 1987.

Heilbrun, Carolyn G., *Writing a Woman's Life*, London, Women's Press, 1989.

Hibbert, H.G., *Fifty Years a Londoner's Life*, London, Grant Richards, 1916.

Higgs, Edward, 'Women, Occupations and Work in the Nineteenth Century Censuses,' *History Workshop Journal*, 1987, vol. 23.

Highfill, Philip H., Burnim, Kalman A., and Langhans, Edward A., *A Biographical Dictionary of Actors . . . in London, 1660–1800*, Carbondale, Southern Illinois University Press, 1973–.

Hiley, Michael, *Victorian Working Women: Portraits from Life*, London, Gordon Fraser, 1979.

Howard, Diana, *London Theatres and Music Halls, 1850–1950*, London, Library Association, 1970.

Jackson, John Arthur, *The Irish in Britain*, London, Routledge & Kegan Paul, 1967.

Jacobs, Arthur, *Arthur Sullivan: A Victorian Musician*, Oxford, Oxford University Press, 1984.

Johnson, Claudia D., *American Actress: Perspective on the Nineteenth Century*, Chicago, Nelson-Hall, 1984.

Kuhn, Annette, *The Power of the Image: Essays on Representation and Sexuality*, London, Routledge & Kegan Paul, 1985.

Lawson, Joan, *A History of Ballet and its Makers*, London, Dance Books, 1973.

Layder, Derek R., 'Occupational Careers in Britain with Reference to the Acting Profession', 2 vols, Ph.D. dissertation, University of London, 1976.

Maas, Jeremy, 'Victorian Nudes', *Saturday Book*, 1971, vol. 31.

McArthur, Benjamin, *Actors and American Culture, 1880–1920*, Philadelphia, Temple University Press, 1984.

McCullough, Jack W., 'Edward Kilanyi and American Tableaux Vivants', *Theatre Survey*, May 1975, vol. 16.

McLuhan, Marshall, *Understanding Media: The Extensions of Man*, New York, Mentor, 1964.

Marchand, Henry L., *The French Pornographers: Including a History of French Erotic Literature*, 1933, reprinted New York, Book Awards, 1965.

Marcus, Stephen, *The Other Victorians: A Study of Sexuality and Pornography in Mid-Nineteenth-Century England*, New York, Basic Books, 1964.

Mayer, David and Richards, Kenneth (eds) *Western Popular Theatre*, London, Methuen, 1977.

Meisel, Martin, *Realizations*, New York, Columbia University Press, 1983.

Miller, Gale, *Odd Jobs, the World of Deviant Work*, New York, Prentice-Hall, 1978.

Murray, Janet, *Strong-Minded Women and Other Lost Voices from Nineteenth-Century England*, New York, Pantheon, 1982.

Neff, Wanda Fraiken, *Victorian Working Women: An Historical and Literary Study of Women in British Industries and Professions, 1832–1850*, 1929, reprinted London, Allen & Unwin, 1966.

Nicholson, Linda J., *Gender and History: The Limits of Social Theory in the Age of the Family*, New York, Columbia University Press, 1986.

Norgaard, Erik, *With Love: the Erotic Postcard*, London, Macgibbon & Kee, 1972.

Oldfield, Sybil, *Spinsters of this Parish: The Life and Times of F.M. Mayor and Mary Sheepshanks*, London, Virago, 1984.

Olsen, Donald J., *The Growth of Victorian London*, Harmondsworth, Penguin, 1976.

Ovenden, Graham and Mendes, Peter, *Victorian Erotic Photography*, London, Academy Editions, 1973.

Parker, Derek and Julia, *The Natural History of the Chorus Girl*, London, David & Charles, 1975.

Pearsall, Ronald, *Public Purity, Private Shame: Victorian Sexual Hypocrisy Exposed*, London, Weidenfeld & Nicolson, 1976.

Pinchbeck, Ivy, *Women Workers and the Industrial Revolution 1750–1850*, 1930, reprinted London, Virago, 1981.

Pollock, Griselda, *Vision and Difference: Femininity, Feminism and the Histories of Art*, London and New York, Routledge, 1988.

Price, Cecil, 'Regulations of a 19th Century Theatrical Booth', *Theatre Notebook*, 1949/50, vol. 4.

Richardson, Joanna, *The Courtesans: The Demi-monde in Nineteenth-century France*, London, Weidenfeld & Nicolson, 1967.

Rickards, Maurice, *Banned Posters*, Park Ridge N.J., Noyes Press, 1972.

Roberts, Helene R., 'The Exquisite Slave: The Role of Clothes in the Making of Victorian Woman', *Signs*, Spring 1977, vol. 2.

Roebuck, Janet, *Urban Development in Nineteenth-Century London: Lambeth, Battersea and Wandsworth, 1838–88*, Chichester, Philline, 1979.

Rosen, Ruth, *The Lost Sisterhood: Prostitution in America, 1900–1918*, Baltimore and London, Johns Hopkins University Press, 1982.

Rosenfeld, Sybil, *The Georgian Theatre of Richmond Yorkshire and its Circuit*, London, Society for Theatre Research, 1984.

Rowell, George, *The Victorian Theatre 1792–1914*, 2nd edn, Cambridge, Cambridge University Press, 1978.

Royde-Smith, Naomi, *The Private Life of Mrs Siddons: A Psychological Investigation*, London, Victor Gollancz, 1933.

Sanderson, Michael, *From Irving to Olivier: A Social History of the Acting Profession in England 1880–1983*, London, Athlone, 1984.

Sawyer, Corinne Holt, 'Men in Skirts and Women in Trousers, from Achilles to Victoria Grant: One Explanation of a Comedic Paradox', *Journal of Popular Culture*, Fall 1987, vol. 21.

Snitow, Ann, Stansell, Christine, and Thompson, Sharon (eds) *Powers of Desire*, New York, *Monthly Review*, 1983.

States, Bert O., *Great Reckonings in Little Rooms: On the Phenomenology of Theater*, Berkeley, University of California, 1985.

Stedman Jones, Gareth. *Outcast London. A Study of the Relationship Between Classes in Victorian Society*, 1971, reprinted Harmondsworth, Penguin, 1984.

Steele, Valerie, *Fashion and Eroticism: the Ideals of Feminine Beauty from the Victorian Era to the Jazz Age*, New York, Oxford University Press, 1985.

Stoianovich, Traian, *French Historical Method: The Annales Paradigm*, Ithaca and London, Cornell University Press, 1976.

Stone, Lawrence, *The Past and the Present Revisited*, revised edn, London and New York, Routledge & Kegan Paul, 1987.

Storch, Robert D., 'Police Control of Street Prostitution in Victorian London: A Study in the Contexts of Police Action', *Police and Society*, ed. David H. Bayley, Beverley Hills, Sage, 1977.

Storr, Anthony, *Sexual Deviation*, Harmondsworth, Penguin 1964.

Summerfield, Penelope, 'The Effingham Arms and the Empire: Deliberate

Selection in the Evolution of Music Hall in London', *Popular Culture and Class Conflict: Explorations in the History of Labour and Leisure*, ed. Eileen and Stephen Yeo, Brighton, Harvester, 1981.

Swift, Clive, *The Job of Acting: A Guide to Working in Theatre*, London, Harrap, 1976.

Tillett, Selwyn, 'Each in His Accustomed Place', *'Ruddygore' Commemorative Booklet*, Saffron Walden, Arthur Sullivan Society, 1987.

Trudgill, Eric, *Madonnas and Magdalens*, London, Heinemann, 1976.

Turner, E.S., *Roads to Ruin: The Shocking History of Social Reform*, London, Michael Joseph, 1950.

Vance, Carole S. (ed.) *Pleasure and Danger: Exploring Female Sexuality*, Boston, Routledge & Kegan Paul, 1984.

Vicinus, Martha (ed.) *A Widening Sphere: Changing Roles of Victorian Women*, London, Methuen, 1977.

Walkowitz, Judith R., *Prostitution and Victorian Society*, Cambridge, Cambridge University Press, 1980.

——, in 'Male Vice and Female Virtue: Feminism and the Politics of Prostitution in Nineteenth-Century Britain', *Powers of Desire*, ed. Ann Snitow, Christine Stansell and Sharon Thompson, New York, *Monthly Review*, 1983.

Webb, Peter, *The Erotic Arts*, revised edn, London, Secker & Warburg, 1983.

Weiner, Deborah E.B., 'The People's Palace: an Image for East London in the 1880s', *Metropolis London: Histories and Representations Since 1800*, ed. David Feldman and Gareth Stedman Jones, London and New York, Routledge, 1989.

Willett, C. and Cunnington, Phillis, *The History of Underclothes*, London, Michael Joseph, 1951.

Wyndham, Horace, *Chorus to Coronet*, London, British Technical and General Press, 1951.

Yeo, Eileen and Stephen (eds) *Popular Culture and Class Conflict: Explorations in the History of Labour and Leisure*, Brighton, Harvester, 1981.

INDEX